Sherrie

Behind the Laughter

SHERRIE HEWSON

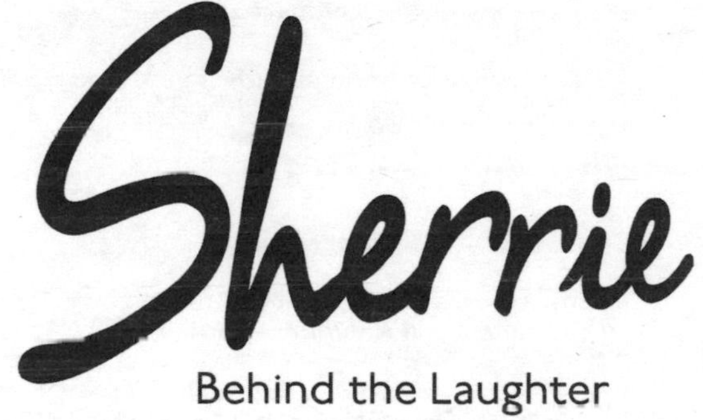

Behind the Laughter

HarperCollins*Publishers*

HarperCollins*Publishers*
77–85 Fulham Palace Road,
Hammersmith, London W6 8JB

www.harpercollins.co.uk

This paperback edition published in 2011
First published by HarperCollins*Publishers* 2011

1 3 5 7 9 10 8 6 4 2

A catalogue record of this book is
available from the British Library

ISBN 978-0-00-741625-7

Printed and bound in Great Britain by
Clays Ltd, St Ives plc

MIX
Paper from responsible sources
FSC® C007454

FSC is a non-profit international organisation established to promote the
responsible management of the world's forests. Products carrying the FSC
label are independently certified to assure consumers that they come
from forests that are managed to meet the social, economic and
ecological needs of present and future generations.

Find out more about HarperCollins and the environment at
www.harpercollins.co.uk/green

To Mum, Keeley, Ollie and Molly

Picture Credits

All images are used courtesy of Sherrie Hewson, with the following exceptions:

Plate section
Page 4 © Mirrorpix; pages 9, 10, 11 (bottom), 12 (top right and top left), 13 (middle), 14, 15 (top), 16(middle) © Rex Features; page 13 (top) © TV Times/IPC+ Syndication; page 16 (top right and bottom) © PA Photos

Cover
Back cover photographs © Rex Features; Mike Lawn (Sherrie reclining on chair); Danny Steer (Sherrie in top hat).

The Author and the Publishers are committed to respecting the intellectual property rights of others and have made all reasonable efforts to trace the copyright owners of the photographs reproduced, and to provide an appropriate acknowledgement in the book. In the event that any of the untraceable copyright owners come forward after the publication of this book, the Author and the Publishers will use all reasonable endeavours to rectify the position accordingly.

Introduction

Nothing is ever straightforward in my life, and writing this book was no exception. In fact, at one point I truly believed there was a force out there similar to Darth Vader that really had it in for me. Each time I opened my laptop, his big glowing tube (OK, light sabre) would gather momentum and strike, causing disasters to happen – I was beginning to think it had all been sent to give me a reason not to do the book.

When you speak to real writers they find every excuse in the world not to write, from mundane tasks such as plants that need watering to 'I have to watch *This Morning* – they're doing a bikini wax on men' or 'I must clean my drains' and even, 'There's a wild Alaskan bear in the garden!' Yet once you've had a wee, brushed your teeth, found something nice to put on (and maybe a bit of mascara just in case), made a cup of tea, found your glasses, tied your legs to the table and started work, it's so satisfying and therapeutic, if humbling and harrowing at times.

When what you're writing happens to be your own story, the whole memory thing can be a bit of a worry. Sometimes you find yourself doubting you were in certain places at certain times and you do have to keep on confirming everything and consulting the reference library – in this case, my lovely mum. The mind is a trickster: it can play games with you. So, did I see The Beatles live in the Gaumont Cinema, Nottingham, in 1962 or was I backstage sitting on Paul McCartney's knee? Did Julie Andrews inspire me to become an actress when I saw her in *The Sound of Music* at the ABC in Derby or was I actually in the film itself? In both cases, I'm sure you can guess the truth. So, you do have to be vigilant and honest, even if the real story isn't quite as exciting as you would have wished.

The only thing is, when you've sat for a long time writing, your bum goes numb, you have to get up and the whole excuse thing starts all over again. I did have a genuine reason not to work on Christmas Eve: I'd had a very bad fall and cracked my ribs and injured my back in the process on a great big lump of ice. Naturally, sitting was extremely painful yet I gave myself every reason to work through the pain. How contrary is that?

It was a good job it happened at Christmas, too, because just before that, five of us – Zoe, Carol, Denise, Andrea and I – were thrilled to be asked to take part in the BBC's Children in Need. I think we have Zoe to blame for the next bit: we were told they would like us to be Girls Aloud and sing 'The Promise' … wait for it, LIVE! Zoe is the only singer, Carol and I scatter cats for miles, Denise is passable and Andrea is, well, very tall.

We rehearsed with the Children in Need team and you could see it on their faces: the look of pain and knowing it was too late to turn back. Meanwhile, we started to love the song and the idea of being pop stars, but the more we got carried away the worse we became. Poor Zoe knew she couldn't do any more with us! Later, we were fitted for our gold sparkly dresses (which were incredible) and then came the night itself.

Sherrie Hewson

We were in a dressing room next to Take That, no less. In 2009 Robbie Williams had been a guest on *Loose Women* and we all fell in love with him. Carol and I went out with his lovely wife Ayda and his mum Jan, who I knew anyway, and got absolutely hammered. The next day Robbie let Carol know that he was very cross with us – he'd never seen his mum so drunk before.

While we waited to go onstage, I went out for a walk to calm myself down and Robbie passed me. 'Hey,' he shouted. 'You OK?' 'No, Robbie – we've got to be Girls Aloud in a minute, we're terrified!' I told him. 'Don't be silly,' he laughed. 'We all think of you as Nanas Aloud, we love you all!'

I told the other girls this and it did calm us down – we didn't have to be the proper Girls Aloud, just us. Of course, Take That went on and stormed the place and we were next up. There we were, the five of us, lined up in our full-length glittering gold dresses, big hair and sexy make-up, microphones at the ready … and knees knocking together in terror. At that moment all we could think was, 'Why on earth did we agree to this?'

We were about to perform before an audience of 12 million people and it was one of the scariest things we'd ever done. As we walked on to a roar from the crowd, the music started up and the atmosphere was amazing. Every time one of us sang solo, the audience went mad – which was just as well because, hopefully, they couldn't hear us then. It was electrifying and for those few short moments we really did feel like Girls Aloud (or as Robbie affectionately calls us, 'Nanas Aloud'). Maybe we could start our own band for Nanas everywhere.

That was one of my highlights for *Loose Women* in 2010 and we know 2011 will bring us many more. The team backstage is wonderful – they work so hard and have to put up with us, too, but whenever we have our end-of-term parties or 'after school' drinks we are very close, a proper team. I'd like to say thank you to them all.

I have written a book before, a short novel called *The Tannery*. It was an extremely dark tale, very disturbing but fictional. This is so much harder because it's the truth: you don't want to come over as all sad or bitter, even pathetic, so you must guard against that. Luckily, seeing things in black and white can be highly therapeutic. They say there's a book in all of us and I truly believe that. You know when your mum or granny says, 'I could write a book'? Well, I honestly believe they can and should – my mum certainly could.

As you will see, I write as I act: from the heart. I don't have any special technique … and I can hear you all agreeing with this. With me, what you see is what you get and I hope it gives you an understanding of who I am, my wacky behaviour, all the hurts and the triumphs along the way. You may recognise some of the things I've been through as being part of your own world because at the end of the day we're all the same – just wrapped up differently. That's why *Loose Women* is such a great show because there's always someone you can relate to.

So, thank you for opening my book. You may well be shocked at some of the things that have happened in my life, but I hope you will laugh reading it just as much as I did writing it.

Chapter One

I was the spitting image of Winston Churchill when I was born; all I needed was a cigar and the appropriate 'V' sign. So pretty, I was probably not. I also had webbed feet à la Donald Duck. I'm not painting an attractive picture here, am I? In fact, I was the chubbiest, grumpiest baby in the world.

My birth, in what was perhaps a sign of things to come, was far from straightforward. Within hours I had to have a complete blood transfusion: the doctors feared I might be afflicted with the same condition which my brother Brett had suffered from when he popped out, 18 months earlier. He'd caused havoc by nearly dying: Mum lacked vitamin K, meaning Brett's blood wouldn't clot and instead poured out of every orifice in his tiny body. She was also desperately ill and too weak to choose a name for my brother – who, the doctors agreed, wouldn't make it through the night. Remarkably, both survived; maybe that's what made them into the strong, resilient people they are today.

I arrived in 1950, five years after the war had ended, but I never felt a thing. Indeed, my life was cushioned from day one.

Shortly after I was born, the family moved from my grandparents' house in the village of Beeston in Nottinghamshire to their very first home – a semi-detached down the road. It had a lovely garden and my mother would place Brett and me in our prams there to get some fresh air. Brett was good as gold, but I wriggled, squirmed and tried to escape until I ended up on at least one occasion hanging out of the pram by my neck.

My mother, Joy, was an extraordinary woman. Her own mother, like most women at that time, had been a housewife and had never gone out to work, but Mum had other ideas. Beautiful, determined and clever, she had energy and vision. And she knew what she wanted: to own a lovely home, send her children to private school and watch us make our mark in the world.

My parents met immediately after the war when Mum was a young woman and Dad was ten years older. Her day job was working for a friend in the clothing industry, but her real passion was ballroom dancing and modelling. She worked for various fashion labels, including Slix swimsuits and Chanel, and she won all kinds of prizes, both locally and nationally, for her dancing. My mother was, and still is, ultra-glamorous, stylish and elegant. Her wardrobe was bursting with beautiful dresses and the most glorious ballroom gowns. She seemed so magical, I used to love to dress up and try my hardest to look like her.

My father, Ron Hutchinson, was born near Sunderland in the North East. His mother died just after his birth and his father skedaddled from the family home, leaving Dad to be brought up by his aunties and uncles. I never knew much about his life up in the North, although I do remember visiting a terraced house where the door led straight into the kitchen and there was a rather large, jolly lady, who cuddled me all the time. It makes sense that she would be related to Dad as he was the most tactile man you could ever wish to meet.

I remember as you looked out of the back-room window of the house there was a large field and a pit, and so I always thought Dad's family must be miners. They were Macams, which means 'Sunderland-born', never to be confused with Geordies from Newcastle. They did, however, have one thing in common: at New Year they had what was called the 'First Footing'. It was one of my most joyous memories: I would sit on Dad's knee and wait as midnight neared. Everything would go deadly quiet and as the clock struck twelve, in came a tall, dark and handsome man – probably a family friend, but to me a glamorous stranger – holding a piece of coal, a coin, salt, bread and whisky. Everyone would cheer and the party would begin. It may have been a superstition, but to me this was truly exciting; to Dad and his family it meant health, happiness and prosperity for the coming year.

Although he was happy at home and loved his family, Dad left at a very early age to discover the world. He had a natural wanderlust and curiosity about life till the day he died. At the age of 15 he joined the Army; that was before the war, which he managed to survive, unscathed. He led a charmed life: he attracted people, especially women, and a certain general's wife took a fancy to him and insisted he become their personal chauffeur. As a result, the closest Dad came to battle was when the General and his wife had a row.

After the war, Dad drove for a General Palmer and had access to all the Army and Air Force bases, including the ones where the Americans were stationed, which meant he could get his hands on the so-called 'black market' goodies. He would turn up at my grandma's house when Mum was at work with nylon stockings, chocolate, bananas and all manner of treats. Dad was so charming and handsome, he looked just like the heart-throb Errol Flynn and no one could resist him.

My mother would come home to find him having tea with my grandmother. Mum wasn't short of suitors and was in no rush to settle down, but Dad was determined to win her over. He even took up ballroom dancing to impress her and became extremely accomplished. Later, he taught me the chacha, which we danced together on many an occasion. Eventually, his persuasive charm won Mum's heart and the two of them married and set up home together.

Dad left the Army and began work for a company called Constance Murray, which made very upmarket men's and women's clothing. As the saying goes, he could sell snow to the Eskimos and so he was in his element in the retail trade. But it was when he sang that he came into his own: he was a Bing Crosby-style crooner and performed with all the big bands across the country.

I adored my dad. He was a warm and loving man and his love for me was unconditional. If I'd murdered ten people that morning he'd have said, 'Never mind, darling – eat your breakfast and we'll find a way.' But he was also a restless dreamer, more often away than he was home, who never really allowed himself to be tied down to family life. We all used to joke that he should never have married and had children. It was only years later when I had my daughter Keeley and he came to live with us that he truly became part of family life and to everyone's surprise proved to be a dab hand at childcare, cooking and housework.

In those early days it was Mum who organised everything and everyone, made the decisions and ran the show. She was the kind of woman who could do six things at once, and frequently did. Although she adored Brett and me, she wasn't a stay-at-home mum but a force of nature, always full of ideas, plans and boundless energy.

I only remember one time when she was ill. She'd been up a ladder – she was always wallpapering or decorating – when she fell off. Her womb collapsed, so she had to have an emergency hysterectomy and then, as was the custom in those days, she stayed in a convalescent home for several weeks. I was still only three and not allowed inside, so my grandparents would take me there and I'd stand in the grounds waving up at Mum as she stood at the window.

My brother Brett was a lovely-looking child, blond and blue-eyed and angelic, while I was chubby and, as I have said, a potential body-double for Winston Churchill. As I grew older I became aware of how Brett's good looks got him attention, or so it seemed to me, and maybe that explains why I became a potential serial killer. At two and a half years old, for some extraordinary reason I climbed out of my cot one night, negotiated the mountainous staircase, navigated my way around the house and picked up a knitting needle from my mother's chair. At that point I discovered Brett sitting on the floor, watching the telly, and proceeded to shove the needle down his throat.

Of course it may have been that I was just plain curious as to how far I could submerge it: who knows what went on in my infant mind? Strangely, Brett – who was a strapping lad of four and much bigger than me – opened his mouth and allowed me to shove the needle in, at which point he started to choke.

The noise brought my mother running from the kitchen. She extracted said needle from my brother's mouth while no doubt checking for puncture wounds and I was taken back to bed with a sore bottom. Peace reigned over the household once more, but not for long: minutes later I was off again and got down the staircase for a second time, found another knitting needle and tried the whole thing all over again. It beggars belief why my brother let this happen twice. This time I was well and truly punished, but I must have got the message because I never tried it again. After that the needles disappeared, although you might say I had my own Weapons of Mass Destruction long before the phrase was coined.

Around the same time, my mother enrolled me in a French nursery school. In those days it was unusual for a child to attend any kind of pre-school or nursery, let alone a French one, but Mum loved the idea of me learning French and so off I went in the nursery uniform of a little white dress with matching socks and sandals.

The nursery was in a big house and we spent the day in a room filled with little wooden chairs. It had elegant French windows and a large stove, where we warmed ourselves while drinking our milk. During our break we played on the lawn outside and at lunchtime we sat at a long table covered in white linen and used proper knives and forks. The staff were strict but kind and insisted on good manners. I remember on at least one occasion being removed from the room after banging my spoon on the table and having to wait for lunch until all the others had eaten.

I soon learned to sing nursery rhymes and recite my times tables in French. We danced and sang a lot, which I loved, and I think of the two and a half years spent at the nursery as a wonderful time. I felt secure and happy there. Perhaps that's why to my mind, ever since then that little white dress, socks and shoes have symbolised all things good, safe and comforting.

At the age of five I had to leave the nursery and move on to a beautiful private school, the Dorothy Grants, which meant swapping my white dress for an extremely smart navy-blue skirt, white shirt and tie, a navy blazer and a posh blue overcoat with silver buttons, topped with a Panama hat. My uniform was very much of that period and I thought it was fabulous. The school was in an elegant old house, the teachers were kind and I was extremely happy in this environment, where I shone and loved every minute of it. On summer days we would take our chairs outside and have classes under the trees in the garden, which was so much nicer than being indoors.

Sadly, though, I was taught a harsh lesson while at this school. One day I waited at the gates for my mother to collect me, not knowing she had sent a message to say she was going to be late. After a bit I decided to walk home. Even in those days this was a daft thing to do, but I was only six years old and I was sure I could find my way. As I walked through the unfamiliar streets, however, I started to panic: all the roads looked the same. I kept on walking and suddenly I became aware of five kids behind me. They began to shout things and made fun of my posh uniform.

Within minutes I was surrounded: three girls and two boys were shoving and pushing me. They pulled at my hair and grabbed my satchel, I lost my hat and then one of them tripped me up and I fell onto the pavement. I knew my hands were scraped and bleeding, but I didn't cry. Instead I jumped up and started to run as fast as my little legs could carry me. The boys kept up with me, still hitting and calling me names, but I just ran and ran. As I turned a corner there was a main road in front and a bus stop with a large red double-decker standing with the door open. I made for that but the driver had already sussed out the situation and shot round to help me, clouting one of the lads as he ran by. At this, I clung to the driver and cried. He was so kind and cleaned my bruises, then asked me where I lived. I told him the address and he sat me down in his bus, closed the doors and drove me right to my house. My mother was frantic but so grateful to the bus driver, who accepted a cup of tea and left after giving me a big hug.

While I loved school I enjoyed my dance and drama classes even more. As soon as I could walk, Mum enrolled me in the local dance school, which was run by a lovely lady called Mavis Levy. By the time I was three I regularly appeared in all the school's productions, singing, dancing and acting. I wasn't shy and I loved it all, especially as it so often involved dressing up in pretty outfits. In fact, such was my passion for the costumes that on one occasion I was willing to turn to crime to get my hands on a particular favourite.

I was standing backstage behind another four-year-old wannabe, who was about to go on for a ballet number. She was wearing the most beautiful pink sequinned tutu, which I had been coveting. In a moment of jealous fury when no one was looking, I gave her a shove. Unfortunately she tumbled down the two stone steps leading to the dressing rooms and sprained her ankle. Her shrieks of pain brought the adults running, and my wish was granted: I was given the tutu and sent onstage to do the dance in her place. I was thrilled, but my triumph was short-lived because as soon as I came offstage I was very aware of fingers pointing from those in the know. My dastardly deed having been discovered, I was immediately suspended from the show for several nights.

Through this experience I learned yet another invaluable lesson in life: envy is bad, get there by your own efforts and not through someone else's misfortune. And so I did: soon afterwards I was doing a regular star turn, wearing a long Victorian dress and a huge hat as 'Little Miss Lady Make-Believe', singing 'You've Gotta Have Heart'. I was very proud of this achievement because I wanted to be a singer like Dad, but sadly, as far as singing was concerned, this turned out to be my finest hour and since then I've never quite matched it. Despite my best efforts, and to my great disappointment, I don't have an amazing singing voice (in fact, people have been known to stuff fingers in their ears when I launch into song) and once I'd outgrown the cuteness factor that was that.

Although singing wasn't my foremost talent, I loved it, and especially when I got to sing with my dad. He was still crooning à la Bing Crosby and sometimes he would take me along to gigs and we'd duet together: our favourite was 'Something Stupid', the song made famous by father-and-daughter duo Frank and Nancy Sinatra. Dad had a wonderful singing voice and so, despite my less-than-perfect pitch, together we were a good act.

I was a good dancer, though, and I loved dancing just as much as singing, if not more. My mother would make me sweet little outfits and I would tap or pirouette my way across the stage in show after show. Mum would drive me to wherever we were performing, my costumes piled in the back of the car. She was very proud and encouraged me to perform not only by making my costumes and ferrying me about but clapping enthusiastically in the audience, too.

My talent for comedy also emerged early, completely by accident. Aged four and a half, I was due to open a show with a tap routine in my little white skirt, red blazer and tap shoes. Unfortunately I was desperate for a wee but there wasn't time for me to go before I had to be on stage. Unable to hold it in, I did a big wee in front of everybody. The audience fell about, but I was in no mood to enjoy it: I fled in tears, my big moment ruined.

It wasn't until years later that I learned to love making people laugh and made my mark as a comic actress. Perhaps this was prophetic because despite my best intentions I was always getting involved in things that went wrong.

When I was six I had a couple more brushes with crime, this time trying my hand at embezzlement. I decided to start a tea club for my friends and managed to persuade five little girls to go home and extract half a crown each (a considerable sum of money in those days) from their mothers. In return for handing the cash over to me, I told them that they would each get a badge made from cardboard, a sugar sandwich and a drink of pop. Delighted with my haul, I stashed the half crowns in my dolls' pram, dipping into the money every now and again to buy one of my favourite sherbet dips – you know the kind, with a liquorice straw – from the corner shop.

I might have got away with this little piece of fraud had it not been for another scheme of mine a few weeks later. One afternoon I informed my friends that we would put on a bring-and-buy sale for Oxfam, which meant they had to extract more money from their mothers. When I told my mother the same thing, she said, 'That's a good idea – I'll help you put up some trestle tables and we'll sort out lots of clothes and bric-à-brac,' and she went on to invite the whole village.

I can't remember now actually how much profit we made on the day but it would have been a considerable sum and everyone believed they were doing their bit for charity. I, on the other hand, had only sherbet dips on the brain and went on to stash the proceeds in my dolls' pram together with the remains of the previous haul. Ten sherbet dips, boxes of sweet cigarettes and many packets of wagon wheels later, I was one very happy little girl.

A couple of weeks on, a friend's mother asked Mum how much money we'd raised. Being so busy, my mother assumed that Dad had taken care of the funds. As they say, the truth will out, and so it did, big time. Everything came to light: my tea-club member scam and of course the great Oxfam scandal. Now in my eyes I wasn't stealing: this was enterprise. With the tea club the girls got treats, and the bring-and-buy would have been potentially worthy had I remembered to send the profit to wherever it was supposed to go. In fact, I had only borrowed a bit for the sweets, which I thought was fair enough given the hard work I'd put in, but that wasn't quite the way my mother saw it. All was paid back, my tea club closed down forever and I was never made an Ambassador for Oxfam – another lesson for this wayward child to learn.

I never was very good at practical matters, perhaps because like Dad I was a bit of a dreamer. From the earliest age I lived much of my life in a fantasy world surrounded by imaginary friends. This wasn't because I was a lonely child or didn't have any other children to play with; it was simply a world of my own that I loved to be in. I used to carry on conversations with people who lived under the floorboards, or in the walls or underneath my bed – I would feel them tugging at my hand or leg, or hear them knocking on the floor. I'd talk to them for hours: there would be tears and laughter and arguments. It sounds strange but it was only the same as the little plays I would write and perform in my grandma's house. I'd be every character, changing hats and voices as I swapped sides in a conversation.

I don't think the adults around me were aware of this private world. While many children have highly creative imaginations, sadly as we reach adulthood we leave that innocence behind. And so I kept my secret friends to myself and chatted to them when no one else was around.

We were lucky to have a television at a time when many families were unable to afford one and I loved watching the children's programmes because they fuelled me with yet more ideas, but books were my real passion: I am a bookaholic. My dream was to one day have my own library – I'm still working on that one. Back then, I would imagine the characters jumping out of the book and me being part of their world before they disappeared back into the pages. I loved all the animated shows and cartoons: I would have liked to work in the world of animation, given the chance. I adored going to the cinema and could well believe I was up there on that screen in whatever film it was: I might be Dorothy in *The Wizard of Oz* or Alice living in Wonderland. At one time I even wanted to be John-Boy in *The Waltons* although that was more to do with the big-family thing than being a boy. Later still, in my teens, I fancied being Doris Day in all those films with Rock Hudson or Ginger Rogers with Fred Astaire, and then of course there was Audrey Hepburn with the wonderful Cary Grant.

Pretending to be someone else was as natural to me as breathing. I couldn't imagine a place where I just had to be myself, and so for me it was a natural progression from a make-believe world into the exciting world of acting.

Chapter Two

When I was six we moved to a large and beautiful house in the pretty village of Burton Joyce, on the other side of Nottingham. My mother had worked hard doing up our last house: walls were knocked down to create larger rooms and she then decorated and improved before selling on for a healthy profit so we could move up in the world. Our new home was detached, double-fronted and gabled; it had its own grounds, outhouses and driveway as well as an impressive flight of steps leading up to the front door. Inside were six bedrooms and spacious living rooms, perfect for the lavish parties my parents loved to hold.

The house cost £8,000, which was a vast sum in the early fifties, but Mum and Dad worked hard and had also been enterprising, plus they'd had a major stroke of luck. My father bought a clothing firm that had gone into liquidation and he inherited all the stock, which filled ten enormous lorries. He saw an opportunity to make a lot of money selling the stock on. At this point my mother held a very senior position at the French cosmetics firm Orlane but she chose to sacrifice her career to help run the business. And so they rented a three-storey factory with a shop underneath, which they named Joy's Boutique.

While Mum organised and ran the new shop, Dad (who could never have stayed in one place for a whole week) hired a team of people and set them up with vans full of stock to visit various markets in the country. On Saturdays I used to go with him. I loved standing behind the stall selling the clothes to shoppers, but we didn't make as many sales as we might have because we would stop for a long breakfast on the way. Mum used to tell me, 'Make sure your dad gets to the stall by seven – you must get there early.' We'd both promise to do so and then Dad would drive us to his favourite transport café, where he would enjoy a full English while I had tea and baked beans. We'd tuck in and Dad would say, 'Don't tell your Mum.' Afterwards he'd play the one-armed bandit while I watched and we'd eventually get to the stall around midday.

Inevitably Mum found out, probably because the takings were not what they ought to have been, but in any case Dad was bored by then and so he let other people take over that side of the business. I don't think he was a lot of help: he would go off in search of new stock or on some other escapade, leaving Mum to do most of the work. She must have felt impatient with him because so much of the responsibility for our lives, our home and our income fell on her shoulders. They did have rows and on one occasion I remember her throwing a boiled egg at him, but it missed and hit a very hot radiator. Fortunately it was painted yellow, as the runny egg stuck like glue and stayed there for a long time.

My parents didn't actually spend a lot of time together – at home they were often at opposite ends of the house and during the day Dad would disappear on some mission while Mum would be left running the shop. She made it into a really successful business and now not only did we live in a beautiful house with a swimming pool, stables and a mini golf course but we had a gorgeous pink and white Cresta with wings on the back, a Mercedes coupé, a violet MGB (custom-built for my mother) and a Jaguar. Little wonder I had a passion for cars when I grew older.

Mum's determination was awesome. We always had a house full of dogs, and one day she decided to breed them. We mainly had poodles so she bred a miniature version, which turned out to be another success. I adored the poodles, especially the puppies, which I would tuck into my dolls' pram and then pet and fuss over for hours. I'm not sure if they enjoyed this quite so much because I was fairly strict and would insist they stayed put, shoving them back into the pram whenever they dared to try and escape.

Dad was a bit of a soft touch around the poodles. When one little white puppy was born with deformed legs, the vet told us that it ought to be put down, but Dad insisted on keeping her as a family pet. We called her Dinkum and although she had to walk on her elbows she managed just fine and lived to the ripe old age of 20.

At the tender age of seven Brett was packed off to a boarding school called The Rodney, a few miles away in a village called Kirklington. I was six when he left home, and after that I only saw him when he came back for the holidays and so for much of the time I felt as if I was an only child. I missed my brother very much when he went away despite the fact that he and his friends often teased and tormented me. They were rough-and-tumble little boys and, although a bit of tomboy myself, I was an easy target. And, to compound the problem, Mum often told Brett to keep an eye on me so I had to tag along with him and his friends. Unfortunately, the 'games' they thought hilarious frequently left me petrified.

One day they took me to the local recreation ground, where some distance from the swings and roundabouts was a large tree covered in gruesome-looking fungus. I had been extremely wary of this tree ever since Brett had told me that the fungus was poisonous and whoever touched it would die a horrible death. Clearly desperate to dump me so they could run off and play, the boys decided to tie me to the tree. They knotted some belts and ties together and after a brief Indian war dance with plenty of whooping, they bound me to the tree. But I wasn't touching the fungus (they had left a small gap and this meant that if I stood up straight I could avoid it) and before they ran off and left me they warned that if I shouted or struggled I would touch the fungus and die instantly.

More scared of the fungus than anything else, I stood straining at my bonds, desperately hoping they hadn't meant it and would come back, but too scared even to shout out. It was Dad who eventually found me, what seemed like hours later. By that time my knees were sagging and I was in serious danger of collapsing against the fungus so I burst into floods of hysterical tears.

Brett couldn't sit down for a week after that incident but it didn't stop him from planning more assault-course tortures whenever he wanted to get rid of me. He used to climb up trees, haul me up after him and then clamber down and leave me sitting on a branch, too high up to get down on my own. Sometimes he remembered and came back for me (once after a game of football, I remember), but on other occasions he forgot all about me and it was some astonished adults passing by underneath who spotted me clinging on for dear life and helped me get down.

And it was another kind adult who came to my rescue on the day when Brett couldn't resist pushing me, fully clothed, into the swimming pool. Mum loved to swim, and long before we moved and had a pool of our own installed she sometimes took us with her to the local pool. On this occasion, aged four, I was standing beside the pool and wearing a pretty cotton dress when Brett gave me a shove and I hit the deep end. I remember the water closing over my head as my skirt floated up around me: I sank down and down until, thankfully, strong arms grabbed me and I was hauled out, choking and spluttering.

The incident so terrified me that I could never bear having water over my head and I refused to take a shower until I was 15, prefering baths. I did eventually learn to swim but despite my best efforts, the phobia has remained with me and even now I won't go in the sea, if I go to the beach.

Of course Brett, who was only six himself at the time, had no idea how much this would affect me. He probably didn't even stop to wonder whether I could swim: he himself was a good swimmer and he and his friends would push one another into the pool without a second thought, to emerge laughing and splashing. I'm sure he expected me to do the same. When my father built our swimming pool in the back garden (which was in itself hilarious as he and a gang of my boyfriends dug the foundations), it was all done to the right specifications but Dad didn't bother to seal it and although it was quite a large pool we would often come down in the morning to find half the water had disappeared. We'd fill it up again and again, but half the water would be gone by the next day – no one ever worked out where it was going. Despite this, the pool gave us a lot of joy and we had many noisy parties.

Funnily enough, my father hated water and never went swimming, so perhaps my fear was genetic and being pushed in simply made it worse. He built the pool for Mum – it was she who loved swimming – and she was an excellent swimmer and even took part in synchronised displays. You know, the kind where you put a peg on your nose and perform a graceful underwater routine in perfect synch with others.

After the swimming-pool débâcle, Brett turned his attention to acrobatics and insisted I join in as his assistant. He liked to make me stand on his shoulders or balance on his knees as he floated on his back and he would also spin me round, faster and faster, by my wrists or ankles. I was always wary of this but he was my brother and so I had no choice. Usually, I would become terrified halfway through the trick, at which point he would insist I carry on.

Things came to a head, literally, one day as I attempted to balance with one foot on his knee. I wobbled about, lost my balance and came crashing down, hitting my head against the sharp corner of a wall. My forehead was sliced open and blood gushed everywhere, but even as I sat howling with pain, I knew Brett was for it and I would get all the sympathy. Most probably terrified, he tried to mop up the blood on my face with the sleeve of his jumper. Mum came running in from the kitchen to witness this gory scene while I of course lapped up every minute of it.

She rushed me off to our local doctor, whose name happened to be Hutchinson (the same as ours). In those days you had the same doctor for most of your life and all the family went to him. As Brett cowered in the corner, the doctor cleaned me up and decided my injury looked far worse than it was. I had to have stitches, though, and I still have the scar. The doctor made sure Brett was well and truly sorry while I revelled in the drama of it all.

Although I liked our doctor (who was stern but friendly), the dentist was altogether another matter. The first time my mother took me to see him I was placed in an huge black leather chair and there were shiny instruments everywhere. A man in a white coat opened my mouth – which I closed again very sharply, catching his finger. He shouted something at me and then the next thing I knew there was a hissing sound and an enormous black mask loomed in front of me. I tried to get out of the chair but an ugly fat woman, sweating profusely, held me down and the mask was put over my face. Then came the smell of the gas – a metallic stench that made me feel quite sick.

The next thing I knew I was waking up with the fat woman poking at my shoulders. As the dentist bent down and peered at me with his foul breath and strangely bad teeth, he said, 'Come on, girl – open your mouth,' and tried to prise my lips apart. The projectile vomit hit first him and then the wall in front of me with such velocity that it must have been the equivalent of a turbo-charged paint stripper. Disgusted, they threw me out and told my mother not to bring her ungrateful little brat back. The whole episode was truly a *Little Britain* nugget.

As for Brett, he could be my tormentor but he was also the big brother who looked out for me. So when he went away looking so small in his smart red and grey uniform, with a big trunk stashed in the back of the car, I felt very sad. Without him there to thump up the stairs or shout down from the landing, the house fell silent and still. More than ever, I began to rely on my imaginary world, having endless conversations with make-believe friends.

I could have asked friends over, and sometimes I did, but mostly I played on my own. And there were always adults around: my grandparents came over a lot and often looked after me when Mum and Dad were out, but they tended to leave me to get on with my own games.

I adored my grandparents. My maternal Grandma Nancy (whom I called 'Nanna') was always very elegant and dressed beautifully. I remember her in a blue dress with a little collar and cuffs, pearls around her neck, her pure-white hair neatly permed. Her skin was baby-soft and remarkably unlined, probably due to the healthy additive-free food they ate plus the fact that she didn't smoke, drink or sunbathe. She was kind and loving and adored dancing, while Granddad was tall, creative and very emotional.

When I stayed with them for dinner Nanna always gave Granddad his meal first. Like the three bears, he would have the biggest dinner, then Nanna and then me. If it happened to be something I really liked, such as mashed potato, I would look longingly over at Granddad's huge portion until Nanna went out to the kitchen, whereupon he would quickly spoon some of his mash onto my plate and wink at me as she came back in. I loved their bed: it was a proper sprung one and when you were in it you rolled into the middle. And I also adored their open coal fire – I have lovely memories of nestling in Granddad's lap in my woolly dressing gown on a winter's night and listening to the sounds of Nanna knitting, the fire crackling and cheeky schoolboy Jimmy Clitheroe on the radio.

Mum was always close to her parents so they came to us almost every weekend and often I would go to their house in the school holidays when she had to work. Nanna and Granddad also came with us to our caravan, which was on a permanent site on the East Coast, between Skegness and Mablethorpe. I absolutely loved that caravan: to me, it seemed the perfect home with everything we needed packed neatly into tiny spaces and seats that turned into beds at night. For me, it was heaven – a proper grown-up dolls' house.

Later, we started to go abroad for holidays and Mum once drove the pink-and-white Cresta all the way to Spain – which took a few days and was quite something then. We used to go and stay in Tossa de Mar, north of Barcelona. At that time it was just a small village with one hotel so they certainly hadn't seen anything like this enormous flashy car with wings on the back driving into the little sandy bay. I think they believed we were aliens because the villagers would simply stand and stare. Our hotel was a gorgeous 1920s building, very glamorous, which was used as a location in an Ava Gardner film. I'm glad I got to see Spain when it was so unspoilt.

When we moved to our house in Burton Joyce, I had to leave Dorothy Grants (which was some distance away) and instead was enrolled in the little village primary school, where I stayed until I was 11. Though saddened to leave the school where I'd been so happy, one consolation was the fact that we now had stables at our house and I soon developed a life-long passion for horses. Indeed, I was crazy about them and lucky enough to have a horse of my own. My first horse was a sturdy mountain pony called Tinto, a bay with a black stripe down his back, and I loved him dearly. Patient and friendly, I felt he was my best friend and, yes, I would talk to him for hours. On very hot days he would sometimes lie down in the paddock behind the house and I would go and lie on his tummy.

I quickly learned to ride, and before I turned 7, I was a competent bareback rider, using only a rope halter and no rein. By then I thought nothing of going off alone on Tinto – in fact, I would often ride him down to the village shop, buy some sweets while he waited patiently outside and then ride back.

When I was 10 my parents took me to visit one of their clothing suppliers, a lady who lived in a village some distance away. She showed me the paddock behind her house and introduced me to her little racing pony, Whiskey. He was very young and hadn't yet got used to a saddle but she let me ride him and we got along fine. Of course I fell in love and begged my parents to buy him for me. Generously, they agreed, and Mum said we could come back the following day with the horsebox to take him home. Typical me, I was having none of it: I didn't want to wait, I was eager to take him home right away.

'I'll ride him home,' I announced.

'But it's 22 miles,' countered Mum. 'That's too far for you and for the pony.'

I wasn't giving up, though, and eventually my parents agreed to let me ride him home, with them following behind in the car. We did it, but what a crazy stunt – it took so long that it grew dark. Whiskey and I plodded along in the car's headlights. Home at last, Whiskey was bedded down in the stable, thankfully none the worse for his adventure because a ride that long might have damaged his legs. As for me, I was jubilant at having made it back with him, but completely exhausted.

The next day I set out to introduce Whiskey to Tinto (who was in the field behind the stables). As we approached, Tinto looked round at Whiskey and then at me. Nostrils flared and eyes blazing, he began galloping towards us. I backed out of the field fast! Tinto was jealous and most definitely not coming over to make friends with Whiskey. In fact, I think he had murder on his mind.

From then on, Tinto was like a spoilt child whose nose has been put out of joint. He was so aggressive towards Whiskey that it was months before we could put them in the field together. When we eventually did so, Whiskey held his own with Tinto (who stopped trying to bully him) and the two became partners in crime. Together, they escaped from their field and destroyed the graveyard next door, something that got them – and us – into all sorts of trouble.

One evening, a couple of years after I got Whiskey, I was mucking out in the stable when I heard a loud thud, followed by a deep shudder and sigh.

'What was *that*?' I asked the friend who was with me, too scared to look.

'It's Whiskey,' she told me, after peering into his stable. 'He's lying on the ground and he doesn't look right.'

I rushed in to find Whiskey lying down, which was unusual as horses seldom do this. Immediately, I convinced myself that he had a twisted gut (which can be fatal) and so I ran back to the house to phone the vet, certain my beloved pony was dying. The vet told me that he wouldn't be able to come out for some time and so I settled down to wait beside Whiskey, gently placing an arm around him and resting my head on one side of his rib cage. He remained perfectly still, not moving a muscle, and after what seemed hours I fell asleep and was oblivious to Mum, who came in every now and then to check on us.

When the vet eventually arrived, early the next morning, I got up to tell him what had happened, and to my amazement Whiskey suddenly stirred, blew through his nose and got up.

After looking him over, the vet said: 'There's absolutely nothing wrong with this horse.'

'But I don't understand,' I said. 'He was so ill and he didn't move a muscle all night.'

'How could he?' he laughed. 'You were lying on top of him and he was clearly too much of a gentleman to disturb you.'

I was so happy to learn that Whiskey was fine that I didn't even mind feeling a complete idiot for calling out the vet to a horse who was apparently just taking a nap.

Not only was Whiskey totally fine, he continued to be in the best of health for the next few years. I rode both him and Tinto almost daily, rushing in after school to see them and take them treats. And I was a totally fearless rider: I loved jumping and would career around the paddock, going over our homemade jumps or take off for long rides in the local lanes.

Sadly, my riding career came to an abrupt end when I was 16 years old and had an accident on Tinto. He had a bad habit of stopping every now and then, lowering his head so that I slid off down his neck. He'd done this a few times, but never when he was moving fast, and so I'd simply scold him and climb back on. This time, though, we were riding by the river when something spooked him. From a gentle trot, he launched into a madcap gallop but suddenly stopped and lowered his head so that I shot straight off him and hit the ground hard. I might have got away with a few nasty bruises, had my foot not been caught up in the stirrup. Meanwhile, Tinto took off again, dragging me along the ground with him. No doubt realising something was wrong, he didn't go far, and once he'd stopped I was able to disentangle myself.

I was hurting all over but somehow I managed to get hold of the reins. Limping and in pain, I very slowly and carefully led him home. Once he was safely in his stable, I told Mum what had happened and she took me to the doctor. Luckily, no bones were broken: I was just grazed, battered and bruised. Unfortunately the accident made me fearful in a way I'd never been before, and although I did ride again I was never able to recapture the same fearless joy. Now I was cautious and the horses could smell my fear and subsequently played up.

Despite the accident, I never stopped loving horses. I haven't lost that addiction to the sniff of a saddle, as I call it – horsey readers out there will know exactly what I mean. Horses are still very special to me and I have a close connection with a horse sanctuary in Oswaldtwistle, Lancashire: Only Foals and Horses. For many of the horses and ponies there, the sanctuary is the only safe place they have ever known. Many have suffered fear, pain and mistreatment. Some, including newborn foals dumped when their mothers were sold, have been rescued from auctions, where they were being sold for meat. I do what I can to help, and when Carol McGiffin (my fellow presenter on *Loose Women*) and I won £75,000 on *Celebrity Who Wants to be a Millionaire?* I was able to donate my half to the sanctuary.

Back in the days when I lived for my horses I couldn't bear to be separated from them for longer than twenty-four hours and so, when my parents decided that I should join Brett at boarding school (at the age of 11), naturally I was horrified.

Boarding school? Not if I had anything to do with it.

Chapter Three

The problem was that I'd failed my 11 Plus. Well, to be fair, I didn't even know the test we took one day was all that important. I'd sit through most lessons gazing out of the window, not listening. To this day, I still have nightmares of sitting at that desk, not having done my homework, with not a clue as to what anyone is talking about. I always blame the teachers and too many kids to a class. It was a shame, though it meant I couldn't get into any of the good local schools, so it was the secondary modern or boarding school for me.

My parents took me on another visit to Brett's school (it was a boys' school, but they were just starting to allow female siblings in) and it was 300 boys to 20 girls. I was shown the dormitory in the small girls' wing, which had been placed as far away as possible from the boys' section of the school.

One look at that dorm settled it: I wasn't going to share a room with several other girls I didn't know. I'd always hated school, so how on earth could I go and *live* in one? My parents agreed that I could attend the school as a day pupil; it involved an hour-long journey each way, but for me this was a much better option. And so it was that in the autumn of 1962, just before I turned 12, I set off for The Rodney School in my smart red and grey uniform. I loved the uniform and the ballet lessons, and once in a while we would have dances in the big hall. The boys would sit on one side of the room, the girls on the other; the boys would have to come over and ask us to dance and it was all very formal but we got to wear pretty party frocks, which was the bit I liked.

The grounds were absolutely beautiful and on hot summer days our school fairs were fantastic. I also remember having choral concerts outside. It's funny how the summers seemed longer and hotter when we were young. It was an amazing school and I wish I could have appreciated it more and enjoyed my time there, but I didn't. In fact, I used to do everything I could to get out of school, including perfecting the art of making myself ill. I was so good at it that I could even throw up when occasion demanded it. I'd then be allowed to skip school – or be sent home if I'd actually made it thus far – and would be put to bed, clutching my stomach and gently moaning. Once I was safely installed and the coast was clear, I'd settle down with a comic or the TV and enjoy my day, then make a miraculous recovery in time to go out and see the horses in the afternoon.

Eventually realising that they were wasting their money, my parents took me out of school and placed me in the local secondary modern. The classes were huge, so I could sit at the back and do nothing, and that's exactly what I did: nothing. My best friend was a girl called Sue Maddern, who was strong and full of self-confidence. I was bullied when I got there because I'd come from a posh school, so I teamed up with her and became a bit of a smart arse. It was self-protection: I'd never forgotten the beating I had as a 6-year-old and I wasn't about to let it happen again. Having said that, I made a few lifelong friends there and have some good memories of those days.

While school felt like a waste of time, once I joined the local theatre club at the age of 11 I absolutely loved it. The club, which was based in the aptly named Shakespeare Street, was great fun and I couldn't wait to go there every week. I also joined a drama class at Clarendon College in Nottingham, run by a man named Allen Tipton, who became a mentor and friend to me. He was a brilliant teacher, who got us kids organised into one production after another and managed to bring out the best in all of us. This was, coincidentally, where Robert Lindsay (who was my boyfriend at RADA) started his drama education, although we didn't know one another there.

By the age of 13 all that mattered to me, apart from my horses, was drama. I was also a member of the Burton Joyce Players in our village and had my first female lead in their production of *The Seventh Veil*, based on the famous film starring Ann Todd and James Mason. I played a young girl – Francesca – a pianist, with an obsessive Uncle Nicholas (played by the vicar, who was brilliant). When she tries to run away, he smashes his cane down on her hands and virtually cripples her, so she is a broken woman.

At the same time I joined the Midland Academy, a local drama school run by a wonderful woman called Miss Audrey Albrecht. This was the beginning of my formal training, in readiness for an eventual audition for RADA. Miss Albrecht was passionate about poetry and insisted I enter all the Poetry Society as well as the many LAMDA examinations, and while this seemed like hard work at the time it stood me in great stead.

After leaving school I attended the Academy full-time, from 16 to 18, and during that time I passed numerous poetry and drama exams. I adored Miss Albrecht, who became in some ways like a second mother to me. She was firm and extremely demanding, but I never minded because she believed in me, and along with Allen Tipton she played a big part in shaping my future. At the same time, my own mother insisted I attend finishing classes, where I learnt how to sit properly and walk beautifully, how to close a door behind me without turning around, how to get out of a car elegantly with no knickers showing and, of course, how to speak properly.

With all this going on my life was incredibly full – I think maybe it was Mum's way of delaying my interest in boys. I had the Theatre Club, Allen Tipton's classes, school, the Burton Joyce Players and the Midland Academy, so I was almost always rehearsing for or appearing in a production. It was a wonderful grounding, and by the age of 15 I was determined to make a career on the stage. Actually, it was seeing Julie Andrews in *The Sound of Music* that finally nailed my decision.

The school had other ideas, though: when I told my careers teacher that I wanted to be an actress she just laughed and told me to stop living in dreamland. Who did I think I was, Doris Day? Well yes, actually. Careers advisers were like that then: they advised the boys to go into engineering and the girls to train as secretaries. They made me feel so ridiculous that I thought, OK, I *will* go and train as a secretary just to prove that I can do it.

Mother was ambitious for me and I'm sure she only agreed to the secretarial training as an insurance policy. She found a private course held in a large Edwardian semi. On the first morning I turned up at the address I'd been given and was shown into a room by a small, rotund lady – not very happy, really quite odd. There was a long table in the middle and six big black typewriters on either side. Three girls were already on one side, two on the other, and I was shown to the empty place. A very tall and sinewy-looking man with a face like thunder walked in, obviously in charge. He stood at the end of the table and lifted one hand up while glancing at a watch on his other wrist. As a clock chimed, he brought his hand down hard on the table, which made me jump and giggle. He then came over and without saying a word showed me what I was supposed to do, and left me to it. I remember he smelled of camphor oil, like bandages.

I started, but the big black keys were very temperamental: you'd hit them and they would shoot back or get stuck. The Lurcher look-alike came over and without looking at me uttered his only word that day: 'Rhythm.' Furiously pulling out all the keys now jammed in the machine, he repeated himself. I did my best to hold in a giggle but as he was walking away he turned sharply and flashed his eyes at me, which stopped me in my tracks. During the allotted two hours I'd asked to go to the loo (which was apparently not allowed), I'd asked for a drink of water (also not allowed) and now my keys were permanently stuck in a criss-crossed heap inside the machine. By this time I was hysterical with suppressed laughter and the other girls were trying hard not to join in. 'Lurch' was red-faced with anger and the small woman who had shown me in (presumably his wife) hustled me out of the room and sent me home, telling me as she did so that I was disturbing the other girls.

Five days later I went back for another try. The small woman opened the door and stared at me with anger in her eyes. She then told me that her husband had died due to stress and the lessons were cancelled, as if it was my fault. After that, I gave up the quest to become a secretary.

It was my one and only attempt to learn a practical skill. Afterwards I told my mother that I wanted to go to drama school and she backed me 100 per cent. I'm not sure which of us was more determined that I would make it, but while I gave my all to acting, other distractions threatened to derail my efforts: boys had arrived on the scene.

I always got on well with boys and seemed to attract them, but until I was 15 I had no romantic interest in them at all. I was a bit of a tomboy and as far as I was concerned boys were pals. They could be fun, sometimes they were noisy and smelly, but mostly I just enjoyed having them around.

My closest male friend from school was Gordon Lewingdon. We got on really well and often he came round to my house. I thought of him as a mate, so it only dawned on me much later that Gordon loved me. I was horrible to him, thoughtless and mean, flirting with all the other boys from the village who used to congregate at my house, but I adored him too. Oh, the fickleness of youth! We both fooled around and kissed a bit, but nothing more – I'm not sure I knew what 'more' was at that stage.

Years later, when I bumped into Gordon, he agreed that I'd treated him badly. He told me he had a doll that he used to pretend was me and he would stick pins in it! He was, and still is, a lovely man and we will always be friends.

But Gordon wasn't my only suitor (I had several) and when I was just 13 he and three other boys actually followed me on holiday to Wales. Gordon had told me that he couldn't bear to be away from me for a whole week and I was happy for them to come along. They wanted to cycle all the way to Wales from Nottingham but their parents insisted they went part of the journey on the train. They arrived soon after my family and me, setting up tents in a nearby field, but a deluge of rain swamped their camp. Late that night they turned up at our hotel looking like drowned rats. Mum couldn't leave them with nowhere to sleep, so she paid for a room, but put them on the train home the next day.

We were a proper gang in Burton Joyce and went everywhere together but mainly hung out at my house because I had the pool. There was Gordon, Chas, Dave, Steve, Ian and John, plus a few others over the years. Every now and then I was asked out by each of them in turn, but I wanted a gang, not a boyfriend. I'd ride my horse and my little entourage would follow on their bikes. I did go on a couple of dates with a boy from school called Dave (because he looked like Paul McCartney) and then there was Rob, whom I adored. Rob had a guitar and was in a band, which was a definite plus. He was a Mod (you were either with the Mods or Rockers and I was a Mod girl), so he was perfect for me, but sadly, young love faded away.

My first real boyfriend was Robbie Tate. Blond, blue-eyed and gorgeous, we met when we were both 15 and I was immediately smitten. We started seeing each other as much as we could and I would often skip drama or ballet classes to be with him. When my mother found out, she did her best to stop the romance, telling me that I mustn't see him because classes were more important. Of course that only encouraged me all the more: seeing Robbie in secret was even more fun, although I didn't dare miss too many classes. He would wait for me outside class and we'd go for a walk, then stop for a kiss and a cuddle.

I worked for several months backstage at the Nottingham Playhouse, helping out with productions and as an usherette. As well as the joy of earning £3 10s a day, I got to see the stars backstage. And there were real stars there because the artistic director was John Neville, a former leading member of London's Old Vic, who had played many big classical roles before becoming a director. He had immense pulling power and brought a series of established actors to Nottingham, turning it into one of the finest repertory theatres in the country. Among many others, I got to meet Elizabeth Taylor, Richard Burton, John

Huston, Ronald Reagan and Charlton Heston. Young and hungry for success, for me it was magical. I remember sitting on the floor in a discreet corner of the stage completely spellbound while watching Judi Dench rehearse her part as St Joan in *Joan of Arc*.

Our junior Theatre Club was also extremely busy, producing a stream of plays and musicals, and I was still involved with Allen Tipton's drama group. The most successful production of Allen's that I was in was *West Side Story* when I was 15. I played Anita, one of the lead roles, when we took it to London in a drama festival, where we beat dozens of other groups to win the Lawrence Olivier Shield.

Soon afterwards we took the play to the open-air Minack Theatre in Porthcurno, West Cornwall. The theatre is constructed above a gully with a rocky outcrop jutting into the sea, and it's a truly spectacular location. We arrived in Cornwall during a hot summer and I remember getting very burnt and phoning home to tell Mum the sun had wrinkled my face so much that I looked really old, probably at least 25, and I was thrilled. Considering my later fascination with cosmetic surgery, it seems ironic that I was so desperate to look older.

All this was immense fun and the perfect backdrop for my budding romance with Robbie, which culminated when I was 16 in me losing my virginity to him in a passionate clinch on the kitchen floor of our house! You have to be 16 for that to seem romantic, but to us it was. After that we'd sleep together whenever we could, though sadly the opportunities were few and far between.

The only experience of sex that I'd had before was at a late-night party my brother had reluctantly taken me to, where a boy asked me to go upstairs with him. We went into the bathroom and he got out some sort of balloon-type thing, then fumbled around trying to undo my bra while reaching down to release the waiting wriggling worm, at which point I just thought, I don't want that thing anywhere near me – and made a run for it!

I thought my romance with Robbie was perfect. He even gave me a ring, which I wore on my engagement finger. Then one day I walked into a bar to see him sitting on a stool, kissing a blonde girl. It wasn't even a peck on the cheek, this was a full-on snog, and at that moment my heart broke. I stood watching them, consumed with the pain of his betrayal.

When Robbie turned and saw me, he had the gall to come over and tell me that I had imagined it. But I hadn't, and for me the romance was over. Loyalty means a great deal to me: I'm a fiercely loyal person and I expect those I love and care about to offer the same loyalty. If I'm betrayed, that's it: there's no second chance, a brick wall goes up and then it's over – I don't even want to be friends.

From then on I barely spoke to Robbie. Deep down I still loved him, but I just couldn't forgive him. One day, a couple of years later when I was at drama school, he turned up. He told me he missed me and asked if we could get back together again, but by that time I had met someone else and I wasn't interested. He then asked for his ring back, but I told him I'd lost it. I'd actually sold it, for a couple of pounds, when he broke my heart. After that I didn't see him again.

There was one other boy I went on a couple of dates with when I was 16. He worked in a shop down the road from Mum's boutique. I used to help out in the boutique on Saturdays and he would walk past the window and stare in. Like Robbie, he was blond, blue-eyed and handsome, but I found his stare slightly unnerving and would look away or busy myself folding clothes. One day he came into the shop, introduced himself and started chatting to Mum. She liked him and invited him to tea at our house.

'Why did you do that?' I asked, after he'd left.

Surprised, she looked at me. 'He seemed like a nice boy,' she explained. 'He's only 19 and he's all alone here, his family live miles away. I thought he might be missing them.'

When he came round, a few days later, he was polite and charming. So when he asked me out I said yes. However, there was something about him, an intensity with which I felt uneasy. But still bruised and suffering over Robbie, I thought it might make me feel better to go out with someone else and so we went to the theatre. After this he continued to come to our house and ask me out. Mum couldn't understand why I didn't take to him.

One evening he arrived and told her that he'd had to leave his lodgings and so she offered to put him up until he could find somewhere else. I was furious, but Mum told me: 'He's only here for a few days – you don't have to go out with him.'

What she didn't realise was that he would come and meet me after rehearsals and performances, telling me that she had suggested he should walk me home, just to make sure I was safe. He was pleasant enough, but somehow I still didn't feel at ease with him. I would say, 'I'm not your girlfriend,' but he'd completely ignore me. Being a nice girl, I politely put up with his attentions, and this was something I would come to bitterly regret.

Chapter Four

Three years after winning the Laurence Olivier Shield, I was offered a scholarship to RADA in London. Words cannot describe how thrilled I was: it was the realisation of all my childhood dreams, but I couldn't have done it without the support of my mother and Miss Albrecht. Mum always believed I had it in me to become a successful actress, and she kept me focused. Whenever I was reminiscing about Robbie she would say to me: 'There are thousands of Robbies in the world but you belong on the stage.' And when I decided that I wanted to go to drama school, she told me: 'Then you might as well go to the best one in the world.'

As for Miss Albrecht – well, she taught me to believe in myself. She would say: 'You're a special girl and you're going to be a great actress.' So, although I wasn't at all academic and had got nowhere at school, I didn't feel like a failure because acting was something that seemed to come naturally to me and I loved it.

RADA (the Royal Academy of Dramatic Art) was regarded as the best school in the world. Its very name commands respect and fuels ambition in young would-be actors and actresses (and I was no exception). And so my audition, in which I had to perform three pieces, was nerve-racking to say the least. I had to wait six weeks afterwards to hear whether I'd made it, and when the letter arrived, telling me that I'd got in, there was huge excitement at home. For the next few weeks life was a frenzy of packing, planning and trepidation, bearing in mind I'd never lived away from home.

For me, the only sad part was that fulfilling my dreams meant leaving my boyfriend behind. After parting from Robbie, I had fallen for a lovely boy called Arthur Moseley. He was gorgeous and looked like a cross between a very young Tony Blackburn and a young Paul McCartney so he became responsible for what became a lifelong obsession with Paul.

Arthur was a few years older than me and already ran a very successful textile business with a partner. He also had a bright yellow E-type Jaguar and used to drive me around in it, which I thought was fab, but what really mattered was that we got on so well. We had great fun and he was kind and tender. Later I came to believe he was the true love of my life, the one I should have married but the one I was foolish enough to let go. Arthur made it very clear that he really didn't want me to leave to go to London, and, although torn, I was far too immature to handle the situation and so I left, dazzled by the bright lights of RADA and the even brighter ones of London. The world was about to become my oyster, or so I believed.

My relationship with Arthur didn't end there, though. We stayed in touch for many years and although nobody, least of all my first husband, knew about it, we remained deeply fond of each other and continued to speak on the telephone on a regular basis. That said, we were very mindful of not hurting other people, so the telephone was as far as it went.

Our relationship was a strange and enduring one. Sometimes we'd be on the phone for several hours and we'd talk until he eventually fell fast asleep. Much later, after we'd both had beautiful children in our respective marriages, we finally realised what we had lost in each other, but before we could do anything about it Arthur very suddenly died of a heart attack at the age of 42. Afterwards I was bereft, yet somehow I realised he was one of those people, like Marilyn Monroe and James Dean, who can never grow any older. I know that sounds strange but I genuinely believe some of us are destined to die while still in our prime, still young and beautiful.

I missed Arthur very much and thought of him often, but many years later the most wonderful thing happened. Having learned we had once been close friends, his daughter got in contact with me and we still write to each other, which is such a comfort after losing the true love of my life.

In January 1969 I started at RADA. The September before I had turned 18, but I was in so many ways far younger. I think my true age at that time was probably closer to 16. As I'd never before been away from home, my mother decided that I should live at the Bourne and Hollingsworth Hostel for Girls in Gower Street, two doors down from RADA. On arrival the day before the course started, suitcase in hand, I was distinctly unimpressed. The rooms were sparsely furnished like nuns' cells, with two iron beds in each one (both covered in puce green bedspreads); there were two sinks and two small chests of drawers apiece. Downstairs was an area where you could get a cup of tea and a few communal tables to sit at while drinking it.

There was a hefty matron, who had a moustache and wore a long, ill-fitting dress with a large chain of keys around her waist. Her shoes had rubber soles and as she stomped around they made a kind of farting noise, so that was the warning she was close by. The hostel had a strict 9.30pm curfew and we were warned that if we were not in by that time we'd be locked out. Every night the farting matron would come round, rap on the doors and ask: 'Are you in bed girls?' I don't doubt she made a note in her little black book if there was no answer. Of course I managed to get myself locked out on a number of occasions but as I had friends who lived in nearby Goodge Street I'd go round and sleep on their sofa. This was 1969, for God's sake. It was meant to be sex, drugs and rock 'n' roll. Not Matrons, boiled cabbage and big knickers!

I only stayed at the hostel for a few months and even then I spent as little time as possible there, so I never really got to know my roommate. As soon as I got the chance I moved into a flat in a tenement block in Camden with two friends from RADA. Sharon Maughan was from Liverpool and came from a big family. She was beautiful, with dark hair and eyes – she went on to star in the 'Gold Blend' coffee ads and married Trevor Eve. Louise Jameson, who starred in the fourth series of *Doctor Who* as Leela the Doctor's companion, had red hair and green eyes. She was the most gorgeous one of us – all the boys loved her.

We three had a great time in that flat, which was always covered in knickers and bras hanging up to dry because there wasn't a laundrette nearby. If boys were ever coming round these offending items were shoved in drawers, cupboards and under cushions. But the place cost a whopping £30 a week, which left us flat-broke and so we relied on friends to bring us food, particularly one boy who was expert at nicking frozen chickens from the local supermarket and somehow managed to smuggle them out to us under his coat. I'd go there sometimes and emerge with a 'pregnant' stomach under my coat, having stuffed everything from peanuts to loo paper in there.

This was the era of bell-bottoms and miniskirts, Beatles and Bowie; also pin-ups such as teen idols David Cassidy and Marc Bolan. People often say to me it must have been great living in London in the late Sixties and early Seventies. Free love, all night parties, a mad crazy time. Well, if it was, I must have gone out that day because I don't remember any of it. The craziest I got was to put cider into a pint of Guiness. I can't remember anyone around me taking drugs at parties either, though it's possible that it happened now and then but I just didn't notice. Certainly a few of my contemporaries have since told me there were drugs about, but no one ever offered me any.

As for sex, the late sixties were supposed to have been a wild time, with everyone at it. Where was I, you ask. Again, I blinked and missed it. But don't get me wrong: I did like boys, especially if they looked like Robbie or were carrying a guitar, and even further back than that I knew how to get an apple in the playground, or better still, a sherbet dip from a boy. It didn't seem to take much – a few bats of my eyelashes, an interest in their marbles, even a loan of my bicycle pump or a go on my rollerskates – but when it came to sex I never really understood what all the fuss was about and I'm not at all sure I do yet. All that mess for so little, as I always say on *Loose Women*.

At school, I remember boys and girls disappearing behind bike sheds but I could never quite fathom what they did back there. When I eventually discovered what it was about, it seemed such a palaver, too – all that fumbling, groping, sighing and squeaking. Maybe, as Michael Bublé might say: 'I just haven't met you yet.' I was much more interested in being Shirley Temple and, later, Debbie Reynolds or Doris Day. All those stars played the perfect girl-next-door – the kind of girl I wanted to be. For them there were no bedroom scenes, and if there happened to be any brief shots in a bedroom they were with Gene Kelly or

Rock Hudson – which was fine by me. And so in the era of 'free love' when London was known as the 'Sexiest City in the World' I appeared to be living on another planet. Now I'm not saying that I was altogether a Miss Goody Two-Shoes – I certainly wasn't that. Neither was I falling into bed with a different man every week or off my head on drugs, though.

In some ways, life was far simpler then. We had no mobiles so I would phone home every now and then from a payphone, and other than that my mum didn't have much idea what I was up to. We had no computers, so no social networking websites – we just bumped into people and got together for parties. The telly still had only three channels so it was pretty boring and, being drama students, we spent our time either acting in plays or going to see them.

Anyway, I loved RADA and soaked up the knowledge passed on to us by all the brilliant teachers, actors and directors there. Early on in my first year, however, I got a bit cocky and began to stretch the rules. I was treating it like high school, taking everything for granted, often going into classes late and sometimes skipping them altogether. I wasn't aware of how lucky I was to be there or how many hundreds of drama students would have loved to swap places with me ... at least not until the day when I walked in very late and was told to go and sit outside the Principal's office.

After leaving me to sweat for an hour and a quarter, Hugh Cruttwell called me in. By that stage I was in an abject state of terror, convinced I was about to be thrown out. With his dry wit, passion for the theatre and an eye for spotting potential, the legendary Principal was held in complete awe by us students, and as I stood in front of his desk he read me the riot act: 'How *dare* you come in late! Don't you know it's an honour to be here? I believed in you, but you've let me down ...' and so on.

By the end of his speech I was left in no doubt just how much trouble I was in. He finished up by saying, '... and if you get yourself together and work hard, I will consider keeping you next term.'

That was the kick up the bum I needed. Believing I was about to end my short time there and determined to show him how wrong he had been, I worked incredibly hard after that. I was never late, attended all my classes, took my acting very seriously and did so well that by the time I left RADA in the summer of 1971 I had won six awards, including the Ronson Award for Best Actress with a prize of 100 guineas. Of course this was exactly the response that Hugh Cruttwell was counting on. Years later he told me, 'I would never have thrown you out – I could see how much talent you had, I just thought I'd give you a fright.' And it worked.

One of the wonderful perks at RADA was that superstars would arrive as visiting lecturers. We met some incredibly famous people, but none more famous – or gorgeous – than heart-throb Steve McQueen, who turned up one day to talk to us about the art of acting. I can see him now. He was standing in front of the desk, and I was at the back. He had a very soft, mumbling American accent and we couldn't understand a word he said. But no one cared, he was delicious. At that time he was one of the biggest stars in Hollywood. A former reform-school kid, known as the 'King of Cool', he had starred in some hugely successful films including *The Magnificent Seven*, *The Great Escape* and *Bullitt*. He was also a dirt-bike rider and racing car driver who did his own stunts. You can't get much cooler than that. So, imagine how overwhelmed I felt after being chosen to show him around London. Of course I was in complete awe of him and fell totally in love: he was just so beautiful and I was dumbstruck.

Steve wanted to go on a London bus and so that's exactly what we did. People must have been gob-smacked to see Steve McQueen on a bus, but I never noticed because I was far too busy staring at him and thinking, I'm sitting with Steve McQueen, little me from Nottingham in my flowery dress and homemade love beads.

That evening Steve decided to take me to the Poissonnerie, a restaurant in Chelsea. Despite my French nursery education I didn't remember that 'poisson' meant fish. Unfortunately, I didn't discover this until it was too late as I'm violently allergic to seafood.

The place was exclusive and classy, all heads turned as Steve walked in and I was so proud to be his dinner companion. Sadly, the evening became memorable for all the wrong reasons. We sat at the bar on high stools, looking at the menus, and, being a gentleman, Steve offered to order for me. I was relieved as the menu was in French and I didn't know what most of the dishes were.

He ordered a stew and it arrived with all sorts of strange-looking things floating in it. As I stared into my bowl Steve handed me a large wooden instrument shaped like a truncheon. I sat there, holding it, but after a minute Steve (realising I didn't know what to do) gently relieved me of it with one of those wonderful Steve McQueen smiles. It turned out to be a pepper mill but I'd never seen one before and I was truly mortified when I realised my mistake.

I dutifully tried the stew and after a very short time, having eaten a rather strange rubbery ring, my stomach started to rumble like a boiler and my face began to swell and burn. I wanted to say something, but I couldn't, and as Steve turned to me, realising something was wrong, the trajectory of vomit hit him square on the chest. I stared at him in horror; knowing I was having an allergic reaction and that there was more to come, all I could do was make a run for the street to throw up in the gutter.

Next thing I knew, I was being bundled into a taxi by the restaurant manager, who gave the driver some money and told him, 'Take her home.' As we took off, my final image of Steve McQueen was of several staff fussing over him and wiping his shirt. Alas, I had almost certainly blown my chances of marrying this particular Hollywood superstar, I realised as I flopped in the back of the taxi.

Chapter Five

After that encounter with Steve McQueen, I felt mortified. I was still smarting when I received some upsetting news from home: my parents were to separate. This was something that would never have occured to me. There had probably been clues leading up to it, but if so I hadn't cottoned on. I always believed they were happily married and the occasional rows they'd had in front of me during my childhood hadn't seemed at all important. I guess I might be forgiven for not noticing that a problem had been brewing. In our house, my father had his bedroom and my mother had hers: having grown up with this, I thought it was the norm.

My mother had the most beautiful bedroom: a proper boudoir, it was full of plumped-up satin pillows, silk cushions and Venetian-style mirrors. There was also a reproduction Louis-Quinze bed and dressing table. Huge walk-in wardrobes had doors decorated with hand-painted French pastoral scenes. Father's bedroom, on the other hand, was a proper man's room with a plain wooden bed and dark brown, masculine-looking furniture that seemed perfect for him.

I'd always been aware that my father went missing on occasion but I thought he was just off in his gown van, selling Crombie coats. When I was 10 I learned how to drive that van up and down our very long drive. My mother is fond of telling the story of how one day she saw the van take off through the kitchen window and, thinking my father had left the handbrake off, she dashed outside only to glimpse my head just below the steering wheel. My grandson Oliver is the same – he's only 4 years old but if there was a van to climb into, away he would go.

Looking back, I'm guessing that Dad (who was always a ladies' man) had a female in every port of call. He was such a good-looking man that no one could resist him: I bet every woman he met fell in love with him. Whenever he came home from one or other of his trips there would be another row and another boiled egg whizzing across the breakfast table to splat on the radiator, but I just thought it was par for the course and never took much notice. And I wasn't surprised when Mum went on holiday with her friends – I just thought that was what women did.

Since those days, however, my mother has told me that the only reason why she and Dad stayed together for as long as they did was because she was determined they would not split up until Brett and I had left home. They had agreed that once we were gone they would separate and sell the house – and that's exactly what they did. Dad got a place on his own in Nottingham and Mum went on to live in a beautiful penthouse at the top of a Nottingham hotel, with a stunning view of the river.

What was lovely about all this was that they remained friends until the day my father died. They didn't even bother to get a divorce until many years later, when Mum met somebody else. Even then she was reluctant to go through the formalities but I encouraged her to do so because I wanted her to marry again, to be happy. I have always thought it was wonderful that she and Dad stayed friendly because I was never able to remain on good terms with my two former husbands.

Like most men, my father hated being on his own, and so although he never lived with anyone else he was seldom alone. Even when he grew older, women loved him. He was an easy man to adore, but at the same time one who should probably never have married or had children. A dreamer, a fantasist, a romantic, he just wanted to live in his own world.

I always thought he was a good father, but he didn't agree. Years later he told me: 'I was never a father to you or to Brett. I was never there, never played with you, hardly ever took you on holiday.' That might have been true but somehow I always knew he loved us: he was never disappointed in me or my brother, his was an unconditional love. By this time Brett had become a successful DJ with his own, extremely busy life working alongside Jimmy Savile and Peter Stringfellow and so we were in separate places. Inevitable, perhaps, but sometimes I felt very sad about it, too.

By then we were nearing the end of our first year at drama school and were all busy with end-of-year productions. As first years we had to go and watch the year above us in their productions, and so one evening I went along to see the second years in Shakespeare's *Romeo and Juliet* starring a young actor called Robert Lindsay. I took one look at his passionate portrayal of Romeo and instantly fell in love. Luckily for me, the passion turned out to be mutual. 'Bob', as we knew him then, had dark hair and dark eyes – he was one of the RADA boys that all the girls fancied. We met at a party soon after I'd seen his Romeo, where we talked and laughed all night. I thought he was funny and talented, while he made it clear that he liked me. He asked me on a date the following evening.

We went to see the musical *Godspell* starring David Essex, who was then (and still is) a major heart-throb. It was at the Roundhouse in Camden. As we sat in the audience, Bob turned to me and said, 'One day, I'm going to be up there on stage, starring in this musical.' And he was right: he did star in it, only two years later, in 1972.

Within weeks of that first date we were in love and decided to move in together, so I left the flat that I shared with the girls and moved into another one with Bob, this time just off the Tottenham Court Road. Our flat wasn't really a flat as such – we couldn't afford anything as grand as that. It was a very old-fashioned room that housed an embarrassingly creaky bed, a couple of shabby chairs, a sofa that had seen far better days and a gas fire. Looking back, I'm sure it should have been condemned for exuding dangerous fumes.

Two steps down from the main room was another small room housing an old sink and a big old-fashioned bath with a tap that only ever produced a trickle of hot water so it was impossible to have more than a shallow bath. The loo was downstairs (freezing on winter nights) and we had a tiny prehistoric cooker that was barely usable. In fact, the whole building (still standing today) ought to have been condemned, but we were in love and nothing else mattered.

The only puzzling thing about the block was that lots of single girls seemed to live there and people would come knocking on their doors at all hours. I had no idea what this was about until one afternoon when there was a knock at our door. I opened it only to realise that the old man reeking of booze and eyeing me up was probably not there to read the meter.

So that was the day when Bob and I worked out that we were not just living in a seedy old block of flats but some kind of brothel and the slimy old sod who had just knocked on the door was a customer. In fact, Bob was standing behind me when I opened the door and he went berserk when he saw the way the guy was leering at me and chased him down the stairs. Afterwards we thought it was really funny and laughed into the night, eating our kebabs in bed while trying to keep warm.

We actually became a popular squat for other students, who used to come and sleep on our floor. This was largely because they got cheap kebabs from the downstairs shop run by Gig, a lovely Greek man: he made sure we all ate well and we loved him for it.

Student days should be romantic, sex-fuelled and fun-filled: for Bob and me, they were. When the summer holidays came, we stayed in London and got jobs as ushers at the Palace Theatre, where the once-seen, never-to-be-forgotten Danny La Rue was performing in a spectacular revue, *Danny at the Palace*. In his big white wigs and diamante-studded ball-gowns, he made the most beautiful-looking, elegant woman. When he first appeared, he'd walk towards the middle of the stage in all his glory and say to the audience in a low baritone, 'Wotcha, mates!' The audience loved him, as did we – although I had many a row with the manager there because I was paid £3 10s while Bob got £4 10s. Talk about inequality! But they refused to back down and in the end I was sacked for being such a troublemaker.

Bob and I had been together in our little love nest for about a year when we decided to get married. There wasn't a formal proposal, we just agreed one day that it would be a great idea. Together we went to see my mum and then on to Ilkeston, not far from Nottingham, to see his. Around the same time, we also told my father. Both our mothers were lovely to us, but I'm sure that privately they thought we were too young and hoped it would fizzle out. I was still only 20 and Bob, nine months older than me, was 21, but we thought we had found real love and would be together forever.

We chose a date in the summer holidays, and despite her reservations Mum bought me a beautiful wedding dress embroidered all over with white hearts and a huge skirt and long train. She also purchased lovely outfits for my bridesmaids, who were children of friends, and the pageboy from Bob's side. Mum and I decided on the venue, while Bob and I chose the guests we wanted to invite and I arranged for our banns to be read.

Everything was in place and I was ecstatic at the prospect of marrying Bob because I thought he was everything I wanted. He seemed just as happy but perhaps he was having private doubts because only a few weeks before our wedding day everything changed. The summer term had ended and Bob, being a year ahead of me, had graduated from RADA and was heading out into the world to begin his acting career. He was in a play in Exeter, at the Northcott Theatre, and I went down to visit, taking with me a little mongrel puppy as a gift for him. While there, I started to feel uneasy. A couple of the girls he was working with were giving him looks that I couldn't mistake and he was very distant towards me, so much so that I became convinced he was playing around.

After I left and went back home to stay with Mum in Nottingham I didn't hear from him. As the days passed I began to realise he wasn't going to get in touch, but then neither did I. I let our romance fizzle out. Thankfully, my mother picked up the signals and quietly cancelled our wedding, having paid for everything.

I thought perhaps his mum had persuaded him not to go ahead because I knew she was unhappy about it, but, looking back, there must have been more to it than that. Bob was fiercely ambitious and perhaps that's what really lay behind our break-up. He used to say to me, 'I'll have my name in lights before you do,' and although it was a joke between us he really meant it. Perhaps he felt we'd always be competing with one another. Of course I felt sad about the end of our romance, but deep down I knew everyone had just got carried away with the idea of the wedding, including Bob and I. He went on to enjoy a career that would see him become a household name, starring in such TV favourites as *Citizen Smith* and *My Family*, as well as appearing on stage in dozens of successful plays and musicals.

At the end of that summer I headed back to RADA for my final year and, incredibly, I didn't see or speak to Bob again until twelve years later when I walked into the BBC to do a radio play. It was the first time that I'd set eyes on him since the day he walked out of our flat, and by then he had married and divorced Cheryl Hall while I was married to my second husband, Ken Boyd. We both said a polite, if slightly awkward, hello, although I couldn't resist a little dig.

'By the way,' I called out over my shoulder as I entered the studio to start the recording, 'I sold the dress!'

Quite rightly, he lowered his head.

In truth, I had given the dress to my cousin Gary Birtles, a brilliant footballer who was a striker for Nottingham Forest in the amazing Brian Clough era. Sandra, his fiancée, looked absolutely lovely in it on their wedding day. Sadly, the dress didn't bode well for them either.

So, am I left with any regrets? Well, no. Regrets are futile and a waste of energy. We were young and silly, it was a student crush and like all holiday romances it should have stayed where it belonged, in the confines of RADA, and not taken out of context. We both made mistakes. I have bumped into Bob in recent times, but it was obvious he had no wish to acknowledge the past. So Romeo really did die in the end.

Chapter Six

In my last year at RADA, perhaps on the rebound from my relationship with Bob Lindsay, I became involved with a director whom I met through one of our productions. He was quite a lot older than me and I thought he was glamorous and experienced. We went on several dates and then he invited me to move in with him. He lived in a beautiful flat in a large Victorian converted house. It was far more comfortable and spacious than my student digs so I didn't hesitate for long.

Everything seemed to be going fine until one morning when he came upstairs and waved a sheet of paper at me.

'Hey, look what I've just found downstairs in the letter-box!' he said.

It was a handwritten note addressed to me. In capital letters, someone had scrawled, 'I know where you live and I don't like the man you are living with.' There was no signature and no postmark, so it had obviously been hand-delivered. It was weird and a bit creepy but, hoping this was some kind of a joke, I shrugged, screwed it up and swiftly binned it. However, the next day there was another, similar note written in the same hand on exactly the same kind of paper. We were both puzzled and slightly alarmed but we didn't know what to do and so once again we decided to ignore the message.

After that the notes began to arrive almost every day: they were all in black ink and capital letters. Gradually they became more aggressive and ominous. The sixth note said: 'I'm warning you. I will kill you if you don't leave this man.'

By this time we were becoming increasingly rattled. Who on earth would want me to leave him? Was there some secret admirer? None I knew about, certainly. Worried the situation was turning really nasty, my boyfriend suggested that I should leave the flat for a time and go and stay with a friend of mine who lived in Islington. I agreed, and the moment I left the flat the poison-pen notes stopped. Clearly whoever it was knew I'd moved out. After a few days I decided to move back, hoping they had given up.

When I was back in the flat, however, my boyfriend looked out of the window and said that he thought he had seen a man coming up the path to our front door. He rushed downstairs only to return with another note. This time it said: 'I know you're back and you are now in danger because I meant what I said.'

Similar messages continued for another week. Seriously concerned now, my boyfriend suggested we should call the police. We did so, and a policeman came to the flat and questioned us both. He took it very seriously and told us, 'You're right to report these incidents. People who behave in this way – write threatening letters – are often very disturbed, unpredictable individuals.' Of course, this only made us feel worse. What on earth was going on and what should we do?

The next day, we were out in the car with a friend who lived in another flat in the house.

'Isn't this poison-pen business awful? It's really getting us down,' said my boyfriend.

'So, what are you going to do about it?' asked the friend.

'I don't know,' he replied, 'but I don't think it's a good idea for Sherrie to continue staying with me.'

'Right, but how are you going to protect her if she moves out?' said the friend.

'I don't know,' he repeated. 'I'll start by going to the police again and see what they suggest.'

That night at my boyfriend's suggestion I went back to Islington.

A few days later my friend said: 'Oh, Sherrie, the police think they've got the man.'

'Oh, thank God!' I said, genuinely relieved after ringing my boyfriend back. 'Who is it?'

'Just some nutter,' he told me, before adding, 'As the police know you're not living with me now, it's not necessary for you to do anything.'

Perhaps partly due to the pressure of the letters and the accompanying drama of it all, he seemed rather distant afterwards and I was utterly confused as to why it had happened – it felt as if we'd been in an episode of a police drama. And so we both kept our distance and let our romance slowly fizzle out, never knowing the identity of the letter writer.

That particular relationship might not have been a great love story but he did take me to one of the famous May Balls at Cambridge. He bought me the most beautiful gown to wear and took me punting. Perhaps more importantly, he did me a huge favour in introducing me to Peter Eade, the renowned theatrical agent. One of the best in the business, Peter represented

– among others – Kenneth Williams, Ronnie Barker and Joan Sims. Actors everywhere held him in awe because, if he took you on, this was guaranteed success.

In those days any agent of Peter's calibre had what was known as 'stables', and his was reputed to be one of the finest. The agents took on few clients, only the ones they believed in, whose careers they could then nurture and steer in the right direction. When Peter invited me to come and see him at his London office in Cork Street, I really should have been a bag of nerves but, completely unaware of just what an honour this was, I was quite relaxed. Instead it was Mum who came with me, who was the one on edge.

The building where Peter had his office was elegant and luxurious: the staircase was of polished wood, heavy doors with large brass handles swung silently open and there were thick carpets throughout. Lawrena, his assistant, met us at the door and brought us tea in china cups while we waited in an anteroom. When we were shown into his stunning office, Peter stood up and shook hands, then invited us to sit down. He was a true gentleman in every sense of the word: his lineage, upbringing and demeanour. What's more, he lived on a country estate with his elderly father and had the kind of cut-glass accent that we were all trying to cultivate at RADA, as was expected in those days. His manners were impeccable and he expected the same from his clients: he was an amazing man and a truly exceptional agent.

The first thing Peter told us was, 'I do not take on new clients any more. I only ever have fifteen on my books at any one time and at the moment I have my full quota. Having said that, I am interested in you, Sherrie: you have a raw talent and that is very rare. If I take you on, you will be guided by me and understand that I have your best interests at heart – you will never let me or the reputation of this agency down – I will mould your career and teach you all about the business.'

The next thing he said was: 'We must do something about your name. Sherrie Hutchinson is too long – we need something shorter, snappier and easier to recall.'

Before I knew what was happening, I had been re-christened Sherrie Hewson. At the time a change of name seemed a small price to pay for getting onto Peter's list, but in truth I always wished I had kept my own name (Sherrie Hutchinson has a far better ring to it than Sherrie Hewson, I think).

But it didn't take long for me to realise just how lucky I had been to be taken under Peter's wing. Not only was he extremely prestigious and highly respected but he also seemed to know absolutely everybody in the business. And everyone I knew was equally impressed that he had become my agent.

'*Peter Eade!*' they kept on exclaiming. 'You lucky little devil – you don't know how fortunate you are.'

But I did: right from the start I realised that Peter was a very special man with a true vocation. His family was wealthy and so he was certainly not in the job for the money – he found it creative, completely absorbing and thoroughly exciting. He loved the world of theatre and genuinely cared about the actors he looked after.

As far as any of his clients knew, Peter had never married. It seemed the only thing he really cared about was his work. While I was with him – and I can't emphasise enough just how unusual this was – I only rarely had to audition for jobs. Everybody in the business of films, stage and TV seemed to know and respect Peter, and if he suggested one of his actors for a part the producers and directors trusted his judgement. And when I did audition I was treated with respect because Peter had sent me.

As part of my 'grooming', Peter used to pick me up in his limousine and take me to the first nights of West End shows. He instilled in me that the way you learn your trade is by watching other actors, and you can never know enough. I still do that today: whether the actors are young or older, you can always learn from watching them. Peter also took me to showbiz parties, where he would present me to famous actors, and to the best restaurants and clubs; also garden parties and Glyndebourne, where he would introduce me to influential entrepreneurs. For all these magical occasions he would buy me beautiful ball gowns and evening dresses to wear.

I know it all sounds too good to be true but that's just the way it was: we lived in a different time with different values. Peter always used to say, 'This is a vocation, Sherrie – it's for the rest of your life, not five minutes of fame.' Sadly, a lot has changed now and many youngsters are indeed seeking instant fame, often through making a splash with a bit of topless modelling or reality TV rather than developing their talent. I'm thankful that I arrived in a different time and had such a good teacher.

I have so many warm memories of those special occasions with Peter. In particular, some of our most wonderful evenings were spent at Rules, the oldest eating-house in London, which is in Covent Garden. Often there would be superb private functions and parties upstairs, with everyone who was anyone in attendance. I remember one particular party there, when Peter and I walked into one of the upstairs dining rooms as a young Wayne Sleep proceeded to jump on the long dining table, kick everything off and do a dance routine, much to the delight of everyone present. The party became very giddy as lots of people clambered onto the table, trying to join in. As it groaned with the weight of them, we feared the worst, but the maître d' burst into the room and somehow managed to throw everyone out.

Frequently, the parties would become quite wild, but Peter was always very protective of me.

Like most students, I was hoping to go into repertory theatre as soon as I left RADA. 'Rep', as it was (and still is) known, meant joining the company of a local theatre for at least a season and performing in lots of different plays, from classics to new productions. The idea was to play a whole range of roles. One week you might be a 20-year-old ingénue in a Bernard Shaw play, then the following week you'd play a 50-year-old mother in a heavy-duty Chekhov production. Drama graduates would hope to work in a number of rep theatres in towns and cities around the country, thereby honing their art and gaining invaluable experience.

But for me, as for every other drama student, the only problem was securing an Equity card. Equity was the actors' union. To work as an actor you had to have a card – producers and directors simply wouldn't consider you without one because it was a closed union. But to get one you must have worked as an actor, hence the conundrum facing every young would-be performer. It was a dotty system, but in those days Equity called the shots.

The solution that Peter came up with was to secure me a part in a commercial. At that time nobody who aspired to being a serious actor or actress would be seen dead in a TV commercial – they were regarded as 'the pits', downmarket jobs signalling the end of your career. How times have changed. Nowadays everybody, from the fresh-faced graduates to headline stars, competes to get into advertisements, which can be extremely lucrative. Back then it was all so different, so when Peter announced that I was to be in a commercial I was slightly concerned.

'The joy of the commercial I have got for you,' he explained, 'is that while it will result in you getting an Equity card, your face will not be seen in it.'

'It's a chocolate-bar commercial,' Peter went on. 'The action is set in the Jacobean period during a jousting tournament and as you have been cast as a young lady in period dress and a wimple who is watching the joust from a box and delicately waving your 'kerchief up and down, with some careful angling your face will not be shown. Then, when the knight comes over, all you have to do is lean over and give him the 'kerchief.'

'It sounds quite a prominent part to me, Peter,' I said. 'How am I going to avoid being on camera?'

'Don't worry, we'll make sure of that at the time,' he insisted.

But he hadn't convinced me. When we arrived at the location in the middle of nowhere, it was a proper jousting scene set in the middle of a very muddy field. Two large horses were dressed in their colours and two knights in corresponding shades. Masses of peasant types were milling about and smoke billowed out of enormous machines all over the field. I was taken into a large caravan stacked with period costumes of various sizes and dutifully dressed as a lady-in-waiting, wimple and all. The dress was fine but the wimple, which consisted of a long, cone-shaped hat with lots of fabric flowing over my head and fastening under my chin, was far too big and had to be fixed on with pins and sticking tape. Even then it didn't stay put and I had to hold it on as I was taken through the mud to the stand that was supposed to be the viewing box for the young ladies while the knights fought.

The director – a thin, weedy-looking man – was having a bit of a hissy fit because the horses couldn't hit their marks. Highly flustered, he came into the box. 'You,' he said, pointing at me. 'You can be number one and you,' pointing to the girl standing next to me, 'you're number two.' Altogether, there were ten of us girls and we were all given our numbers.

'Number one, come here,' he called, and he instructed me to sit on the middle of the front bench. I could see Peter looking on at the side of the box and gestured that this was disastrous, but there was nothing I could do. We all sat there as the director, now looking extremely silly, ran up and down the field pretending to be the horses, trying to show everyone what he wanted. He galloped towards me and reached up. 'Number one,' he kept shouting, but with the wind and the wimple I wasn't sure what he wanted me to do.

He jumped up and grabbed my hand, at which point I lost my footing and catapulted over the top of the box, only to be saved by a burly security guard who happened to be standing by. It was not a pretty sight – me with my dress over my head, the guard holding my legs, and meanwhile the prissy director was down below the box with a face full of bosoms, trying to get out from below me. Somehow the guard managed to yank me back up onto the box, but by that time I was definitely not the director's favourite. Shooting me a filthy look, he gave each of us a chocolate bar.

'This is why we are all here,' he said, gazing at the bar as if it was the Crown Jewels.

By that time we'd been there for ages and I was starving. Without thinking, I unwrapped the chocolate bar and devoured the whole thing. As I popped the last piece into my mouth, the director – now almost frothing at the mouth – screamed, 'Number one, *STOP*!'

He flew at me, grabbed the empty chocolate paper and shouted, '*What* did I say? I said *not* to eat the chocolate bar! *What* did I say?'

'Not to eat the bar,' I replied, bursting into tears. As I did so, the tape at the back of my head pinged. The wimple and the rest of the headdress fell forward across my face and then slid to the floor. At this, he could hardly contain himself. He leaned towards me and hissed: 'You are no longer number one, you have been nothing but trouble: you are now number *ten*!'

I was led to a seat at the back as those around me glanced sympathetically in my direction. Poor girl, they probably thought, she's lost her chance to star in this commercial. Little did they know I was thrilled and equally relieved; Peter smiled.

My final humiliation that day was when I was given a block of wood, which had been coated with brown paint as a replacement for the chocolate bar. Unbelievably, they didn't have any spares. Throughout the shoot I had to pretend to nibble on it joyously. At least my face didn't show in the final commercial and I got my Equity card – but I've never liked chocolate since.

After that, I headed off into rep, which meant staying in lodgings in whatever town I happened to be working in. One of the first places I went was Cheltenham, and Peter, who was looking after me like a mother hen, told me that he had found me some very nice digs there.

Off I went to the address he gave me, where I met the owner, his wife and two children. I was shown to an extremely pleasant if somewhat spartan bedroom with only two blankets on the bed (which was a bit of a worry for me because I always feel the cold).

I was told to come down to breakfast the next morning at eight o'clock, sharp.

'We are quite informal so there's no need to dress, added the man of the house.'

That was kind of him I thought, but I didn't think it polite to go down in my dressing-gown. Before leaving me in my room, he showed me the bathroom.

'Now, let me explain the system,' he said. 'You can have six inches of hot water, no more ...'

'Right!' I gulped, trying hard to disguise my astonishment.

'… and your days for a bath will be Tuesday and Friday,' he continued.

As it was a Monday, I was thinking, oh God! I'll have to wash today and look forward to a bath in six inches of water tomorrow. All this seemed very strange to me, though not so odd as what was to come.

The next morning I went down to breakfast just before eight o'clock to a cheery 'good morning' from my host. As I walked into the breakfast room I had the odd feeling that something wasn't quite right. It was then I noticed that the host, his wife and two children were all sitting at the table completely naked. Except when I walked in, the host stood up and moved towards me, to direct me to the chair. Now the naked body isn't a particularly pretty sight at the best of times, but with Coco Pops and Sugar Puffs it just isn't right.

'What would you like for breakfast?' he asked. 'Egg, bacon … and a sausage, perhaps?'

This was too much for me. I struggled to control a burst of nervous giggles as he brought over the serving dish and with his tongs picked up the most enormous sausage. I was about to say, 'That's too big for me,' when I glanced down and thought better of it. It was a chilly day and my host's manhood had shrunk to the size of a mini-chipolata. The sausage was deposited on my plate along with two fried eggs. His wife was sitting right opposite me and I couldn't help but think her breasts and my eggs made a perfect matching foursome.

Staring at my plate, I kept my head down and tried to tuck in. I have to say I did not cut the sausage. Soon I had to give up the struggle to eat anything and, claiming I was late for work, I bowed my way out of the room, my eyes fixed on the floor as if I was a royal lackey. In a complete daze I went off to rehearsals thinking bloody hell, but when I came back they were all in the sitting room, still without any clothes.

'Do come and join us,' the host convivially told me. 'We're toasting crumpets.'

With a muffled, 'I don't think so,' I disappeared into my room, leaving a very strange image in my head.

The next day I made up some tale about a long-lost relative who I'd suddenly discovered lived in Cheltenham. It wasn't a highly plausible excuse but I had to leave – one can only take so much naked flesh with every meal, especially when it's freezing cold!

As I made my way down the path, the parents stood at the window, waving a cheery goodbye. I often wonder if their children carried on with the same tradition after they left home. Goodness knows, but one thing's for sure: I've never been able to look at a sausage in quite the same way.

Chapter Seven

Having been issued with my prized Equity card and after starting the rounds of repertory theatres, I was thrilled to land not one part but three different roles in three different episodes of the biggest series then on television: BBC1's *Z Cars*.

Set in a fictional town on the outskirts of Liverpool, *Z Cars* was based on the police teams who patrol in cars and it went on to become a top-rated weekly programme for sixteen years. The series broke new ground and showed the police in a far more realistic light than the previous, rather gentle police drama, *Dixon of Dock Green*. Dozens of highly successful actors had made appearances in *Z Cars*, so I was extremely lucky to land these roles fresh out of drama school.

'This job,' Peter explained, 'is a terrific opportunity for you.'

I was nervous, appearing alongside established stars such as the Irish actor James Ellis. He had a reputation for being a bit of a hell-raiser but I loved him: his talent was immense. Douglas Fielding was another regular, who was also very talented. I had a real crush on Doug – it was the blond hair and blue eyes that did it for me every time.

But if I thought the acting was to be my biggest challenge, I was wrong. That was fine, but what actually drove me loopy was another member of the cast. Between takes he was always chasing me around the studio, trying to pinch my bottom. There I was, just 21, fresh out of drama school and being forced to run away from this man, who clearly saw me as fair game. Sadly, the situation was often par for the course in those days. Only the other day an aged actor said to me: 'Don't understand young actresses these days – they get so het up if you as much as touch their bottoms. In my day the young chorus girls never batted an eyelid if I gave their titties a good old feel. Gave me a boost and they didn't care!'

I bet they damn well did, but were much too scared to tell on the old lech. That reminds me of a voice doctor, whom we all visited when we were students. A small man, he had a unique way of healing your voice so quickly you didn't have to miss a show. He was a miracle worker – and he knew it. The first time I went to see him was on my own. I was waiting to go into his office when the lady behind the desk asked, 'Haven't you got anyone with you?' 'No,' I said. At this, her brow wrinkled and she mouthed, 'Oh, *dear*!' But before I could question her, out he popped.

'Hello, my dear, come in,' he told me, extremely dapper in his grey suit, black tie and highly polished shoes. I told him my throat was sore and that my glands felt swollen. 'Right,' he said, 'let's have a look.' He pulled up a stool and sat directly in front of me. 'Open wide,' he instructed. He shone a light into my mouth. 'OK, you need a mouthwash and I'm going to spray your throat with this.' He reached over for a small aerosol can. 'Close your eyes, we don't want it getting anywhere else, do we?' he continued. The next moment his hands were all over me, up my sweater, nearly down my trousers. I opened my eyes and leapt up.

'Pay on your way out,' he told me. Stunned and completely shocked, I wasn't sure if it had happened or not. As I passed the receptionist, she could see my face. 'Bring someone with you next time,' she said, smiling sympathetically. From then on I took Mum with me: she thought he was a sweetheart but I knew what he really was.

Back on the *Z Cars* set, I was becoming completely fed up with my fellow cast member's obsession with pinching my behind. Fortunately I was a lot younger and faster than he was, so he never did catch me. If I'd complained, it would have been me who wasn't hired again, not him. But it seemed no one had any sympathy for my plight, even though they could all see what was happening – they all thought it was funny.

In those days not only would some of the chaps pursue us girls onset but the 'casting couch', as it was called, was also commonplace. It meant that sexual favours would be expected in return for a job. One of the times when I found myself subject to the unwelcome attentions of a potential employer was when a highly successful director came to talk to us at RADA. Afterwards I was delighted when he invited me to go for a meal with him.

Anyway, there we were, this mega-famous director and little me, driving towards the King's Road, Chelsea, which was considered to be *the* place to go. This was at the tail end of the Swinging Sixties, the anything-goes time, when the miniskirt and thigh-length boots were all the rage and the King's Road was the parading ground for the coolest people ever. It was such an exciting place to be, with the music of the day playing everywhere: Mungo Jerry's 'In the Summertime', Smokey

Robinson's 'Tears of a Clown' and Freda Payne's 'Band of Gold'.

The director steered me into a restaurant, which was all scrubbed tables and candles in Mateus Rosé bottles. He made it clear this was his treat and he did all the ordering, which was fine by me: one, I had no money, and two, this was a proper big-time director and I didn't want to look foolish. When our food arrived, it looked like a pile of shrivelled bones covered in brown sauce. Not far off the truth, it was spare ribs, but I'd never seen them before. Also, I had no idea that the little white bowl placed next to me and containing water and lemon was for rinsing my hands in after I'd eaten them.

Anyway, I thought I'd better have a go and stuck my fork in. Rather too enthusiastically, it turned out, as it became jammed in one of the bones and slid along the plate, knocking against the others. It was like a game of skittles except all the ribs shot up into the air before landing in my lap and sliding over my knees onto the floor. Said director looked slightly miffed and muttered something uncomplimentary as he shuffled me in my sauce-stained clothes out of the restaurant.

I hadn't planned on ending the meal by leaving prematurely, with my skirt and knees covered in sticky brown sauce and my face the colour of a tomato, but there was worse to come. He had offered to drive me home but as we walked down the street, he pointed up towards a window. 'That's my flat,' he told me. 'I can't take you home in that state. Come in and clean yourself up.'

This seemed like a good idea – I was just so innocent. Inside, he sat me down in his very smart lounge and asked if I would like a drink. I didn't drink alcohol in those days, so I told him that I would love a glass of lemonade or Coke.

'*Really?*' he said. 'I've got something you'll like better than that. The bathroom, by the way, is upstairs and you'll find a dressing-gown in there if you want to take off those stained clothes.'

I should have made an excuse and left at that moment. Instead I meekly accepted a glass of lemonade. When I asked why it tasted so funny, he told me that it contained 'a bit of Pernod'. I didn't know what that was, but it tasted quite nice and so I had a second glass, after which I started to feel a bit strange.

'I'd better go home,' I hiccupped.

'I can't take you home in this state,' he said, 'but don't worry – you can spend the night here on my very comfy sofa.'

And he sauntered out of the room to fetch a pillow and some blankets, which he placed in a heap beside me.

'You'll be fine there,' he told me. 'Don't worry about a thing. Good night.'

Moments later, I heard his bedroom door close and quiet descended over the flat. Having managed to strip down to my bra and knickers, I wrapped myself up in the nice soft blanket and snuggled down on the sofa. Just as I was dozing off the door burst open and there he was: stark naked, with his bits and pieces swinging and ready for action. I gaped in horror, but before I could unravel myself from the blanket he was on top of me.

For the next fifteen minutes or so, after I had succeeded in wriggling and squirming my way from beneath him, the scene turned into a Keystone Kops' routine. As I ran out of the room, he and his jiggling equipment sped after me in a true bedroom farce. In and out of the various rooms I went, hiding in wardrobes, behind doors and curtains, under beds. At one stage we both stopped to catch our breath, and then we were off again: up and down stairs, round the kitchen table, back into the lounge. Eventually he cornered me and I opened my mouth to scream.

'Don't you dare scream, I've got neighbours!' he hissed.

Perhaps that brought him to his senses because suddenly he backed off and disappeared from the room. Left alone, I sank down into a corner and, wide awake, there I remained until daylight when he appeared (fully clothed, thank God). He threw some money down on the table and said coldly, 'Get yourself a taxi.' Back in my sauce-covered skirt, sleepless and extremely shaken, I left, hoping never to see him again.

There was a postscript to all this, however, for I did see him again when I auditioned for a very prestigious theatre company. I was there early, well prepared as I knew they would ask me to act out two contrasting pieces, and I walked into the rehearsal room to find at least ten people on the panel waiting for me. As I worked my way along the line, they all shook my hand and introduced themselves.

'Lovely to meet you. Don't be nervous – well, not of me anyway. It's this man you should be nervous about!' one woman said. I turned my head with a big smile, which immediately sank to the floor, for there he was. He took my hand, pulled me towards him as if to give me a peck on the cheek and whispered, 'Not a fucking chance in hell!' He then smiled broadly as I carried on down the line. Of course I didn't get the job.

I came to think of this kind of outrageous behaviour as an occupational hazard because it was incredibly common back then. I'd arrive at an audition or walk onto a set, see the middle-aged male 'star' or director eyeing me up and think, here we go again. Right from the start, I made up my mind if anybody treated me like that, I'd kick them in the balls. From time to time this attitude has cost me jobs, but I stuck to it and became quite good at getting round the situation.

When I went up for one of my first film jobs, the director (a chubby chap with white hair) didn't even bother to look up as I walked in. 'Sit,' he snapped, and carried on writing. 'Name, age and what size are your tits?' he continued. Shocked, I remained silent. 'Oh for *God's* sake, you're not going all coy on me, are you?' he said, looking up. But I still said nothing, more out of fear than belligerence. 'Look, just show me your tits or fuck off!' he told me, standing up. And that did it. 'You show me your cock and I'll show you my tits!' I snapped back. He was so surprised: all he could do was hiss at me to get out – which I gladly did.

A few years later when a well-known older actor invited me to his caravan for lunch on the set of a TV mini-series, I asked four of the make-up girls to come with me. Just as well, because the actor opened the caravan door wearing nothing but a flimsy silk dressing gown! Naturally, he wasn't best pleased.

In 1971, the year after I graduated from drama school, I went back to my home town, Nottingham, to do a season in rep. I was due to appear in *The Tempest* and *The Homecoming* with John McEnery and his then wife, Stephanie Beacham. It was an extraordinary feeling, appearing at the Nottingham Playhouse, where I had sat so many times at a corner of the stage watching and learning from great actors. I felt incredibly lucky to be able to come back, just a few years later, as a professional actress and be paid for the privilege. I got £22 a week, which was a very good wage then for an inexperienced actress of my age.

John had recently won a BAFTA for his role as Mercutio in Franco Zeffirelli's film *Romeo and Juliet*, while Stephanie had just appeared alongside Marlon Brando in *The Nightcomers*. Barrie Rutter, who now owns the fantastic Northern Broadsides theatre company, was also in the cast, so I was in exalted company.

During the season there we went to France and Germany for three or four weeks on a British Council tour. We started with a bumpy Channel crossing: Barrie and I sat up all night on the ferry and were the only two not to become seasick, but when we landed in France I hadn't quite got my land-legs back and I fell off the pavement and was instantly sick. Welcome to France! Trust me to do everything in reverse.

I have two abiding memories of that trip. The first concerns the rather old, extremely whiskery member of the cast (an old Hollywood star), who unfortunately took rather a fancy to me. A renowned actor of stage and screen (and until then someone I had respected greatly from a professional viewpoint), he chased me around with a lecherous twinkle in his eye so often that by the end of that tour I could have become an Olympic sprinter. His wife, a highly eccentric grande dame, was sympathetic. One day she whispered: 'Don't worry, child – he's riddled with gout. He can hardly lift his leg up, let alone get it over!'

My chief memory of the trip, though, was of one of the actors giving me what I thought was a strange-looking cigarette. I didn't smoke, but we had all gathered in his room after going out for a meal and the air was blue. 'Do you want a puff?' I was asked and he handed me a long, thin cigarette. Not realising this was cannabis and not wishing to appear silly, I took it. The trouble was, I didn't know you were supposed to take a puff and hand it on, so I kept hold of it. He had instructed me to take a long drag, hold it in my mouth and then let it go, so I kept on doing this until it was all gone.

Of course I went sky-high, so high the next thing I remember is climbing out onto the window ledge, looking down and seeing the pavement rise up (we were on the seventh floor). Convinced I could fly, I stepped off. In the nick of time, John – I *assume* it was him – flung himself across the room and dragged me back in. I remember blankets, lots of shouting and then sleep.

One of the nicest things about that time was getting to know the lovely actor Reg Bundy. He never became a household name but he was an extraordinary character. The alter ego he created a few years later, Regina Fong, was groundbreaking and attracted a huge following. Along with Paul O'Grady (who also became a dear friend of mine), Reg broke the mould of female impersonation. Regina Fong and Paul's creation, Lily Savage, were a million miles away from the music-hall 'dames' or dramatic Shirley Bassey-style divas of the past. Funny, irreverent and topical, they brought female impersonation to a whole new audience.

When I met him, Reg was simply in rep with the rest of us. We had a lovely brother-and-sister relationship: we behaved like naughty kids, winding each other up and constantly landing ourselves in so much trouble. Reg, who was four years older than me, was worse than me. Crazy, wild and always up to no good, he was forever in trouble or the cause of it. Once, for example, when we were in the middle of *The Tempest*, Reg came on stage carrying Stephanie Beacham. When he saw me and I made him laugh, he simply dropped her. Poor Stephanie!

On another occasion he very nearly got us both sacked. I was doing a serious scene on the set of a living room with a window at the back, with a well-respected actor called Paul Freeman. Reg appeared at the window in drag, with a fag in his mouth. In full view of the audience, he started to clean the window and sing like Hilda Ogden! I couldn't stop laughing – and I couldn't go on.

It was while we were in France together on the British Council tour that Reg proved he really was there for me, though. The morning after the night when I had smoked that 'funny' ciggy, I was still feeling decidedly groggy as I sat next to him on the coach, and unfortunately the inevitable happened. When you're sick in someone's lap, you soon find out who your true friends are, and Reg, bless him, proved himself a real treasure. He barely batted an eyelid, cleaned us both up and gave me a comforting hug.

Reg and I stayed friends for many years, but when he contracted cancer a few years ago in 2003 I didn't cope at all well. Through good times and bad he'd always been there for me, and now I wanted to be there for him too. Often we'd get together and have afternoon tea in one of the London hotels – it was our favourite thing to do. But as the months went by I was forced to watch my beloved friend deteriorate in front of my eyes, and there came a time when I felt distraught at seeing him and I know he felt the same way too. He would say, 'I can't do this,' and I couldn't either, yet we had always been so close.

It was our mutual friend Paul O'Grady who looked after Reg and nursed him right to the very end. He took care of everything – doctors, carers and eventually the funeral itself. Reg was adored, and to this day people talk of him fondly and laugh as they think about him – he would have loved that. I have never forgiven myself for being so inept towards the end of his life and I often say, 'I'm so sorry, Reg,' hoping he can somehow hear me. He was a massive talent with a very big heart. The memories of Reg that Paul and I share are very precious and will always be a special bond between us.

Chapter Eight

While I loved appearing at the Playhouse and being in Nottingham, the move back there also signalled the beginning of a traumatic and painful time in my life. One evening, when the cast went out for a drink after the performance, I got talking to a man who was charming, funny and very good-looking. I almost always fall for blond, blue-eyed men, but John Rowlands had dark eyes and olive skin. He told me he worked in a bank and at the end of the evening he asked to see me again. I'd had a lovely time and happily said yes.

After that we went on two or three more dates. John was charming and attentive but it wasn't long before he started to behave a little oddly. One night when I was telling a story, laughing and waving my arms around, he snapped at me, 'Stop being such a show-off!' It was so sudden that I stopped, mid-sentence, and stared at him. He was scowling angrily at me and I felt a chill run down my spine. A second later he laughed and said, 'You didn't think I was serious, did you?' I laughed too, but later

I was to wish I'd trusted my instinct and called a halt to things then and there.

At the time I was staying with my mother in her penthouse flat and John would often call round. He was always charming to Mum, as he was to everyone, and she was pleased that I'd found someone new, but I was beginning to feel a tiny bit uneasy. John was becoming slightly too attentive: he would turn up at the theatre most nights, offering to walk me home. It seemed like concern and affection but I didn't understand why he wanted to know what I was doing all the time. Whenever I had a day off he immediately arranged for us to spend the whole day together, without consulting me about it. I told myself he was being masterful and passionate but I was starting to feel uncomfortable.

With hindsight I can see that he became obsessed with me from the first moment he laid eyes on me. At the beginning I felt flattered and charmed by his attentions, though. I didn't understand that the kind of obsession he had is not healthy and usually goes hand in hand with being jealous and controlling, as I was about to discover. I had no idea then what an obsessive personality can be capable of or that I was in fact way out of my depth.

Meanwhile, John wooed me with romantic gestures and compliments as well as promises of a wonderful life and gave all the appearance of being completely besotted with me. And to cut a long story short, I fell for it. I was young, extremely naive and had not yet learnt to trust my own judgement. Deep down, I knew not only did I not love him, I didn't trust him either, but despite my misgivings I let myself be convinced I was wrong. I had already been through a break-up with Bob Lindsay, so perhaps I was more vulnerable to any new suitor who swore undying love and a lifetime of devotion. It's easy now, almost forty years later, to say what a silly, innocent and trusting girl I was, but so many of us are at that young age. The upshot was that I allowed him to virtually take over my life for the next few months, and as time went by, the cracks began to show. Behind closed doors he would be controlling and unkind, but this rapidly escalated into physical violence.

By the time I went on the British Council tour, only a few weeks later, I was already desperate to get away from John, and so when I came back I moved into Dad's little flat. Since my parents' separation he had been living quietly in Nottingham and I hoped that I might find refuge with him. John knew Mum's flat, but I had never told him where Dad lived. It didn't take him long to find out where I was, though, and when he came looking for me I felt I couldn't involve Dad in my troubles and so I reluctantly left with him.

As the violence escalated, I struggled to cope. John would hit me until I was bruised and battered but somehow I still got myself together and went to the theatre. It was partly pride and partly because at the theatre I had my only respite. Immersing myself in the production and my own role, for a few short hours I could pretend that John and the nightmare of my life with him didn't exist. Of course I've asked myself many times why I didn't get away from him at this stage, but I had taken on the beliefs of so many battered women: blaming myself, accepting his apologies and promises to change, feeling helpless to escape because my confidence was so low. At work I could pull off a demanding role, but away from the stage I was an emotional wreck.

By this time I had begun to realise the full horror of what I was doing: getting involved with a man who had stalked, battered and controlled me. Perhaps the survivor in me knew that if I allowed this to go on my life would be over because one night when we were in a pub together, as soon as John went to the bar to get some more drinks, I got up and fled.

Sobbing, I ran to my father's flat, and this time I told him the truth about what was going on. Horrified, Dad comforted me, but when John arrived the next morning and demanded I come with him I told my father to go to work and let me sort it out. Dad was reluctant to leave me, but I didn't want John to turn on him too, so I urged him to go. Once he had left, John cornered me in the front room: he was furious I had run away and for the next hour he knocked me from one side of the room to the other. Then, as I cowered in terror, he announced that we were going to stay with his parents in Eastbourne.

Numbly, I went with him. The production at the Playhouse had already come to an end and his parents seemed perfectly pleasant people. I went through the motions of being polite, but I was just waiting for another chance to escape. A few days later John took me out to a bar. From the moment we walked in he never took his eyes off me and refused to let me out of his sight. By this time he had become fanatically jealous, so much so that I didn't dare raise my eyes and look around me, instead keeping them firmly fixed on the table in front of me.

Eventually, feeling as if I was going mad with claustrophobia and starting to suffer from stomach cramps, I stood up and said, 'I've got to go to the loo – I'll only be a minute.' A minute out of his sight was clearly too long, though, because while I was in the loo I heard footsteps and knew it was him. He began trying each of the cubicle doors and, having found the one that I was in, he began to rattle it and hiss, 'Open the fucking door!' He must have repeated this a dozen times before two women came in and he was forced to leave.

When I eventually came out of the loo, terrified as to what he might do next, I started to make my way back to our table only to see John in a passionate clinch with a girl. As I stood there, shocked and humiliated, some adrenalin finally reached my legs and I turned and headed out of the bar. I was on my way down the stairs towards the street door when he came at me from behind, wielding a cricket bat – God knows where he'd got it from – which he smashed over my head. The first blow was forceful enough to knock me unconscious, but I later heard that he continued to hit me with the bat until some of the other customers succeeded in dragging him off me and called the police.

Minutes later, I came round to find a woman holding an ice cube to my right temple and trying to clean some of the blood from my face. John was standing next to me, two people holding him by the arms, and talking to a policeman. 'It's just a domestic,' he was saying. 'She's my wife, you're not needed here.' Horrified, I watched as the policeman nodded, before saying: 'Well, if you're sure – we don't like to get involved in domestics, but don't do that again, sir.' He was going to be let off! I couldn't believe it. As I discovered during this whole awful episode, at that time the police steered well clear of what they called 'domestics' – in other words, if you were married to your abuser then they didn't want to know, which is why John pretended we were husband and wife.

Convinced I was about to be murdered, I rose shakily to my feet still clutching my bleeding head, and made a run for the door before anybody could stop me. Out of my mind with fear, I ran into the road, raising one hand to a car that, by some miracle, just happened to be a taxi. Inside were two burly male passengers, but as it skidded to a halt beside me, I was past caring. Having squeezed into it, I shouted to the driver, 'A man back there is trying to kill me! Please help me and just drive, as fast as you can.'

Without asking any questions, he did just that.

I was so lucky that night. The two men, slightly the worse for drink, just treated me like a slip of a girl who had got herself into some kind of trouble and sat there commiserating until they nodded off. Once they'd been dropped off, the taxi driver asked me where I wanted to go.

'London,' I said. 'Please take me to London.'

'Are you sure?' he asked, shocked. 'It's 2am.'

'Quite sure,' I replied. 'It's where my brother lives.'

Goodness knows what he must have thought, but that kind man didn't ask another question. He simply drove through the night as I dozed fitfully in the back. Arriving in Vauxhall, the following morning, Brett was at a friend's. Thankfully a friend of his came down from the flat above to let me in and I was able to pay the taxi driver and give him some breakfast before he left.

When Brett came home he found me lying on the sofa, exhausted and traumatised. He was shocked by my story and immediately called our mother. She came down from Nottingham and between the two of them they cleaned me up, packed me a case and booked Mum and me seats on a flight to Cyprus for two weeks.

Mum was angry with me for getting involved with John, but mostly she was concerned that I should get away from him and start afresh. She had taken me to Cyprus because she loved it there and she hoped I would rest and recover some of my fighting spirit.

I was in Cyprus for my twenty-second birthday, on 17 September 1972, and as Mum and I celebrated quietly that night a charming Greek man came over and introduced himself to us. Mamas turned out to be a lovely man – kind, generous and very wealthy. He fell for me and invited me to go and live with him in his gorgeous villa, marry him and have lots of children. My mother thought he was a great catch and I was tempted: a life in the sun, with a good man who would look after me, sounded pretty attractive, but I wasn't in love with Mamas. Apart from anything else, I was still far too shocked and traumatised by what had happened with John to want to get involved with someone new. Besides, Mamas was already 32, which I considered far too old for me.

Naturally disappointed, Mamas was kindness itself. As well as his villa, he owned a flat on Famagusta beach, which he said I was welcome to use any time. I took him up on that offer, going back several times over the next few years to visit Cyprus. Mamas became a good friend and would come to visit with his dog Smoky, a Weimaraner. At one point Smoky – a big, sleek dog with a noble bearing and a gentle temperament – came to live with me in the flat for several weeks. I loved him so much that a few years later I got a Weimaraner of my own.

After I returned to Britain from Cyprus, I stayed with Brett for a couple of months. During that time I was constantly looking over my shoulder for John, but I didn't hear from him. I hoped and prayed he was out of my life.

Chapter Nine

In January 1973 I was due to start a season in rep in Harrogate and I couldn't wait to begin working again. The first play I did was *Julius Caesar* with Martin Shaw, who later starred in the hugely successful TV drama series, *The Professionals,* for five years. Martin was playing Mark Antony and I was Portia. Needless to say, I immediately fell for him – as I always seemed to do with my leading men – but he wasn't the slightest bit interested in me. Back then, he was happily married and his son Joe had just been born.

How time flies! A few years ago, in 2006, I played Joe Shaw's older wife in *Murder Mistaken* at the Windsor Theatre. He was a lovely young actor and we had great fun. My first encounter with his dad – Martin – all those years ago proved to be very educational, however. Martin was a vegan and when I told him that I didn't know what a vegetarian was, let alone a vegan, he took it upon himself to enlighten me.

One memorable night he said to me, 'Come back to my place tonight, I want to show you something.' When I turned up at his rented flat he entered the room. My heart skipped a beat as he smiled and said, 'I'm going to cook for you.' How lovely, I thought. I hadn't come across this particular chat-up line before and I thought it was very romantic. There were even, I noticed with a pleasurable shiver, candles on the table. Perhaps, after all, he was interested in me – not that I would ever have got involved with a married man, of course, but Martin was gorgeous so it was nice to think that he found me attractive, too.

While he was busy at a small stove that was just out of sight, we chatted about macrobiotic cooking, which was something I had never heard of. I wasn't actually all that interested in it either but I didn't want to appear rude and so I asked all kinds of questions, all the while wondering what he was cooking up.

Minutes later, Martin reappeared and presented me with a boiled egg.

'It's a boiled egg!' I muttered, astonished.

'Yes,' he replied, 'but *look* at that boiled egg, Sherrie!'

I hadn't a clue what I was supposed to be doing, but I sat, staring intently at the boiled egg.

'Now I want you to think about this,' and Martin's tone was grave. 'Every time you eat a boiled egg, Sherrie, you are killing a baby chick.'

'Oh my God!' I said, with a sharp intake of breath.

'I just want to make you aware,' he continued with all the intensity of a new convert, which he was. At this, he sat down at the table and proceeded to educate me on veganism and animal welfare for what must have been a solid hour. I listened intently, and although I respected him for his strong beliefs, I still had no idea what he was talking about. But that didn't matter, I fancied him anyway and always have.

It was during the next production that my happy sojourn was shattered, however. I opened the door of the tiny flat where I was lodging and there was John, sitting waiting for me. He had taken some time off and had somehow tracked me down and persuaded the landlord to let him in. Shaking with fear, I did my best to hold my ground and told him to go, but he refused and nothing I said or did made any difference. With frightening speed, I once again became the abused and battered girlfriend. Cowed and submissive, I allowed him to stay in my flat for the rest of the run (which was several weeks). I didn't mention to a soul that he was there, and if my fellow actors and the theatre crew noticed I had become quieter and rushed off every night after the curtain fell instead of going for a meal or a drink with them, they didn't say anything.

Each night as we got to the last scene of the play I would begin to shake with nerves, knowing that John was waiting outside the theatre for me. He expected me to come straight out and would march me home, where I would stay until it was time to go back to the theatre the next day. He watched me constantly, never – not for one moment – taking his eyes off me.

By the final night I knew I had to escape, but I was desperately afraid that wherever I went he would come and find me and make my life even worse. I didn't think of asking for help. At that time the first women's refuge had recently been opened by Erin Pizzey in Chiswick, though I'd never heard of it: the concept of a safe house for women in my position was a new one. Besides, if I stayed in hiding then I wouldn't be able to work again. An actress is so easy to track down, but I wasn't about to give up my career to escape this man, so there had to be another way.

It was during the last performance when I made my bid for freedom. That night I glanced towards the side of the stage and saw John standing in the wings, staring at me with hatred in his eyes. He had slipped into the theatre and the resulting fear that

I experienced very nearly knocked the breath from my body. I was afraid that if I delayed leaving him any longer he would completely lose control one day soon and kill me.

As I turned to deliver my next line my voice dwindled and then faded altogether. Fortunately, the actor I was addressing realised I was in difficulty and carried on as if nothing had happened. Moments later, having come off the stage, I turned to a friend and fellow actress to say: 'I need to get away from someone so I'm going to skip the curtain calls and go out the back entrance tonight. Will you cover for me?'

'Fine, Sherrie – no problem,' she replied at once, instinctively realising that I was in some kind of trouble.

So while members of the cast were getting themselves in line for the curtain calls, still dressed in my costume I ran for my life – down the long backstage corridor, out the back door and down the road. Almost throwing myself in front of a taxi, I leapt inside it and begged the driver to take me to Nottingham.

'*Nottingham*!' he repeated, astonished. 'That's *70 miles*!'

'Yes, I know,' I said, 'but please, *please* take me there.'

I had no money on me and I must have looked an odd sight in my costume, sniffing away tears, but a kind-hearted cabbie came to my rescue for the second time. 'All right, love,' he told me. 'You sit back and I'll get you there.' And so for the next couple of hours I sat slumped in a state of nervous exhaustion in the back of his taxi.

At that point my mother had moved out of her penthouse and was staying with a friend while she had a new house built. When I arrived at her friend's house, hoping to find Mum, no one was in. Luckily I had a set of keys to the house and knew where the spare cash was kept, so I was able to pay the driver.

'Good luck, young lady,' he told me solicitously as he left. 'You take care of yourself.'

Those kind words reduced me to tears as soon as I had closed the door.

Moments later, my mother arrived home with her friend. Shocked at my state, she fed me hot tea and put me straight to bed, where I lay wide awake, unable to close my eyes. But the drama was not over yet: John managed to track down my taxi driver on his return and threatened him until the poor man had no choice but to tell him where he had dropped me off. It was early morning when John arrived outside the door in another cab.

My mother had been woken by the sound and, realising it must be John, she bundled me into a wardrobe. It was full of children's clothing, a row at the top and another at the bottom. I squeezed into the back behind the little rows of dresses and rompers, trying to keep as still as possible, hardly daring to breathe, but I was shaking so hard that it felt as though the whole wardrobe was shuddering.

Meanwhile, John banged loudly and repeatedly on the front door. Eventually, Mum opened it and he pushed his way in.

'Rest assured,' I could hear my mother repeating over and over again in the firmest voice she could muster, 'Sherrie is not here and has not been here for weeks.'

Minutes later I heard John enter the room where I was hiding. Then, to my horror, I heard him say in a mocking tone: 'You haven't shut the wardrobe door properly.'

As I squeezed myself further back behind the coats, he came over and flung open the door. Heart pounding, I held my breath and then for one brief and awful moment I found myself gazing straight into his eyes through the row of baby clothes in front of my face. Convinced he could see me, I very nearly screamed, but somehow, with the light behind him, he couldn't. At that moment my mother came over and, slamming the wardrobe door shut again, told him, 'I've had enough of this, John

Rowlands. If you don't leave right now, I will call the police and have you arrested.'

For some reason – and I really did not expect it to work – that did the trick and he left.

When Mum and her friend were absolutely sure he had gone, they returned and opened the wardrobe door.

'It's OK, you're safe now,' Mum's friend kept saying, as I tumbled out and collapsed in a flood of tears on the floor. But I didn't believe for a moment that I was safe: I stayed there for a few days, not daring to leave the house before going back to London, where I found myself a flat in Covent Garden and got back to work. Extraordinarily – and I will never know why – John gave up hounding and chasing me after that. In fact, he seemed to have disappeared altogether and it was not until 1992, almost twenty years later, that I heard from him again.

I was in a show with the comedian Russ Abbot on Blackpool Pier when I received a call, asking me to go to the stage door. When I got there the doorman said, 'Sherrie, there's someone on the phone for you.' Thinking it would be a friend, I took the receiver.

'Guess who?' said a voice which caused the hairs on the back of my neck to stand up.

'Where are you?' I asked.

'That's not for you to know,' he replied and the menacing tone in his voice took me instantly back.

I took a deep breath. 'Then get off the phone,' I said firmly. 'You are of no interest whatsoever to me, Mr Rowlands. Never, *ever* ring me again!'

That call – and my response to it – changed things forever for me: I had found the strength to tell him to get lost, and it freed me. No longer did I have to be a victim: I knew it, and now so did he.

Left: Me and Brett in the pool in the garden in Nottingham, just before another circus trick.

Right: Doing my best Winston Churchill impression. 'We will fight them on the beaches on my elephant.'

Left: You don't have to ask me twice, I'll sing anywhere. I love the sunglasses.

Right: My first professional appearance. Shyness was never a problem.

Right: My dad and granddad. Eat your hearts out; they were Errol Flynn and Humphrey Bogart to me.

Above: A fringe, a Poodle and Brett's girlfriend, in 1956.

Left: My grandparents, Raff the Poodle and me, aged seven.

Aged 15, in one of my first period dramas, *Our Town,* at the Theatre Club, Nottingham. Who chose those hats?

Left: Two peas in a pod. Me and my lovely Nana in Spain, 1963.

Right: The swinging sixties. Check out that coat!

My wedding day, 1983. I am wearing a 1910 period dress accompanied by Madonna lilies from the Queen's florist. How posh is that?

The happy couple. A sign of things to come!

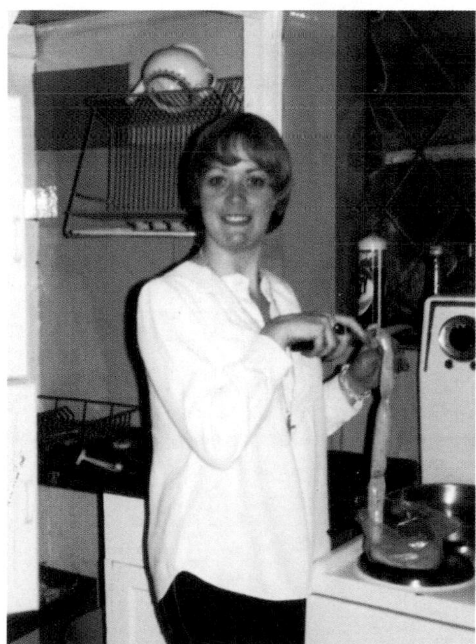

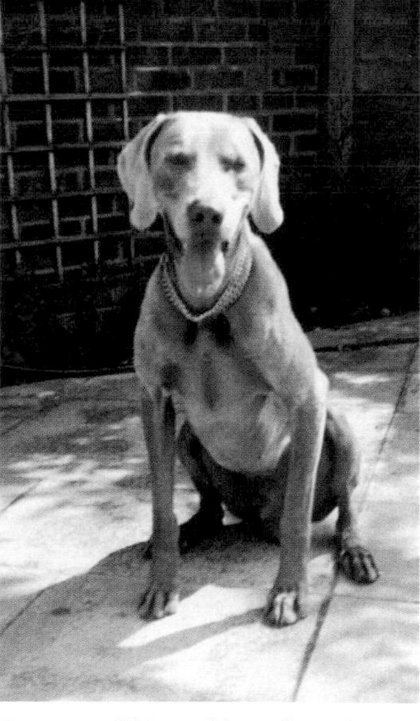

I never said I could cook. At least Caius never complained!

Left: The generations. Nana, Brett, Mum, Annie, Ken, Keeley and Chloe.

Below: Like mother, like daughter. Keeley was always ready to have her photo taken.

Below: The dreaded fringe makes another appearance, this time on Keeley. What was I thinking?

Right: I made this outfit for Keeley's Caribbean school day. She didn't take her arms down for the whole day!

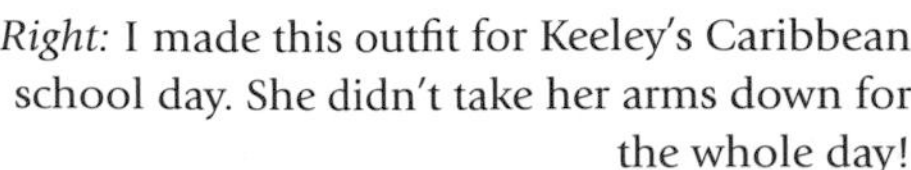

Above: My glamorous model mother.

Right: My lovely dad. Our last cuddle together.

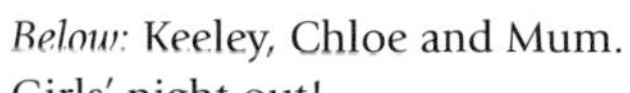

Below: Keeley, Chloe and Mum. Girls' night out!

Right: Keeley with Ollie, only a week old. Such a beautiful moment – my baby with her baby.

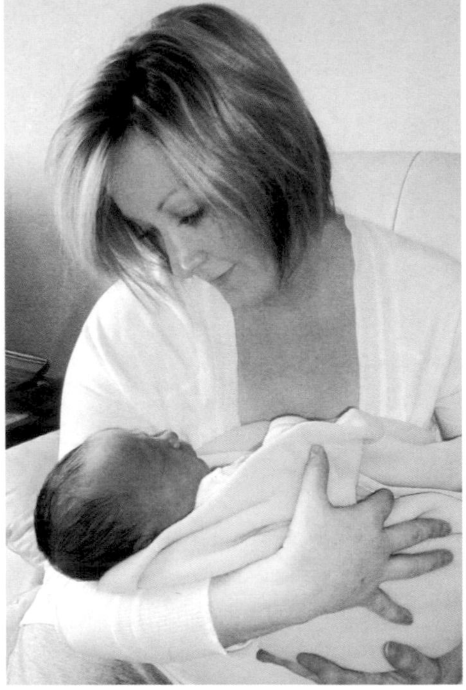

Below: Keeley and Simon. I'm so proud of both of them.

A proud Nana, with Keeley and new addition Molly. Now they are a complete family.

I was, however, to see John one more time. Two years later I was a regular in *Coronation Street* and doing a public appearance for the show, signing autographs for a long queue of people, when a voice that I recognised said: 'Just sign this one, "John, to you."' I looked up to see him standing in front of me and I felt sick. Without signing it, I simply handed the book back to him and turned to the next person in the queue.

And that, thank God, was the last I ever saw or heard from him, although he left a painful legacy. For many years afterwards I would look over my shoulder whenever I went out, and it's really only during the last fifteen years that I have started to relax and stopped doing that. To this day, if somebody standing near me suddenly raises a hand, I flinch.

Chapter Ten

As has been the case many times, work was my salvation as I picked myself up, all the while feeling I had somehow made a terrible mess of my life after that brief and horrendous relationship. Although it really wasn't my fault, I couldn't help but blame myself for allowing John into my life. Luckily for me, with the backing of my wonderful agent Peter, the offers of work flooded in, and for the next couple of years I was kept very busy indeed.

In 1974 I was offered a part in one of the famous *Carry On* films. As I have already mentioned, Peter represented Kenneth Williams and Joan Sims (both *Carry On* stalwarts) and when he suggested that he might have a word with the director about getting me a part I jumped at the chance. Peter felt the experience would introduce me to Pinewood, ranked then and now among the world's most famous and prestigious film studios.

The *Carry On* movies are British comedy classics – full of farce and innuendo, good-natured and beloved by the public. I was offered the part of camper Carol in *Carry On Behind* and very excited at the idea of my first chance to be on a film set. Altogether, there were twenty-nine original *Carry On* films and I was in the twenty-seventh, so by that time they were a British institution. Most of the actors had appeared in the *Carry On* series before: Kenneth had been in twenty-four of them, while Joan featured in almost as many, but there were other newcomers, too, including German-born film actress Elke Sommer, who played the sexy lead, Professor Vrooshka.

Elke was extremely glamorous and a proper Hollywood star at that time. Being so young, I saw her as an older, sexy femme fatale. All the boys loved her and fancied her rotten. I was intrigued to see someone walk around without a bra, her nipples clearly on show – I think my granddad would have said she was quite brazen. She had a proper dressing room, with all the comforts of a shower and a settee, while most of us just had your bog-standard rooms with a sink and window. It was intriguing to watch how she would have all the young boy runners in the palm of her hand. All day long they would fetch and carry for her – the only thing she had to do was bat her eyelashes, wiggle her chest and they were there. Lunchtimes, we would traipse off to the canteen but she would have the prettiest boy runner deliver food to her room. I thought when I was her age – she was ten years older than me – that I would call on the cutest runner to come and rub me down with a scented palm in my lunch break. Sadly, all I want these days is a cup of tea and a chocolate HobNob!

When I first left RADA Peter took me to meet Joan Sims at her house in Parsons Green, West London. It was a beautiful, three-storey Edwardian property with memorabilia all over the place. On the walls were posters from all the plays and musicals she'd ever done, plus photos galore of the stars she had worked with, from Hattie Jacques and Kenneth Williams to Katharine

Hepburn and Laurence Olivier. It was magical for me, just out of RADA – which Joan had also attended quite a few years before. Joannie was down-to-earth, funny and quite lovely to me. I have glorious memories of nights round her dining-room table with the *Carry On* team relating endless wicked tales of the goings-on behind the scenes of the other films. One by one, they would get up and do rude little ditties, which became ruder and ruder, the more they drank.

One particular night Joan and Kenneth did a mock striptease as we all la-la'd to 'The Stripper'. Kenneth climbed up onto one of Joan's beautiful Georgian chairs and, as if in slow motion, turned while dropping his trousers to expose his backside. Suddenly, the seat on the chair gave way and he dropped through, but we were all laughing so much that no one attempted to help him. Immediately, he picked up the chair so it was round his waist. Meanwhile, his trousers and pants were now round his ankles. With the chair hiding his bits, he carried on with the routine and made a big exit through the sitting-room door. Following this, we heard the biggest crash as he collided with something but we were all screaming with laughter. 'Don't fucking worry about *me*!' he bellowed, which rendered us completely useless.

Magic memories.

As she went upstairs to bed, Joan always used to ask me to be a sweetie and bring her some water. Every night, I would dutifully take a cut-glass jug of water to her. Propped up by big, plumped-up pillows, she'd be snug as a bug. I'd pour her a glass of water, then sit and talk for a while. I loved this time with Joan. It wasn't until many years later that I found out that the water was in fact vodka and I shouldn't have been giving it to her – by then she had an implant to stop herself from drinking. I felt so guilty.

If a *Carry On* movie had the word 'camping' or 'caravan' in the title, they were all filmed in March on the same muddy field on a back lot at Pinewood studios. The field would be a mud bath, there were no leaves on the trees and snow was always imminent. A lot of blue bodies in shorts or bikinis, including me, would be running around and doing their best to pretend it was summer. Early spring was freezing cold, and between takes we had to wait in tatty old caravans – our 'dressing rooms' – parked at the side of the field. One day I was in a caravan with Joan, who desperately wanted to wee. There was no loo in the caravan and the Portaloos were right across the field, so Joan said, 'Darling, pass me your empty cup.' I handed her the small polystyrene vessel and she lifted her skirt, pulled down her knickers and proceeded to wee into it. Just at that moment Kenneth Williams walked in. He took one look, slammed the caravan door, threw back his head and said with a withering sniff, 'No tea for me, thank you!'

While I loved Joan's lack of vanity and great sense of humour, Kenneth was altogether a different kettle of fish. Wickedly cutting and cruel at times, he was a master of the icy put-down and invariably turned his spotlight on me. I was what they then termed his 'whipping boy'. Young and unsure of myself, I didn't know how to cope with his contemptuous and savage jibes, yet Carol Hawkins (my friend in the story and in real life) could handle him beautifully, but then she had done quite a few films with him and knew his ways.

It was Peter Butterworth, another *Carry On* great, who became my mentor and protector. If Peter was there, Kenneth wouldn't torment me, but the moment he left Kenneth would ask me some obscure question about an eighteenth-century painter or Greek philosopher. When I invariably didn't know the answer, he'd ask, 'Did you *actually* go to school? You're a philistine!'

Then again, I didn't know what one of those was either. Later, I wished I'd stood up to him as some of the others did. It was a pattern with him: he'd be cruel to someone, tire of them and move onto the next, almost as if he wanted to see how far he could push before they cracked. I certainly let him push me around but I didn't have the courage to stand up to him and tell him what I thought, so he just went on pushing. He soon tired of me, too, and moved on, though. Having said that, I believe he was a genius, an extraordinary talent the like of whom we will never see again. I only wish I hadn't been so young and obtuse then: I might have had the chance to get to know the real Kenneth Williams.

All in all, I loved being in a *Carry On* film, even the chilly discomfort of the caravans. It was all so wonderfully tongue in cheek, with its trademark saucy-postcard humour. How amazing to have appeared in a film which is now a part of British cinematic history.

It was not long afterwards that I got to know another *Carry On* great: Barbara Windsor. Barbara had starred in nine of the films, but she wasn't in *Carry On Behind*. We met when I was asked to take part in the only TV series ever made by the *Carry On* team: *Carry On Laughing*, which went out on ATV in 1975. It spoofed all the major TV shows of that time such as *Upstairs Downstairs* with wonderful names like 'The Case of the Screaming Winkles' and 'The Case of the Coughing Parrot'. For me, this was another chance to work with a brilliant team, who taught me so much.

I liked Barbara enormously – she was warm, funny and excellent company. One day she told me about a private drinking club owned by her husband, Ronnie Knight, in London's Tottenham Court Road. Barbara had been married to Ronnie for eleven years and by this time the rumours about him being a gangster, whose associates had included the notorious Kray Twins, were rife. Ten years later Ronnie fled to Spain and he and Barbara parted, but all that was to come. Now I knew none of this: I just thought how nice and I'd never been to a private club where the licensing hours were non-existent.

And so three of us turned up at this very old Victorian building and went up several flights of stairs until we reached the top, where there was a door with a panel in it. Not sure what to do, I knocked on the panel. Just like in the movies, it slid back and a very large man stared at me. 'Yuh?' he grunted. 'We are Barbara Windsor's friends,' I spluttered. At this, the panel slammed shut and I heard a clunk, clunk, clunk as the bolts were released. When the door finally opened, it was amazing: we walked into jazz playing and a long bar, and it was mostly full of men in suits. The door slammed shut, it was locked again and we were escorted to a table facing the main windows at the front of the building.

'You know what Ronnie Knight does, don't you?' my friend whispered.

'No, what?' I asked.

He then proceeded to tell me the whole story of Mr Knight and all that entailed. It was the most exciting thing I'd ever heard. 'He's over there,' my friend muttered out of the corner of his mouth. He nodded towards the opposite corner from us and sitting with his back to the wall in a white polo neck and black trousers was the extremely handsome Ronnie Knight. He had about ten men sitting round the table with him. Now I won't get carried away and say they kissed his ring – it wasn't *The Godfather* – but it was still exciting for a girl from Nottingham with Robin Hood as her only point of reference as to this kind of world.

Suddenly Ronnie got up, the men stood up, too, and then dispersed. He came over to us and we also got up. He went to shake my hand, saying, 'I know who you are, Sherrie. I just want to say, you are all very welcome here as friends of Barbara. Anything you want, just ask – it's all on the house. Stay as long as you like.' He was very gracious and warm towards us. With his entourage in his wake, he strolled past the bar through a door and then he was gone. We stayed quite a few hours and ate and drank as much as we could – never tell an actor the food and booze are free or they will eat you out of house and home! My imagination ran rife that day and by the time we left I had conjured up all kinds of scenarios. It felt as if we were in the middle of a 1920s' film set – Al Capone and me, what a team.

Almost as soon as *Carry On Behind* wrapped, I was incredibly lucky and landed another film role: the wonderful *Slipper and the Rose*. How this came about was that while I was filming *Carry On* Peter came down for lunch. Now lunch at Pinewood was held in their Baronial Hall and always an opulent affair, with its oak-lined walls, highly polished wooden floors and long refectory tables, each dedicated to different film casts. As I sat at the *Carry On* table with Peter, Kenneth and Joan, I felt privileged.

After Kenneth and Joan had gone off to the sound stage, Peter said: 'I want you to come with me to meet someone very special.' We went upstairs and were shown into an office, where sitting behind the desk was Bryan Forbes, the brilliant director of films such as *Whistle Down the Wind, The Railway Children* and *The Raging Moon*. I was there to meet him and talk about *The Slipper and the Rose*, a musical based on the story of Cinderella. He told me the part was to play one of the Ugly Sisters – except this wasn't the usual panto sister for she would be evil, not ugly. Bryan was so charming and filled me with confidence by offering me the part then and there, which was very unusual. I thanked him, and as we got up to leave he told me: 'You have beautiful ankles.' I had a pair of strappy shoes on, and gazing at them he said: 'Very nice.' I never dared mention this when I got to work with him.

I must add that I came to love Bryan because he taught me so much about acting: I remember him taking me to see the rushes one night – those are the raw, unedited scenes filmed that day and shown on a big screen for the producers and director to watch. As I sat there with him, he told me: 'The person I want you to look at closely is Kenny More.' Now he was the most consummate actor of his time and I already admired him. 'What is it he's doing?' asked Bryan, as we sat and watched him. 'Nothing,' I said. '*Precisely*, and that's the greatest lesson you will ever learn about acting: if *you* believe it, we will see it. You don't have to act it.'

I treasure those memories of Bryan, his direction and also getting to know his gorgeous family: I'm so grateful for the chance he gave me. And it was quite a coup to land this part because the cast included some very big names. It was the last film ever made by Margaret Lockwood, star of dozens of Hollywood films including *Lorna Doone*, *The Lady Vanishes* and *The Wicked Lady*. Michael Hordern, Kenneth More, Edith Evans and Annette Crosbie also appeared, and the young star was Gemma Craven as Cinderella. Richard Chamberlain played Prince Edward and was the most beautiful man I have ever seen – he took your breath away.

When we assembled for our first read-through, Richard came over to say hello. I was a bit too young to remember *Dr Kildare* but I had seen him in many films, too numerous to list, but among them were *Lady Caroline Lamb*, *The Towering Inferno* and *The Three Musketeers*, although it was too early for every woman in the world to have fallen in love with Ralph de Bricassart from *The Thorn Birds*. As he held out a hand, saying in the deepest, darkest American voice, 'Hello, I'm Richard,' my legs turned to jelly and I collapsed at his feet.

'Are you OK?' he asked, as he helped me up.

'There's nowt wrong wi' me,' I muttered.

He stared at me, unsure of what I'd said.

'Would you like some water?' he continued.

'No, you're all right, me duck,' was all I could say.

After this he gave me a pitying smile and moved on. Standing nearby was Gemma Craven, who asked: 'Why are you speaking with that odd northern accent?' 'I don't know, I've lost the power of speech – that's all that would come out,' I explained. 'Well, get over it! You sound stupid and seriously weird,' she told me in a fierce whisper. Goodness knows where he must have thought I was from, certainly no Northern town I've ever been in. In the end, I managed to control my accent but I never got over my obsession with Richard or the overwhelming desire to marry him.

Despite this unpromising beginning, we became great friends but I was always a foolish, giggly girl around him to the point of doing painfully embarrassing things: while filming in Salzburg, for example, if we all went for a walk into the town then I would slip my hand in his. He never once said, 'For God's sake, what are you doing?' and I didn't realise how silly I looked. He played really naughty tricks on me, though: he once told me that we were all going to have lunch in the dining room at Pinewood. Usually, most of the tables were booked for each film and so anyone else wanting to eat had to queue near the door, although they could see into the restaurant. Richard told me that we had the largest table and so we leant about twenty chairs into the table so people would know they were taken. He then instructed me to sit at the table and wait for the others while he left, saying he would make sure everyone else was coming. Needless to say,

I sat there for what seemed like days and no one arrived. Eventually, the Maitre d' approached and asked me to leave as some other diners had been waiting for an hour and a half. Little did I know that watching me with a few of the others behind the long windows outside was Richard!

I still would have married him except for the other thing I learned about him: he ate raw steak for nearly every meal – he must have smelt like a cow. Inside and out, Richard was absolutely beautiful. He was always kind and courteous and although of course we were never more than friends I convinced myself that he could love me as I loved him. It makes me squirm now to think I could ever be that dense.

We made the film in the famous Pinewood studios in Iver Heath, Buckinghamshire. In the next studio to us were Trevor Howard and Terry Thomas, who were starring in *The Bawdy Adventures of Tom Jones*. I had to try and get on the set to watch Trevor because as far as I was concerned he was film royalty. Sadly, this was late on in his career and drink had taken its toll – he struggled to remember lines and seemed disorientated. Later, I watched him walk off the set and into the bar, where the crew stood with him and he was throwing money at them to buy drinks. I walked away, thinking you should never meet your heroes because the last image is what you always remember.

Over in the next studio to them were the inimitable Jodie Foster and Scott Baio, who were having a fantastic time making *Bugsy Malone*. I will never forget standing at the back of the set with one of the sound boys, watching Jodie sing, 'My Name is Tallulah'. It was spine-tingling: she was only 14 years old and yet somehow you knew a star had been born. Scott later played Charles 'Chachi' Arcola in the TV sitcom, *Happy Days*, among many other TV and film roles.

At the end of *Bugsy* they all have guns, and as they fire them cream pies come out instead of bullets. They then start throwing pies at each other – brilliant! Some of us from our set snuck in to watch behind the scenes, and unfortunately we were found lurking and got caught up in the fun, too. We got in terrible trouble with our wardrobe department but it was worth it just to have those wonderful memories.

Richard and I spent a lot of time together during the nine months we were filming. We became really good friends, and towards the end of filming he invited me to his home in America and gave me his address and phone number. On the last day I was so excited that I couldn't resist telling everyone on the set. I then showed them his details, just in case they didn't believe me. Not an 'ounce of nous', as my dad might have said.

Margaret Lockwood, who had taken me under her wing as a surrogate mum, shook her head sorrowfully at me and said, 'Sherrie darling, you are the most imprudent girl I have ever known.' Seeing my confusion, she added, sadly, 'Never mind.' At first I didn't know what she was talking about … until I got back to my dressing room. Every last vestige of Richard – his telephone numbers, photos and keepsakes – had disappeared from my room. I was extremely hurt.

I didn't really understand what I had done and it was only years later, after I'd joined the cast of *Coronation Street* in 1993, that I realised how frightened stars can become, paranoid almost, about the possibility of people misinterpreting their kindnesses and of attracting the sort of attention that might lead to stalking. It was a lesson learned too late for my friendship with Richard.

Much to the delight of everybody who worked on it, *The Slipper and the Rose* was chosen as the Royal Command Performance for 1976, to be screened for the Queen Mother, and it was then nominated for two Academy Awards: a Golden Globe and two BAFTAs. It felt wonderful to be part of something so successful.

After *Carry On Behind* and *The Slipper and the Rose* my career was on a roll, but it wasn't all successes – I had my share of mishaps, failed auditions and blown opportunities, too. One of my worst moments ever was when I threw away the chance to appear with Robert Redford in *The Great Gatsby* (1974). I attended the audition, knowing they were casting for a big Hollywood movie, still so top secret that we weren't even told what it was going to be. I walked in and had only just opened my mouth to talk about my CV when I spotted Robert Redford sitting in the corner – in general, you don't walk into an audition to find a movie legend sitting there. In the previous five years he'd starred in *Butch Cassidy and the Sundance Kid, The Way We Were* and *The Sting*. Now I found myself face to face with a Hollywood legend and my mind became a total blank.

The producer conducting the audition asked what acting work I had done, but all I could recall at that moment was playing the third witch in *Macbeth* at RADA. 'Yes,' he kept on patiently saying, 'but you must have done more than that.' Of course, I had done so much more, but all I could see was Redford looking over at me and helplessly I kept on repeating, 'I played the third witch in *Macbeth*,' over and over again.

Naturally, they thought I was potty and eventually I was told I could go, whereupon they virtually had to pick me up and throw me out. Outside, I came to my senses and begged the casting director to let me back in to at least let them know I had a brain, but I was told in no uncertain terms to go home: I had blown it. Robert Redford, for God's sake, what an idiot!

Luckily for me, I landed a major TV series soon afterwards. *Love for Lydia* was a 13-part television series for London Weekend Television, based on the novel by H. E. Bates. It's the story of Lydia Aspen, a young heiress growing up in the 1920s, and her transformation from shy teenager to wild young flapper. Along the way, several young men fall in love with her only to have their hearts broken as Lydia flits from one to the next.

Many prestigious actors, such as Rachel Kempson, Michael Aldridge, Beatrix Lehmann and David Ryall, all starred alongside up-and-coming newcomers like me and Peter Davison (who later went on to become the fifth *Doctor Who*), Mel Martin and the very new Jeremy Irons. Peter and I played brother and sister Tom and Nancy Holland, who were the country bumpkins of the piece, living on a farm and not understanding the Bright Young Things, yet in a very naive way joining in. I adored Peter and we became quite close in a brother-and-sister kind of way. In fact, I still think of him as a brother to this day.

The male lead was Christopher Blake, who played the part of Edward, the young reporter who is the first to fall for Lydia. My character (Nancy) was supposed to be in love with him, too, and for this I hardly needed to do any acting at all. Chris was very handsome, extremely funny and so talented. We had a great relationship, much like the characters themselves. Nancy fancied Edward and he found her funny but ever so slightly annoying – you know, when you really like someone but you are already attached to another person and so you flirt in the only way you can? In my case, this was to hit Chris – just whack him one as I passed him or jump out from behind a door in a scene and say 'Boo!' So, now you can see why he found me irritating. If I'd been single, God only knows what I might have done – certainly try and snog him – he'd have had to prise me off. Makes you shudder to think, doesn't it? We stayed friends for many years and Chris just got better looking and became an excellent writer for drama and comedy. Sadly, he died much too young (55, of non-Hodgkins lymphoma) in 2004, but it still makes me smile now to think of the fun we had – and the fun we might have had.

The girl playing the part of Lydia was a young actress called Mel Martin, who was a couple of years older than me. We became very good friends and spent a lot of time together, on and off the set. When I introduced her to my brother Brett, much to my delight they hit it off and began dating. Then, as I have already mentioned, another newcomer was Jeremy Irons, who had an air about him of such self-confidence. There was no doubt where he was going: the boy done good.

The outdoor film set was on an old airfield in Wisley, Surrey, and for many of the scenes we were supposed to be skating on a frozen lake. Part of the field was covered in a surface that looked like ice and the cast were given skates with little wheels rather than blades on them so that we could look as if we were ice-skating. The whole area was covered in what looked like snow, but of course it wasn't real. I believe it was a sort of salt and it looked bleak and wintry. Alan Clarke was our director and he became one of the most influential directors of our time, creating a whole host of controversial TV plays and films, such as *Scum* (1979), *Made in Britain* (1982) and then *Rita, Sue and Bob Too* (1986), among others. Revered by all who worked with him, we were lucky to have him as our first director.

Alan was extremely innovative in his approach, and although we were mostly newcomers in *Lydia* he wanted to film long shots of us skating, so no one could be sure who we were. The pretend mist and smoke puffed over the fields and set an eerie scene, very filmic. We filmed all the skating scenes over several weeks and we just knew it would look stunning and that it really was something quite special. At the time, the head of London Weekend Television (the company making *Lydia*) was Cyril Bennett. This was the man who disliked the first episode of

Upstairs Downstairs so intensely that he did all he could to prevent it from going ahead, declaring the series wasn't commercial enough and no one would watch it. He couldn't stop the filming and so he tried to hide the show in the schedules, hoping no one would discover it. Thankfully, his efforts proved fruitless and it became the most successful series in television history.

In a similar way, he stopped all filming on *Lydia* and called an emergency meeting at the studios the following day. Everyone attended, including Alan and other directing greats who were already starting out, such as Piers Haggard, Tony Wharmby and John Glenister. As we sat down, we knew something ominous was afoot. Cyril Bennett stood up and proceeded to say exactly what he must have said to the *Upstairs Downstairs* cast and crew. Because Alan had shot all the scenes in long shot and this being a commercial studio, he wanted every shot, in full close-up and not this fancy filmic nonsense, therefore all footage would have to be scraped and re-shot, with or without our director. He knew full well that Alan would never compromise – and certainly not for a lame excuse such as this. No apology, no discussion, no reprieve, he had made his decision and this time no one was going to flout his orders. It was devastating news for all those involved in the production. That day in September 1976 one of our greatest directors walked, and we missed him. Two months later Cyril Bennett took his own life, which was shocking and upsetting.

Despite the tragedies, upsets and false starts which meant filming took over two years to complete, I loved every minute of making *Love for Lydia* and feel lucky to have been a part of it. One of the most expensive drama series made at that time, it was set in the thirties and so the vintage cars and the Art-Deco sets must have cost a fortune. It was a major TV series and a big breakthrough for me.

Chapter Eleven

The summer of 1976 was scorching and broke all records. In fact, the heatwave was so extreme there were water shortages all over the country and James Callaghan, the British Prime Minister, was forced to appoint a minister for drought.

At the time I was working on the last episodes of *Love for Lydia*. It was so hot that it was difficult to do anything. Under cloudless skies we all fried and dreamt of rain and snow. Despite this, I was very happy – I had just attended the royal première of *The Slipper and the Rose* and had been offered a part in a TV drama-series called *My Son, My Son*, starring Michael Williams.

I was still living with my brother Brett in the flat in Vauxhall and he continued with his modelling, as well as working as a DJ in a club called Cactus, which was attached to the Regent Palace Hotel. I used to go down there sometimes to see him and it was Brett who introduced me to the club's doorman-cum-cashier, Ken Boyd.

Ken was a good-looking, blue-eyed blond, four years younger than me. He was so attractive I thought he must be gay, but I soon discovered otherwise. At the club he was always surrounded by girls and chatting them all up. I really fancied him and he made it clear that he liked me, too, but he seemed unavailable and made me do all the chasing. Of course, I became more and more attracted to him, as you do when someone seems disinterested. Then, it seemed, Ken stopped chatting up the other girls and decided he wanted to be with me. We got together, and he and I made up a foursome with Brett and Mel. After the guys finished up at the club and we had wrapped on set, we used to go back to Mel's flat in Brixton, order takeaway curry, put on some music and talk and laugh for half the night.

Ken and I would also meet outside the Regent Palace Hotel and go for long romantic walks all the way down the King's Road in Chelsea – which is a very long road. As we strolled along, we'd look in the trendy boutique windows and end up in The Trafalgar pub, where we'd sit holding hands and share a drink. Neither of us had much money to spare, so we couldn't go out for expensive meals, but it didn't matter. We were in the first flush of love and just being together and walking, hand-in-hand, was enough.

We spent hours swapping life stories and Ken told me that he was born in Ireland, although as his father had been a navigator in the RAF he had spent his childhood travelling all over the world. Eventually his parents settled in Padstow, Cornwall, and he had gone to live in Spain, returning a short while before he met me.

Within a month of our first meeting we decided to move in together. We wanted to find a flat, but while we were looking for one we took a room in a little hotel called the Arundel, between Hammersmith and Barnes on London's South Bank.

The temperatures used to rise to boiling point in our tiny room. I remember sitting by the window when I woke up in the mornings, gasping for oxygen like a fish out of water. It just seemed to get hotter and hotter – Ken and I used to have a cold shower at night just to get our body temperatures down. He was still working at the Cactus Club in the evenings, so I would be left to swelter at home. If anything ought to have finished our romance off, it was that heatwave, but I was convinced Ken was the love of my life and nothing would deter me: a Saveloy sausage, a can of lager and that little room was all I needed.

When I introduced Ken to my mother, she did her best to put me off, though. 'He's a waster, Sherrie,' she kept saying. 'Think twice before you get too involved.' After he met Ken, Dad also tried to warn me, saying: 'He's a chancer, Sherrie. I don't trust him – be careful.' I was certain my parents were wrong but the truth is that even Ken tried to prepare me: 'I'm not the kind of man you should be with, Sherrie,' he said, after I told him that I was in love with him. 'I can't be faithful to one woman.'

He then added that he had always planned to return to Spain and was thinking of going back there soon.

'Why?' I asked, distraught.

'Because I'm not the sort of person who's ready to settle down,' he replied.

Ever the optimist, I refused to give up, saying: 'I can change you, Ken.'

'No,' he insisted firmly, 'you can't, Sherrie.'

'Then let's both be unfaithful,' I suggested.

'No, absolutely not,' he exclaimed. 'I couldn't stand that!'

'Then why don't we go on as we are and try and make a go of it?' I pleaded.

'All right,' he said at last, 'but don't ever say I didn't warn you.'

So, did I listen to any of the warnings I had been given? Of course not, but Ken was telling the truth, and later I would discover to my cost that he and my parents were right all along:

he couldn't be faithful and I wouldn't be able to change him. But at the beginning I felt so sure that being in love was enough. As far as I was concerned, everyone was wrong, including Ken, and I was so sure that I could change him, given time.

Why do women do that? It's such a waste of energy.

From the Arundel Hotel, Ken and I moved into a flat in Barnes for £132 a month. It was in a house owned by a woman who was terribly well spoken, somewhat aristocratic. She had obviously fallen on hard times and been forced to rent out rooms – 'PGs', she used to call us (paying guests). We soon discovered she was totally eccentric. Very old, rather wizened and a bit like Bette Davis in her latter years, she lived in the back part of the house, which we were never allowed to see. She was friendly with Lord Longford, who used to come to tea with her once a week. On days when he was coming she would leave a note, warning us not to make any noise out of respect for his title! We used to watch him arrive – a rather strange-looking man, we thought – and he would disappear into her part of the house. Ken and I often used to joke that Lord Lucan (who had gone missing a year or two earlier after the murder of his children's nanny) probably made up a happy trio.

We tried to come and go without our landlady seeing us because her behaviour was unpredictable and often rather scary. If she spotted us, she would frequently scream obscenities at us all the way down the stairs and out into the drive. The next day, however, she would be utterly charming and offer us fresh fruit from her garden.

Ken and I had a little Mini that we called Spit because it was literally held together by a spit and a promise. We paid just £40 for it, but the MOT cost us a crippling £80. By the time we moved to Barnes, Spit's bonnet was just about clinging on and the doors (not the originals) were prone to work themselves loose as we were driving along. One morning we were sneaking out of the house when our crazy landlady saw us. As we were getting into Spit she put her head out of the window, started to yell the usual obscenities at us and then tipped a bowl of dirty washing-up water out of the window, drenching both us and the car! Far worse was to come for poor old Spit, though.

Not long afterwards, we were driving down the motorway one afternoon at 35 miles an hour – much to the fury of other drivers, Spit couldn't go any faster – when a gust of wind suddenly lifted the bonnet and it flew up, obscuring the windscreen. To add insult to injury, both doors flew off and Ken put his foot through the floorboard. Just at that moment, as we were struggling along at snail's pace and still hoping to reach our destination, a police car – lights flashing – drew up alongside us.

Having wound down his window, the policeman nearest me yelled, 'Pull over before that vehicle totally disintegrates!' In fear and trembling we did as he asked. We had no insurance or road tax, but fortunately the two police officers had a sense of humour. Having slapped the equivalent of a 'not to be driven' notice on Spit's flapping-in-the-wind bonnet, they arranged for our beloved car to be towed away and trashed.

'Goodbye, Spit,' I whispered tearfully.

Our next car was a little red Viva, which had a diva-ish engine. In cold weather the only way we could get it to start was to wrap two hot-water bottles and a duvet round its insides. To make matters worse, in those days we often used to go to Padstow to visit Ken's mother and father, and believe me, it was a long, slow drive down the A30 in those days. Before we could set off the Viva had to be defrosted for hours, and as we had no heating in the car I would wrap myself in a duvet and was constantly pouring tea from a flask to keep us warm and awake on the journey once we finally set off. To this day I love travelling with a flask of tea and some sandwiches on my lap.

During our first years together Ken and I were very happy. We loved our little flat, loved our trips to Padstow to see his parents and eat crab sandwiches, loved each other and had a lot of fun. We didn't stay long in the tiny flat in Barnes. Desperate to escape our deranged landlady, we moved to a flat in Mortlake. It was a bit bigger and was on the ground floor, which was how I came to have a pet snail called Brian.

Friends thought Brian was disgusting because he left slimy silver trails everywhere, but I adored him. He lived outside, but in the mornings when I opened the kitchen door he used to amble in and wander around, looking for his lettuce leaf or bit of cabbage, whatever treat I'd got for his breakfast. Sadly, this relationship was to end in tragedy. One day he didn't appear and when I went to look for him I found a wet, mashed-up mess with bits of shell in it – someone had trodden on him. I kept on saying, 'It's not Brian,' but Ken insisted, 'It is.' By the time I had accepted the inevitable I was so upset I didn't even consider another pet for ages – not until we bought our first house in Ham, Richmond, a couple of years later when we eventually got a Weimaraner puppy.

Ken always wanted to be an RAF pilot. His father had been a navigator, but Ken was keen to fly the planes themselves. Unfortunately, tests showed he had a lazy eye, which put paid to any hopes of this. He then thought about becoming a policeman but decided against it, which was why when I met him he was directionless and working in a nightclub. After we'd been together for a couple of years he decided he needed a proper job, and he got one, working as a project manager for British Aerospace in Ham, Surrey. I was delighted that he had decided to do something worthwhile, and his new role also meant that we could buy a house together. It was a sweet little place and felt like our first proper home.

One day when I was looking out at the garden I said to Ken, 'Why is our lawn not flat, like everybody else's? Ours is all bumpy.' When we started to investigate, we could not believe our eyes: every time we dug the spade into the soil, out came another object. We dug up books and newspapers from the 1950s, a pram, bicycles, dolls, lamps, clothes, a huge roller and a lawn mower. We ended up with such a variety of objects that our garden looked just like the conveyor belt featured in *Bruce Forsyth's Generation Game* – except these items were old, filthy and worthless.

By the time we finished removing it all, we were left with a huge crater. I kept saying to Ken, 'We'd better stop before we find a body!' We just couldn't understand why anybody would dump so many of their precious possessions in that way and remained convinced that they must have left in a tearing hurry for one sinister reason or another. In fact, we never did solve the mystery, but once we got rid of everything and filled in the crater we had my much-longed-for, perfect lawn.

After that, we started on the kitchen. Having decided we wanted to enlarge it, Ken (who fancied himself as someone who could turn his hand to anything) decided to knock down the wall on his own. Once it was down, we had a room twice as big and were rather pleased with ourselves until a friend looked up and asked, 'What's holding that ceiling up?' We gazed up to see the now-unsupported ceiling had developed huge cracks and a strange sag; it was about to come down. 'That's it,' I declared. 'We're getting a builder in!'

That was not the last of Ken's DIY disasters: his next project was to build a partition wall by the hall doorway to make space to house a fridge-freezer. Having created one huge mess, splashing cement everywhere and laying a few rows of bricks that reached calf height, he totally lost interest in the project. Indeed, the 'wall' remained as it was for the next three years until we sold that house and moved into our next one. The trouble was, Ken thought he could do anything and in those days I was still seeing him through rose-tinted spectacles, so I thought so, too.

By this time I was longing to have a baby: Ken and I felt settled. I dreamed of a little boy or girl to make us a complete family, but despite the fact that I hadn't used contraception since we'd been together, nothing happened. Much as I wanted a baby, I had also made up my mind that if I didn't become pregnant then I would accept it and wouldn't have any intervention or fertility treatment. After a while, and many disappointments when I thought I might have conceived only to find I hadn't, I became convinced that I would never have a child. Ken didn't seem to mind – he wasn't longing to have children in the way that I was and he agreed we should just accept it if I never became pregnant. Instead we decided to get a puppy and I wanted a Weimaraner because of Smoky, Mama's dog in Cyprus. We chose a gorgeous little puppy from a breeder and I named him Caius – a noble-sounding name for a noble-looking dog.

From the moment he entered our home Caius became my baby, and I do mean 'baby' because he was the child I had not been able to conceive. I loved him to distraction and he returned my affection with an amazing unconditional love. He was utterly impossible and would never come back when let off the lead, but he could do no wrong in my eyes.

As Weimaraners do, Caius kept on growing. By the time he was a year old and fully grown, our cute little puppy had turned into a strapping hunting dog. Worse still, he was impossible to train. Caius needed routine and discipline – something he wasn't getting from us – and so I did what I thought was best and offered him to the police to be trained as one of their working dogs. A dog handler came round to the house and took him off for a half-day's training, but he was back within two hours.

'You have made this dog into your baby, you've ruined him!' he explained. 'He's useless to us and will never make a working dog. In the short time I had him, he refused any order or command I gave him, so I knew there was no point in carrying on. He just wants to be kissed and cuddled.'

'Oh, Caius!' I cried, and smothered him with cuddles and kisses as he wagged his tail and slobbered all over me with pleasure. It was true love. Soon we were back to the way we'd been before: my 'baby' and me on Ham Common for walkies every morning and once again locked in a battle of wills, with me bawling at him to come back while he delighted in giving me the run-around. Despite his size, I swear he could out-run the wind if he saw me approaching with his lead – he knew perfectly well that I had no choice but to wait until he felt like ambling back to me. Of course he eventually grew out of his naughtiness, as all babies do. Certainly no dog has ever been quite so loved as he was: I adored him, but he knew it and returned my love sevenfold.

I decided that we should sell the house in Ham when I found a beautiful, round Art-Deco property in Hinchley Wood, Surrey. By this time we had been together for almost six years and although we didn't know it then we'd had our happiest years together and the honeymoon period was gradually giving way to resentments and difficulties. Ken was eyeing other women while I was painfully aware of it and unsure whether he loved me as much as I loved him. I hoped desperately that he did, but my heart sank every time I saw him smile at a pretty girl. To this day

I cannot go to a party without scanning the room and being aware of who my rivals might be.

Full of fears and doubts, I turned to the one thing that always helped: work.

Chapter Twelve

I may have been in love with Ken but that didn't stop me from fancying my leading men. It's a professional hazard, I suppose. I never have been able to help it, perhaps because I've been lucky enough to work with so many good-looking, funny and talented actors. One of the very best was Michael Williams, with whom I worked in *My Son, My Son* (1978), which we made for the BBC. Alas, he was already very happily married to the brilliant Judi Dench, but at least I got to be his wife in the drama.

Anything can – and does – happen on sets, whether they're in the theatre, or in TV or film studios. I've had stools, chairs and tables collapse beneath me, curtains fall around my ears, walls buckle, shift or tumble down and doors jam just as I'm about to make a dramatic entrance or exit. In *My Son, My Son*, it was the curtains, followed by the curtain pole, followed by a wall – all just at the moment when Michael and I were right in the midst of a tragic scene about the death of our son. With cameras rolling, I entered the room dressed in severe funereal black and went to pull the curtains only to have the whole lot – curtains, pole and wall – come down around me.

Michael and I were reduced to hysterical giggles. We tried once more and then several more times, but every time we began the scene the two of us collapsed in fits of laughter all over again. The production team were not amused – they rarely are when something like this happens because you're wasting time and money. The trouble is, laughter is so contagious, and if you have two gigglers there's no control. We were both helpless and hopeless and so the director had to get very cross with us indeed before we could pull ourselves together.

In *My Son, My Son* I played Nellie, the estranged wife who dies in a car crash at the end. As it was a 1930s drama, I was of course given a car from the period. The problem was that I really didn't know how to drive it and the brake was only a hand brake, not exactly adequate for stopping.

'Don't worry,' I was told. 'All you have to do is drive along this tiny bit of road, avoid hitting any of the lights or cameras or crew, of course, and turn the car sharply onto the grassy verge.'

'OK,' I agreed, enthusiastically.

And so I got behind the wheel of the gorgeous little classic car they'd lined up and, having succeeded in getting it moving, rolled gingerly forward. The trouble was, I was concentrating so hard on not hitting the lights, the cameras or the cameraman that although I did turn onto the grassy bit and applied the hand brake I spun the wheel so hard that I ran the car off the road and managed to crash it into a ditch. Fortunately, the cameras were still rolling and caught the whole thing. 'Brilliant!' the director shouted. 'Keep Sherrie in there till we set up the next bit of the scene.' They sort of checked that I was OK, but as the light was going they just wanted to finish the set-ups and end the day.

The next bit showed me on the grass, as if thrown from the crash with blood dripping from my mouth. It was now early evening, getting cold, and there I was, lying on damp grass, trying to keep still, with blood pellets in my mouth ready for me to bite. They did one shot of me very still as blood dripped from my mouth, down my chin and into my neck. It wasn't quite right so we did it about five or six times, by which time I was really cold and the blood was everywhere. 'Too much blood now,' shouted the director. 'She looks like she's been massacred!' So they wiped it off and started again. I was dying for a wee but didn't dare say. Eventually, they got the shot and I was well and truly dead, thank God.

Once I had departed this world, Michael's character had to lean over my body, look devastated and kiss me tenderly on the lips. As he was leaning over me, waiting for the shot to be lined up for the camera, he asked, 'Are you OK?' 'Yes,' I whispered, 'but if I don't get up soon I'm going to wet myself!' At this, Michael began to laugh, which started me off. 'Don't make me laugh, Michael – I can't hold it any longer!' I hissed, which only made him laugh more.

As the director called 'Action!' we were both doing our best to stop laughing. Michael leant over to kiss me but instead of the tender peck that was supposed to happen he came straight in with a full-on snog. It stopped us giggling, but shocked me so much that my bladder gave way. Thank goodness no one noticed – by then I was wet through, anyway. 'Sorry,' said Michael, still laughing. Meanwhile, the puzzled director was telling us that the kiss was a bit over-enthusiastic as Michael's character hadn't really loved his wife any more, but to my relief he said he wouldn't make us do it again.

Michael was one of the loveliest and most talented actors with whom I have ever had the privilege to work. The next day I met Judi Dench for the first time when she visited the set. I had admired her ever since I watched her play St Joan in the Nottingham Playhouse, when she was already well known and successful while I was a teenage hopeful. Just in case she heard about it and got the wrong idea, I thought I'd better be upfront about the previous day's shenanigans and so I told her the tale of the innocent snog. She thought it was very funny and we had a good laugh together. I knew she, too, was a terrible giggler, so she sympathised with our plight.

Both Judi and Michael were superb actors and a joy to be with. I was terribly sad when in 2001 Michael died of lung cancer at the relatively young age of 65. By then he and Judi had enjoyed one of the most successful marriages in showbiz for thirty years, and my heart went out to her.

Soon after *My Son, My Son*, I made a wrong decision that still breaks my heart: I turned down a starring role in a six-part drama called *Pennies from Heaven*. It was written by Dennis Potter and went on to receive enormous critical acclaim and make a star of Bob Hoskins, who played Arthur Parker. *Pennies from Heaven* also won a BAFTA for Outstanding Drama and was eventually voted number 21 in the British Film Institute's Top 100 TV Programmes.

The story revolves around Arthur Parker, a man with a fistful of dreams and a roving eye for the ladies, who is a sheet-music salesman in 1930s Britain. Frustrated by his frigid wife (the part I would have played) and the cynical shopkeepers he meets on his travels, he begins a desperate romance with a schoolteacher and lives almost exclusively in the fantasy world of songs. For Arthur, life is all about 'Looking for the blue, innit, and the gold … the patch of blue sky and the bleeding gold dawn, and the light in somebody's eyes …' It was a brilliant piece of writing and the cast included Nigel Havers, Cheryl Campbell and Peter

Bowles. So why did I turn down a role in something so clearly destined to be a classic? The answer is modesty or stupidity, you decide. My only excuse is that I was young and naive; also easily shocked in those days.

It was during a read-through of the script with Bob that I realised that as Arthur Parker's frigid wife I would have to bare my nipples onscreen and, worse still, paint a circle around them with lipstick. I was so horrified that I broke down and cried.

'But your reaction is exactly right,' Dennis Potter kept saying to reassure me, all the while handing me tissues. 'Don't you see, that's exactly how we want your character to feel, would expect her to feel ...'

But I couldn't bear the thought of doing any such thing. The producer continued doing his best to persuade me until Bob swiftly led me out of the room, saying: 'Leave this to me.' We both ended up in a small office down the corridor, he shut the door and told me to sit down. We talked it through, then he placed an arm around me and said he totally understood how I felt. He was really wonderful and I've never forgotten him coming to my defence in that way.

Arriving back at my agent's office, I told Peter what they wanted me to do and he handed me yet more tissues and agreed with me.

'I don't want you upset,' he said, 'so don't do it, Sherrie. I'll phone them and tell them that's our decision.'

At the time I was grateful to Peter for his support but now I can see that it would have been far better for my career had he simply calmed me down and said, 'For heaven's sake, Sherrie, this is a part to die for! Don't be put off by one tiny scene which will be over in the blink of an eye, just get a grip and do it.' However, that was not Peter's style: he was a gentleman in every sense and was concerned for me. Later, I realised that I had made a terrible mistake in backing out and my refusal to paint my nipples red remains one of my biggest regrets. In the end, Gemma Craven (who starred in *The Slipper and the Rose*) played the role brilliantly, although she actually had a lot of trouble after the scene was transmitted. Times are different now, but in the late seventies the scene was considered very raunchy and attracted a lot of the wrong kind of attention.

A couple of years later I had another chance to work with Bob Hoskins in a period drama about the early days of silent films. Called *Flickers*, it co-starred Frances de la Tour as Maud Cole, the wife of Bob's character Arnie (they made an oddly matched couple) and I had an amazing part playing a whore. Letty was Arnie's girlfriend and we had some wonderful scenes together. One was when I had to shave him. As it was set in the twenties, a man would have used a cutthroat razor – you know, the type with the sharp blade and a leather strap. We rehearsed the scene with a pretend one. I had most of the dialogue and so concentrating on the shaving proved impossible. We rehearsed several times, and had it been a real cutthroat by then I would have sliced off Bob's head several times!

We all laughed about it and Bob kept saying, 'It's a good job she's not got a real blade or I'd be dead now!' 'Don't be ridiculous,' the director piped up, 'we wouldn't do that, but make it look as if Sherrie has and she's scary.' 'No problem, she *is*!' cracked Bob.

Just before the take, I was led to one side to have my make-up checked and the director gave me a real razor with a fierce-looking blade but told me not to let Bob see it until we'd started the scene. So he was sitting in a chair and I straddled him, whereupon the director shouted, 'Action!' I started the dialogue, covered him in soap and then suddenly produced the real cutthroat. As Bob saw it he let out the most enormous scream, grabbed my wrist and yelled, 'No bleedin' way!' The crew collapsed with laughter, he jumped out of his chair and pointing to them all said: 'And you can all fuck off!' He then dissolved into fits of laughter but still looked terrified, thinking what might have been.

We filmed in the ATV studios at Borehamwood (now home to *EastEnders*) where, for the second time, Bob did me a great favour. In one scene I was in period underwear (camisole and bloomers, and sporting a large, curly red wig) and I was supposed to be having a fight on a bed with Bob's character. The scene was very emotional as Letty finds out that she's being dumped for Frances de la Tour's character. Instead of hogging the scene – which some actors might have been tempted to do – Bob slowly turned himself away from the camera and turned me towards it so that every one of my emotions would register on screen. Quite literally, he gave me that scene, and it's something I have never forgotten. I thought it was really generous of him, particularly as I'm an actress who relies on my emotions rather than any technical or method-acting techniques.

While we were at Borehamwood there were two extraordinary incidents. The first happened as Bob and I were walking down a corridor on our way back from the canteen. A very tall young American stopped in front of us and said hello. We got chatting and he told us that he was making a TV series that was doing quite well in the States and he hoped it would take off in England. He asked us to come into his studio to see some of his work. As we were due back on set any minute, we very nearly didn't, but I'm so glad we accepted his invitation.

'What's your name?' asked Bob.

'Jim,' replied the American, as we followed him into the studio.

'We can't be long,' Bob explained. 'We'll just have a quick look and then get back to our set.'

Walking through the studio, we passed set after set on stilts: men were standing underneath, their arms reaching up through the bottom of raised floors.

'Up here,' Jim beckoned. We followed him up a staircase and looked down over a vast array of different sets.

'I'd like you to meet someone,' smiled Jim, and reaching up to a shelf he brought down a green puppet.

'Meet Kermit the Frog,' he grinned.

Absolutely enchanted, we stayed on to meet Miss Piggy, Gonzo, Fozzie and the rest of the Muppet 'cast'. I've never forgotten that day and I'm sure Bob hasn't either. Jim Henson went on to become phenomenally successful and his Muppets are familiar to adults and children around the world.

The second extraordinary moment during filming came when the legendary impresario and media mogul Lew Grade arrived on our set. Baron Grade of Elstree was an extraordinarily influential figure in the world of television. It was he who brought Jim Henson over from the States and allowed him to make his show, and he created many, many stars. Despite his stature, he never passed a single person without a kind word. It didn't matter if you were the tea-lady, carpenter, sound recordist, floor-sweeper, star of the series or a humble jobbing actor, he would always say hello and give a word of encouragement. Visiting us, he knew everybody's name and walked around the studio, enquiring: 'All right, Phil?' and 'Things OK with you, Joanie?' and then, 'Is your hubby all right now, Stella?' and 'How's that son of yours, Martin?' When he got to me, he said: 'I've just watched that scene of yours, Sherrie, and I loved it.' I was gob-smacked that he knew my name. It was a great time for the studios and very exciting to be part of it all and to work with such amazing people.

With some of the auditions, it's best to make a careful study of the character they are seeing you for because often those doing the casting go on first impressions when you walk through the door. Well, I was once up to play the part of a prostitute in an American film and so I thought that I'd make an effort and dress accordingly in a tiny skirt, laddered fishnets, stilettos and a plunging neckline. I slapped on masses of lippy, big eye make-up – lashes, the lot – and mussed up my hair and held a fag. Off I went, although luckily I did have a coat on top to cover this creation.

The audition was held at the Dorchester hotel in London. I realised once I had arrived that my outfit might be a teensy problem and so I slipped in by a back door and entered the lift (Peter had already given me all the information as to which floor and what room). Walking into the audition room, I took off the coat to reveal my character. As I entered, the three men opposite me just stared. For one second I began to feel smug, thinking at least this has made them notice me.

'What on earth?' the producer nearest me spluttered.

Listening to my explanation, they began laughing.

'Well done for trying, but do you really think she'd get any punters dressed like that?' asked the first man.

'Well ... yes,' I replied, though my voice was beginning to waver.

'Go and get yourself cleaned up, Miss Hewson. You might think you look like an old tart, but you don't! And in any case you're far too young for this part,' I was told.

At this I felt so stupid, and got out of there as quickly as possible. I could hear them sniggering from the audition room, and I was devastated. Wrapping my coat around me, I walked up and down endless identical corridors in search of the lift I had used before. Catching glimpses of myself in mirrors, I definitely looked like a tart. I had to keep on flattening myself against walls and hiding in crevices whenever I heard somebody coming. Meanwhile, I just couldn't find that bloody lift or any back stairs. In the end there was nothing for it but to jump into the nearest lift, hope for the best and make the quickest exit I could when it came to a halt on the ground floor. As the doors opened I stepped out into the front lobby reception area, where there were two officious-looking doormen, whose eyes swivelled in my direction.

As I gulped nervously, they advanced towards me. With one on each side of me, they gripped me by the arms and almost lifted me off the floor.

'Let me explain ...' I said, doing my best to sound dignified.

'Now you know better than to come in here,' one of them muttered quietly in my ear, obviously trying not to attract the attention of other guests. 'We suggest you be a good girl and leave quietly – now.'

'But you don't understand ...' I began. 'I'm working, I'm an actress ...'

'Yes, of course you are,' the doorman hissed. 'Out of here!'

I burst into tears of frustration.

'It's no good trying that,' he muttered. 'We've seen it all before.'

And on that note they frogmarched me to the revolving door, almost carrying me through, and put me out on the pavement. The way I looked, I was lucky to get a taxi – I think the driver just felt sorry for me. I never knowingly dressed as a tart again.

Another memorable audition was with the British actor-turned-director Kenneth Ives, who was married to Marti Caine, the comedienne. Ives, who had appeared in *The Lion in Winter* and *The Last of the Mohicans,* was about to direct a TV play called *Butterflies Don't Count.* Having listened to me read for minute or so, Kenneth put up a hand and said, 'I'm sorry, you're not right for this part.'

'Why?' I demanded, shocked. 'Why am I not right?'

Now it was his turn to look perturbed – he was not used to having his judgement questioned in this way.

'Well …' he began. 'I hadn't thought of the character having dark hair.'

'*Dark hair!*' I gulped. 'Why can't she have dark hair?'

'Well …' he looked stunned. 'No reason, really.'

'And don't tell me she is also taller than I am,' I continued, 'because I can be as tall as you like. I can wear heels and be six foot, and I can be blonde too, if that's what you want.'

I've never been one to give up easily.

'How can I not be right for this part?' I demanded. 'I am exactly right for this part – I *know* I am!'

'Oh, for God's sake,' he exploded, throwing his script at me, '*have* the bloody part!'

And so I did. Having put up such a determined fight, I actually felt I deserved it.

Chapter Thirteen

Towards the end of the seventies I took on some exciting and challenging roles. The first was in a film with up-and-coming screen idol Harrison Ford, who had just made the original *Star Wars* movie, in which my brother Brett actually played one of the now-famous storm-troopers.

Hanover Street was a romantic World War Two drama in which Harrison Ford plays an American pilot and Lesley Ann Down takes on the role of the married British nurse who falls for him. I landed the part of Phyllis, girlfriend to another of the Yanks and played by Richard Masur.

We made the film at the iconic EMI studios in Borehamwood, which has sadly closed despite having housed such amazing works as *The Shining, A Clockwork Orange, Star Wars* and *Indiana Jones,* to name but a few. Some bright spark decided to rip out all the memorabilia, knock down the building and build a soulless supermarket on the site. They tried to do the same with the historic Ealing Studios, but we all fought hard to keep them, and won. I do believe Pinewood Studios was actually under threat at one point – utter madness.

Anyway, back to the gorgeous Harrison. He was (and still is) a real looker, with a brooding, dark character, which of course is always intriguing. All the girls fancied him – he had that dangerous charisma that women find unable to resist. He proved to be quite a deep thinker and a method actor, which was way above my head, but then his mind was not the only thing that interested us girls. I certainly respected his irrefutable talent on the set but never felt I could approach him. Unlike the other actors, he didn't really mix with us socially, and so imagine my astonishment when out of the blue he asked me out to lunch.

I was so excited. On the date arranged, I had my hair done and I had bought a glamorous dress for the occasion. When I got to the restaurant I proudly told the Maitre d' that I was there to meet Harrison Ford for lunch. 'Miss Hewson?' he said, having glanced at his list. I was so impressed that he knew my name. He smiled knowingly as he showed me to the table, something I didn't really pick up on. As it happens, I was in for a bit of a surprise.

There was Harrison seated alongside twelve other women from the production team. Just like me, they were dressed up for the occasion. He had invited us all to lunch – he thought it was hysterical, though not in a nasty way. Each of us had believed we were the only one to be singled out for his attentions. Luckily, we all saw the funny side and had a great lunch, and at least I managed to sit next to him. All through lunch I 'inadvertently' touched his trouser leg and I can still see that sideways benign smile of his as I enjoyed the Harrison Ford moment in my life.

And if Harrison was not available, Richard Masur (who played my boyfriend in the film) clearly was. One day on the set he whispered to me, a twinkle in his eye: 'Do you play around, Sherrie?' Being very naive, I wasn't even sure what he meant and so like some twonk I asked, 'What do you mean?' As his hand slipped round my waist, the light went on and I quickly added, 'Well, I have a boyfriend.' 'It's OK, that's allowed,' he chuckled and walked off, smiling to his other buddies. I felt such a dork. Given that he went on to star in over forty films, including *The Burning Bed* with Farrah Fawcett, maybe I should have said yes.

After *Hanover Street* I moved on to something that couldn't have been more of a contrast when I was offered a part in *Afternoon Off*, a television play by Alan Bennett. Alan had been commissioned by London Weekend Television to write a series of six plays and this was the fifth. It starred a young actor called Lee Man, along with established stars such as Thora Hird (who many critics have said was at her finest in Alan's plays), Pete Postlethwaite (the wonderful actor who died in early 2011), Stephen Griffiths and Alan Bennett himself. The director was Stephen Frears, who I believe is one of the best directors in the world. At that time he was widely respected within the acting world but wasn't yet famous – that came with *My Beautiful Laundrette*.

In *Afternoon Off* I played a prostitute called Iris (this time, I got the role *without* attempting to dress the part for the audition!) and my first scene was in bed with a lovely actor called Philip Jackson. I thought the make-up girls had done a pretty good job of transforming me into an old tart. We were filming in a hotel and Philip had already got into bed in the room we were using as our set. I was standing outside, wearing a dressing gown with only knickers underneath, well aware that the whole crew were in this cramped little room waiting for me, so I felt rather wobbly. At that moment Stephen approached along the corridor, ready to direct the scene. As he reached me, he studied my face for a few seconds and then took me by the hand and said, 'Come with me.'

He led me to the nearest bathroom, where he proceeded to wet a towel and wipe my face with it, smearing mascara, eyeliner and lipstick everywhere. 'That's it, now you look like a tart,' he told me. Then he took me back to the bedroom and made the whole crew turn to face the walls while I disrobed and climbed into bed. He even created a little barrier in the bed between Philip and me, so we didn't have to touch each other's bare skin.

Just before we started the scene, Stephen gave me a lit cigarette to hold. It went well, but the moment he said cut, Philip let out a cry of pain. Apparently the ash from my cigarette was falling onto his bare chest: in fact, I had thought I could smell burning hair but was too nervous to stop the scene and say something.

Stephen was a joy to work with and he was also a lot of fun. After filming one day, we all returned to the hotel where we were staying, but as it was very late the kitchens were closed. Some of the others went out in search of curry but Stephen said to me, 'Let's not go out, we'll raid the kitchen instead.' When we thought the coast was clear, we crept down the corridors until we found the right door. We went through every fridge and cupboard to put together a feast of cold chicken, bread and other goodies. Soon we were stuffing ourselves and giggling like naughty school-kids until suddenly the door opened and the hotel manager marched in with a face like thunder. Mouths completely full, Stephen and I could only stand there looking horribly guilty. The next day it all had to be paid for (apparently we had contaminated the whole kitchen), but it was still a great midnight adventure. I was particularly sad to finish the shoot as I adored and was very privileged to work with the incredibly talented Mr Frears.

Soon afterwards Peter introduced me to the indomitable Michael Elliott, one of greatest theatre directors ever produced in Britain. Michael ran the Royal Exchange Theatre in Manchester, which was and remains an amazing theatre, very similar to a time capsule. He was known for attracting big names to the Exchange, and in 1979 he put on Henrik Ibsen's *Lady from the Sea* starring Vanessa Redgrave and offered me the part of Bolletta, stepdaughter to Vanessa's character. It provided a wonderful opportunity for me as a young actress. Vanessa was playing Ellida the mother, Graham Crowden (later famous for the BBC series, *Waiting for God*) was Doctor Wangel, Terence Stamp played the stranger and Lindsay Baxter was my sister Hilde.

The play turned out to be an amazing theatrical experience for me, not only because we opened in Manchester but also because Michael then transferred it to the Roundhouse in Chalk Farm. Vanessa was, and remains, an extraordinary woman. In those days she was known for her radical left-wing politics as much as for her acting. I hadn't heard of the WRP (Workers Revolutionary Party), but Vanessa was much involved with them. She'd be up all night campaigning and demonstrating somewhere, then arrive at the next day's rehearsals not having slept and still be organising – and this before the internet, emails and such like. I had no idea what it was all about as I was politically unaware, back then.

One night at the Exchange before the show opened, she brought us all shoeboxes and said she wanted us to go round the audience and beg for money afterwards. We didn't agree to this, but we watched as she approached each person in turn. Sadly, people just looked bemused. She was extremely committed to the cause, so much so that when we moved to the Roundhouse in London she hired two coaches to bring Welsh miners to see the play. We didn't understand the reasoning for this as they arrived with lamps in their miners' gear. Backstage, she'd set up trestle tables with mugs of tea and jam sandwiches. They stayed for the first half and had a sandwich or two in the interval, but then disappeared to the pub. Despite the setbacks, Vanessa's zeal was never dampened, however.

The other amazing thing for us young ones was seeing the theatre and film royalty who frequented the show. Every night when Lindsay and I were in our dressing room there would be a knock at the door and in would walk the most illustrious star-studded characters. Of course, we weren't the draw – it was Vanessa Redgrave and the delicious Terence Stamp. Almost every star they'd ever worked with came to see the play and the bonus was that, having visited Vanessa, they all called into our dressing room to say hello and congratulate us on the way out. We were so star-struck – I don't think we closed our mouths throughout the entire run of the play. Night after night, we were in a permanent state of being completely and utterly star-struck.

One night, for example, it was Paul Newman and his wife Joanne Woodward who came to see us, and I couldn't help noticing three things about them. The first was that Joanne did all the talking while Paul remained smiling but completely silent throughout, the second was that Paul was surprisingly short, and the third was that he had the most amazing violet-blue eyes I had ever seen.

Of course every member of Vanessa's family came too, including her mother Rachel Kempson, her brother Corin and her sister Lynn. All the family were charming and very warm towards us. Others luminaries included Jane Fonda, Judi Dench, Sir John Gielgud, Dustin Hoffman and Richard Gere, so you can imagine the surreal world in which I found myself.

As for Terence Stamp, it wasn't just me who fell in love with him – we all did. Terence was so gorgeous, he was mesmerising. His film career has been extremely diverse: from playing Freddie Clegg in *The Collector* to General Zod in *Superman* and

Bernadette in *The Adventures of Priscilla, Queen of the Desert.* He had dated legions of women, including Julie Christie, Brigitte Bardot and Jean Shrimpton. By the time I met him he was 40 and into everything holistic, including meditation and vegetarian food.

'When you have a cold, Sherrie,' he told me on one occasion, 'don't eat rubbish, just eat black grapes, water and honey.' The next time I had a cold I tried this tip, and I can confirm that it works like magic. 'Bananas, Sherrie,' he told me another time, looking deep into my eyes. 'Always remember that bananas are full of potassium, which is good for the heart. I never saw a banana for a long time because I was a kid during the war, but when I did I realised how important they are in life.'

I think I must be the only person who knows exactly what he means: bananas are brilliant.

Lindsay and I would watch from the window of our dressing room at the Roundhouse as an open-top sports car glided to a halt outside. Behind the wheel would be a stunningly beautiful girl, waiting to collect Terence for what we could only assume was a night of steamy passion. The thing was, every evening it was a different car and a different girl (or so it seemed). For us, that period at the Roundhouse was a glimpse into another world – a world of glamour and celebrity that we found ourselves caught up in. It was both fascinating and tantalising, a proper peep into British theatre and Hollywood film royalty, thanks to Peter.

Soon afterwards, I was in a television play called *Kate the Good Neighbour* and once again worked with one of the Redgrave dynasty. This time it was Vanessa's mother, Rachel Kempson, a wonderful actress who was then 70. She played Kate Dawson, an elderly English spinster who lives alone but will not accept help and is thoroughly disliked by everybody. However, Kate had kept diaries and the film goes back in time to her youth in the 1940s. This is when we start to see the real Kate and begin to understand why she has turned into such a dreadful old woman. The part I was to play was the young 1940s Kate. This was another occasion when I decided to attend an audition dressed for the role, so I bought what looked like a 1940s suit, copied a photo for the correct hairstyle and took some advice on the make-up. I loved the look, and what's more I landed the role.

I had worked with Rachel a few years earlier when she played an elderly aunt in *Love for Lydia* and I was absolutely thrilled to be working with her again. However, two days after the part was confirmed I was celebrating with Ken when Peter phoned to tell me that the producers had had a change of heart and they had now cast Rachel's daughter, Lynn Redgrave, to play the part of the young Kate. Of course I was devastated, but what could I do? Lynn was a brilliant actress, who had starred in a number of great films including *Georgy Girl*, and I could understand she might seem ideal to play a younger version of her mother. For three days I walked around, utterly gob-smacked, but then came the twist in the plot. Peter called again to say there had been yet another change of plan and now the part was mine again. I've no idea what went on behind the scenes to bring all this about but I was, to say the least, beside myself with joy.

We were filming on *Kate* for about a couple of months and in that time Rachel and I became very close. She would tell me such stories and anecdotes that it was just as well we were playing the same part and didn't have scenes together because we were both really bad gigglers. One day Rachel invited me to lunch to meet her husband, Sir Michael Redgrave. He had been a matinée idol in his day and starred in dozens of films including *Oh! What a Lovely War*, *Goodbye, Mr Chips* and my favourite, *Dead of Night* (when he becomes obsessed with a ventriloquist's dummy) and so it was a great honour. We had a lovely lunch and he couldn't have been more solicitous or charming. Sadly, he was suffering from Parkinson's disease and was rather confused, although he had many lucid moments when he regaled us with amazing stories. I did mention *The Lady Vanishes* as I had worked with Margaret Lockwood on *The Slipper and the Rose*. He seemed thrilled about that and said he loved her, which made me feel as if we had a little in common. His moments would come and go through the day but I was just mesmerised by this truly fascinating man, an enormous talent.

As we said goodbye I knew he had slipped into his other world, but Rachael said, 'He won't know you now – he needs to rest – but thank you so much for coming.' Thank *me*! It was such a privilege. They say you should never meet your idols for fear of being disillusioned and disappointed – well, I was neither, and although very poorly by this time, the great man was also enigmatic and glorious. That memory will stay forever with me.

Kate the Good Neighbour won excellent reviews. One critic said Rachel's performance was 'extraordinary and wrenching and her finest work', while another declared it her 'crowning achievement' – quite something, given how illustrious her career had been. As for myself, I couldn't have been more pleased when I read the following review in *The Times*: 'Two beautiful performances by Rachel Kempson and a newcomer, Sherrie Hewson, made *Kate the Good Neighbour* one of the most watchable television plays in a good long time. Who, after all, could match Rachel Kempson's performance? But there was Sherrie Hewson, a brilliant actress and possessed of the same sort of strong face as Miss Kempson.'

The review meant a great deal to me, as did the charming letter that I received a couple of days later from Lynn's husband, John, in which he said: 'Lynn and I have just watched the rough-cut of the play and we think you are absolutely wonderful in it. Lynn particularly wants you to know that she thinks you were the perfect choice for young Kate. Well done!' Some years later after Rachel sadly died, I was also extremely touched when her granddaughter Jemma (Corin's daughter) came up to me at a party and said, 'We all want you to know that Rachel loved you and we all thought you were so good when you worked with her in *Kate the Good Neighbour*. We are so pleased to have that play as one of our memories of Rachel.' I was thrilled to think I had some little part in the memory of Rachel as we were very close at that time and I often laugh when I remember our naughty escapades together.

For me, the saddest thing was that my lovely agent Peter Eade never saw the wonderful reviews for *Kate*. He would have been so proud and I, in turn, would have felt that I had repaid him for all his hard work and dedication and that I hadn't let him down. I was utterly heartbroken when, out of the blue, he died of a heart attack in the spring of 1979. He had been sitting at his desk and had told his assistant that he had a headache and asked her to get him an aspirin. When she returned he was dead. He wasn't old (in his fifties, I think) and he seldom drank and never smoked more than the odd cigar, so it was a terrible shock for everyone who knew him. For his elderly father it was heartbreaking. I remember going down to see him in his big old country house – he was confused and lonely.

Peter had only represented me for eight years, yet in that time he kept me constantly in work. Thanks to him, I had covered a huge range of parts from comedy to classics, television series to films and theatre work. He had given me the best start any actress could ever wish for and had always treated me more like a daughter than a client. I owed him so much and I grieved for him terribly. Most days, I still think about him and consult him on important matters. 'Integrity at all times' was his legacy to me, and I have always tried to honour that maxim. Although I went on to work with some fine agents, Peter was irreplaceable.

Chapter Fourteen

In the early eighties my career took an interesting and unexpected turn when my agent told me that a producer at London Weekend Television had asked to see me about a role in *Russ Abbot's Madhouse*. Russ had taken over the 'Madhouse' from Freddie Starr and he was rapidly becoming a Saturday evening institution. Hugely popular, the show was comedy magic: a series of sketches, impressions and crazy characters such the Glaswegian 'CU Jimmy', 'Basildon Bond' and 'Julio Doubleglazias'. His characters were so loved that comic annuals of the show came out every Christmas, children used to imitate them in the playground and in a Scottish poll CU Jimmy was only narrowly piped by The Krankies for the title of Best-known Scottish Person in the World.

Although I knew Russ's show, I wasn't quite sure why the producer would want to see me. Russ Abbot, Les Dawson, Morecombe and Wise, Tommy Cooper and Frankie Howerd were all brilliant stand-up comics of the day – a world I had always admired, but never had the guts to attempt nor indeed ever thought that I might be asked to become a part of. I had never done anything remotely like this. Restoration comedy and Feydeau farces at RADA were roughly the extent of my comic acting.

My new agent was the highly esteemed Jeremy Conway, who had taken me on after Peter passed away. It was he who rang me about the request.

'It's from a producer called John Kaye Cooper,' he told me. 'He seemed very keen to see you.'

'Jeremy, tell him he's made a mistake,' I said. 'He must be mixing me up with someone else.'

A few minutes later Jeremy called back: 'There's no mistake, Sherrie,' he told me. 'He says he met you when you were at RADA. He thinks you'd be perfect for the Russ Abbot show and he's sending you some tapes to watch.'

Still puzzled, I sat down to watch the tapes when they arrived. Russ reminded me of Tommy Cooper in that he had exactly the same kind of stage presence: he could walk on, stand still, not say a word and the audience would just fall about laughing. Their laughter would crescendo to almost hysteria and yet he hadn't done a thing. Still later, I watched this happen from the side of the stage one night as he walked on. I thought someone must have been doing something that I couldn't see, but it was just Russ, standing there. He had an amazing control of an audience.

Eventually, Jeremy advised: 'Why don't you at least go along and talk to him about it, now that you've watched the tapes?'

So off I went to the studios, where I met John Kaye Cooper. He reminded me that he had once come along to talk to us at RADA and had taken a group of us to a television studio.

'You did a little piece to camera,' he said. 'I've always remembered you.'

Well, that remark was flattering in itself.

'Can you do impressions?' he continued.

'No, of course not,' I quickly replied.

'How do you know?' he persisted.

'I just do,' I shrugged.

'Well, I think you can,' he told me. 'How about having a go at an impression of Janet Street-Porter?'

'No *way*!' I laughed, all the while thinking this man is mad – impressions, Janet Street-Porter, *me*?

Despite my protestations, John persuaded me to go home, have a practice and then decide. I wasn't sure if I'd done the right thing but when I told Ken about it he thought it sounded like a great idea.

The following day I woke up and thought, This is madness – I *can't* do impressions! I phoned Jeremy and asked him to call John Kaye Cooper and say no, thank you. A little later I received a telephone call from Jeremy: John was offering me quite a lot of money. Light entertainment paid so much more than drama, it seemed, and I was completely gob-smacked. All right, I'll have a go at this, I thought. Luckily, it wasn't until later that I learnt the choice was between Tracey Ullman and me – or I'd have felt even more daunted.

The following Monday, John wanted me to do the impression of Janet Street-Porter in the rehearsal rooms in front of Russ and the rest of the cast and crew.

'That's *so* cruel!' I protested.

'Oh, and by the way,' he added, 'could you have a go at Lorraine Chase, too.'

What? Suddenly I had not one impression but two to master, and within a couple of days as well. That weekend I practised Janet's toothy twang and Lorraine's cheeky cockney lines, made famous in the TV ad for Campari, in which the hunky Italian asks her: 'Were you wafted here from Paradise?' and Lorraine, elegant and beautiful as ever, opens her mouth to say in broad cockney, 'No, Luton Airport!'

Ken listened to me practising and assured me I was a dead ringer for both. I wasn't so convinced, but on the Monday I turned up and did my impressions in front of Russ and the rest of the cast, which included Les Dennis, Susie Blake, Dustin Gee, Bella Emberg and Michael Barrymore. To my astonishment, they all clapped and told me I was fantastic. And that was that: I joined the regular cast for the third series of the show in 1982.

Russ Abbot was so easy to work with. Multi-talented, he was always very professional, and what he didn't know about comedy wasn't worth knowing. I have to say, I have been in bed with Russ more often than any other man in my life. In fact, we got so bored with our bedtime frolics for various sketches in the show that I would play noughts and crosses on his back while waiting to start a scene. I'd play either the wronged wife or the sexy girlfriend or the enigmatic spy: I was 'Miss Funny Fanny' to his 'Basildon Bond', 'Gertie Lawrence' to his 'Noël Coward', 'Arkela' to his 'Naughty Boy Scout'. For me, this was a massive learning curve, an incredible baptism of fire, and all the while I was learning the art of comedy performance and timing from the very best.

Les Dennis and Michael Barrymore had been winners on the TV talent show of the day, *New Faces*, and they joined at the same time. Both were extremely gifted and very naughty, too. Michael was incredibly talented but only stayed with us for one season – he was destined for greatness. But the tragic side of Michael that eventually led to his downfall and disgrace wasn't apparent then – he was just full of fun and we witnessed many a mad moment.

One particular day when we were just finishing rehearsals Michael, Les and I all decided to go for a drink on our way to get the tube home. There was a pub down the road, and having finished early we thought we'd treat ourselves. 'I'll get these,' said Michael as we walked in, and he leapt over to the bar in a gazelle-like way. Within seconds he was on top of the bar, doing a tap routine. Everyone just stood and stared, including the bar staff. He then jumped down behind the bar and started pouring drinks for everyone in the pub. At that point things turned a bit sour. Thinking him a total nutter, the landlord grabbed him and threw him out, with us following behind. We never mentioned a thing and carried on to the tube, where Les and I sat discussing the morning's work with Michael sitting opposite us.

When we came to the first stop, Michael went over to a man who was quietly minding his own business, grabbed him and said in a John Cleese-like fashion, 'Time to get off now!' As the doors slid open, he threw him off the tube! As we pulled out of the station, the man now standing on the platform looked totally shocked and confused. At the next stop, Michael did the same to two more people. No one challenged him. Meanwhile, Les and I were both hysterical, if a little stunned. At the next stop we decided to slip off in case things grew ugly. Michael spotted our quick exit and flew off the tube just as the doors were closing. However, nothing was mentioned and we all just went home. Those of us who knew him came to accept this kind of behaviour as 'just Michael' – he was an exhausting, intangible and incontestable genius.

Among all this incredible talent was me: trying not only to do sketches that I'd never done before but impressions, too. In readiness for taking off Janet Street-Porter, imitations of her teeth were specially made for me. On the night after rehearsals, I was walking down the corridor at the studios still wearing the set of teeth when to my horror I spotted Ms Street-Porter herself coming towards me.

As I dived into the nearest loo I heard her snap, 'Who's that fuckin' girl wearing my fuckin' teeth?' She didn't sound as though she was joking, so I stayed where I was until some kind soul came and told me that she had left the studios.

In the course of that season I played not just Janet and Lorraine but a whole range of other characters. I was 'Soyah', Toyah Wilcox's sister who couldn't sing, and had a song specially penned for her called, 'Please Come Up Here and Stop Me' – something I think would resonate with a lot of people today. Then I was the tiny singer with a vast beehive, 'Mari Wilson', 'Marylyn Monroe', Ingrid Bergman in *Casablanca* and Joyce Grenfell. You name it, I played it – fat, thin, tall, short, animal or mineral, we all took on an enormous variety of roles. We even did one sketch set in the 1900s when everyone just had gums and no teeth. Always big lavish productions, the musical numbers were like West End shows. On the studio night we would have our dressing rooms under the stage and so above us were at least 400 people. All the different wigs would be lined up, plus rails and rails of costumes. We would run on in Girl Guide and Boy Scout uniforms to sing a silly version of 'Ging Gang Goolie' and then run off to don a whole range of costumes for various characters, often going through ten or fifteen different sketches. It was so fast and furious, you could almost see the burn-marks on the floor.

Our costumes and sets were fantastic: every set was a masterpiece, every costume just perfect – which helped a lot when we were trying to create different characters. We had enormous fun making the show because we laughed non-stop: the writers were brilliant and there was a wealth of great material. The show went from strength to strength and when I was invited to stay on for the next series and then the one after that I had no hesitation in saying yes.

While I discovered that I wasn't bad at comedy, the same cannot be said of my singing. Russ used to do a pop-star character called 'Vince Prince' and Les Dennis, Dustin Gee, Susie Blake, Jeff Holland and I were 'The Tone Deafs', his backing group. Everyone could sing but me, so they had to pretend they couldn't sing while I just sang. Having said that, I continued to believe – as I had ever since I was a little girl – not only could I sing, but I was also a great, undiscovered singing talent in the Judy Garland or Doris Day vein. It was obvious to me, though somehow not to other people. Then came the day when I was due to play a singing mermaid on Russ's show. The song was 'No Two People Have Ever Been So in Love' from *Hans Christian Andersen* (which I sang with Russ, all the while supposedly sitting on a rock by the sea).

We used to record the songs in a studio in the week ready for the show on the Saturday. In those days there would be a 40-piece orchestra costing a fortune, so no time for mistakes and no time to waste. Usually, everyone would sing together and I would hide behind Susie Blake (who was great), but this time it was just Russ and I. Away we went and I thought I sounded wonderful, but Ray Monk, the musical director, sidled over and said, 'Sherrie, you're off-key. Can you hear it?'

'No,' I said, surprised.

So we started again and I sang my heart out until Ray suddenly raised a hand and said, 'Stop! Sherrie, you're off-key.'

Now I must confess that I didn't know what he meant, although I pretended to understand.

'Yes, I see, Ray – sorry,' I muttered.

And so Russ would start, 'No two people have ever …' and then I would sing 'been so in love, been so in love …' and so on.

Meanwhile, Ray would raise his hands and the whole orchestra would grind to yet another halt.

By then Russ was getting slightly frustrated, Ray remained strangely calm and the sarcastic comments of the 40-piece orchestra could be heard throughout the studio. But I was convinced that whatever was going wrong was someone else's problem.

In the end, Ray (by now a broken man) said, 'OK, I think we've got it.'

'But we haven't done the whole song yet,' I protested.

'No problem,' he insisted, 'we've got all we need from you.'

'*Really*?' I said. 'That's fantastic!'

Russ told me I'd finished for the day and could go home. Happy with my day's work, off I went, humming the tune we'd been singing – 'No two people …'

Two days later, when I went on to the studio floor, it was a different story. I arrived as they were playing the song back.

'Funny,' I said, 'that doesn't sound like me.'

'Really?' replied John, innocently enough.

Then the penny dropped: they had had the cheek to get in a session singer to perform the song for me. When I found out I burst into tears.

'Look,' said John, doing his best to console me, 'I hired you to be an actress, not a singer.'

Even so, I couldn't understand why people didn't hear what I heard. One day, I thought; it's just not my time.

That wasn't the only time when I came a cropper singing with Russ. We were just finishing one of the TV series and Christmas loomed, when at rehearsals the producer (who clearly hadn't been around for the mermaid sketch) said: 'You sing, don't you, Sherrie?' 'Of course,' I replied, as I still believed this to be the case. 'You should be in Russ's panto,' he suggested. 'I'd love to,' was my reply.

The next day I received the script. I was to play Russ's boy sidekick, wearing short jacket, lots of thighs, long boots – you know the kind of thing. I had the opening number, a pop song of the day, and I was wildly excited. This was my chance to show just what I could do. It was in a big theatre that held 3,000 people. We didn't have a lot of time and rehearsals were frantically busy so the producer phoned to say he was sure I'd be fine. I knew Russ so well, and as long as I learned my lines, everything would be OK. The song was on tape, he added, so no problem.

How considerate of them to send me a tape to learn it from, I thought. I wasn't worried at all. Blissful in my ignorance, I learned the song and practised as much as I could. When we went through the rehearsal, we always skipped the opening number. The fourteen dancers taking part in it rehearsed separately and I was told that I just had to stand in front of them and sing, so there was no need to rehearse.

Come opening night, the theatre was full and the band warmed up while I was backstage with the dancers, ready to go on. A message was sent round to tell me that the click track had gone down. Now I didn't know what that was, but apparently it was the tape of the other girl singing that I was supposed to mime to. This, it seemed, had been the plan all along but I hadn't understood that – I thought I was going to sing live and have my big moment. And as it turned out, because the tape wouldn't work that's exactly what happened.

The curtain went up and 3,000 people clapped and shouted for joy. Children's eyes sparkled and the mums and dads were happy. I walked on and the orchestra started to play the intro to the song. As I looked down into the orchestra pit towards the musical director, he made a slicing movement with his hand to his neck and mouthed, 'Click gone, you sing live!' And so I did. To be fair, at first the audience simply looked bemused, but then as the dancers started to bump into each other as I carried on, disbelief crept over their faces. It wasn't until I got to the part, 'I'm so excited, I just can't hide it,' that I heard a dancer behind me say, '*We* can!' At last, I got to the end of the song and in the auditorium you could have heard a pin drop. Thankfully, there was a lone clap and a few people joined in out of sympathy. I came offstage and Russ was waiting in the wings to go on. Ghostly pale, he stared at me as I grabbed one of his arms and muttered, 'Think that went well – you'll be fine, good luck!'

As that story shows, I have an amazing capacity to survive setbacks and soon bounced back to sing another day. A few months later my agent said, 'You've just had a request to go for an audition for *Carousel* but as you can't sing you'd better give it a miss, eh?'

'*What*?' I protested, shocked. '*Of course* I can sing!'

By then I'd had at least fifty singing lessons, and as I was paying £50 a time the coach had buttered me up and told me I really could sing.

'OK,' said Jeremy, shifting uncomfortably in his chair. 'Off you go, then.'

So off I went to this big West End theatre packed full of singers trilling away.

'What have you brought to sing?' asked the producer when it came to my turn.

'What do you mean?' I replied.

'Have you not brought any music?'

'Music? *Me?*' I answered, perplexed. '*Why?* Haven't you got any?'

Really, I was thinking, what is it with this lot? Meanwhile, alarm bells were obviously ringing.

'Why don't you go to the pianist and talk to him?' suggested the producer.

'Oh, all right,' I agreed.

'Hi,' said the pianist by way of a greeting, 'so what key?'

'What *key*?' I repeated, utterly bewildered and looking at all the keys on the piano.

'What *key* do you want to sing in?' he explained, looking slightly worried.

'What key have you got?' I answered, deciding it was better to indulge him.

'What key do you normally sing in?' he patiently pressed.

'I don't normally sing,' I confessed at last.

'*Oh!*' His eyebrows almost hit the ceiling. 'But this is an audition for *Carousel*, and *Carousel* is a musical.'

'Oh yes, I know *that*!' I told him. 'I *love Carousel*.'

'Do you know any of its songs?' he asked.

'No, not really,' I admitted.

'Well, what song *do* you know?'

'I Feel Pretty' was the first song that came into my head. Too polite to point out that I was in the wrong musical, he told me that he was just going downstairs to talk to some people.

When he eventually came back, he said: 'OK, please sing "I Feel Pretty"'.

At last, I thought. And so I started singing, 'I feel pretty, oh so pretty …'

'Thank you,' he said, interrupting me, 'that's absolutely fine.'

'But I …' was all I could manage to say.

'Thank you, Miss Hewson,' said the producer.

'Oh, thank *you*,' I said, thinking they must really like me.

Back home, I put in a call to my agent.

'I did the *Carousel* audition,' I told him breezily.

'Yes, isn't it a shame?' he said in his most sympathetic voice. 'You didn't get the job.'

'*Really*?' I said, astonished. 'Are you sure? They seemed so pleased with me.'

Delusional to the end, deep down I still thought I could sing like Barbra Streisand and I was convinced the reason why I wasn't sought after for musicals was simply because the right people hadn't found me yet. My attempts to sing in other shows, including one Tom Stoppard play and a panto, have always ended with similar responses. Despite all the evidence to the contrary, there's a teensy bit of me that still believes I'm a singer.

Somebody will discover me one day, I always tell myself.

Chapter Fifteen

After six years together I still loved Ken and we both adored our round Art-Deco house and our dog, Caius. We hadn't got much money, but with his job at British Aerospace and my income we were all right.

Both of us had an obsession with cars and we bought a good few of them over the years, whether we had money or not. We lived in car showrooms – I've sometimes thought that if only I'd been a Ferrari Spider Ken would have loved me forever, but unfortunately in his eyes I was more of a Mini Clubman. We were as bad as each other when it came to cars – you name it, we had it, from Triumph Stags to the innovative Mazda Wankel engine car, the VW Scirocco, Aston Martin DB4 Vantage, Ferraris, Jags, an old Daimler, a Porsche 911 and so on. Of course, all total madness when we couldn't afford any of them. Those were the Thatcher years – 'What you want, you shall have' regardless of the consequences. When I look back, it makes me so angry that neither of us appeared to have half a brain and we wasted so much money on ridiculous cars but I would have done anything to make Ken happy and at the time this seemed to be the way to his heart.

Despite this, we still had good times together. We could make each other laugh and we both loved giving parties for our friends. Our social circle was an eclectic mix and they all got on extremely well. Ken had colleagues from British Aerospace and the Spanish Navy, while I had a bunch of crazy, off-the-wall actors – a great combination. Some of Ken's friends were quite formal and so when I turned him into a zebra one day they were quite disconcerted.

Let me explain. I've always had a passion for hairdressing – in my fantasy world I'm a fabulous hairdresser. At one point I even blagged my way fraudulently into a hairdressing wholesalers and managed to get my hands on a discount card. This I used to buy every colour of hair dye, foils, plastic pots, colouring brushes, highlighter caps, hooks, capes, back-washers, hair separators, hair extensions, hairpieces, dryers, brushes and, best of all, a stool that swivelled up and down.

I was delighted one day when Ken agreed to let me put some highlights into his hair to 'lift' the colour. He was an unexciting mousy brown and I knew I could change all that, as the adverts assured me. I used the special highlighter cap (a bit like a shower-cap with holes in it, which hairdressers use for creating streaks). The idea is that you pull the cap on and then with a little hook tweak strands of hair through the holes and apply dye to those strands. While Ken was absorbed in a TV programme, I got to work, carefully applying the bleach that I had mixed up. According to my calculations he would emerge with subtle highlights to blend in perfectly with his own hair colour. I just loved it – better than sex any day!

By the time we went to rinse the bleach off I was getting quite excited about the results. I had visions of all Ken's friends queuing up for me to give them a similar look. With the cap off and the bleach washed out, I left him to towel-dry his hair until a shriek from the bathroom brought me running.

'Look at me,' he yelled. 'I look like a tiger!'

It seemed I may have slightly overdone the bleach for the 'streaks' were white, which had the effect of making the rest of his hair appear darker so that the finished effect was a bit like a zebra.

'Sorry,' I mumbled, 'I can't think what went wrong.'

'*Sorry?*' Ken was spitting mad. 'I've got a meeting tomorrow with the Spanish Navy chaps to talk to them about a vital contract. I can't go like this – you'd better do something, *fast*!'

It was now seven o'clock at night and in those days the shops were shut at that time. I went to our local chemist, banged on his door and begged him to open up and sell me a hair dye to get Ken through the next day. Very sweetly, he did as I asked, but he only had a dark brown dye in stock. Better than nothing, I thought, grabbing it.

'This'll sort it out,' I panted, rushing in to mix up the dye.

How was I to know that the second dye would turn the bleached streaks in Ken's hair green? When we washed it off and he emerged looking like the not-so-jolly Green Giant, he was horrified.

'I had no idea it could do that,' I muttered, while Ken sat with his head in his hands, groaning loudly. 'Didn't know brown on bleach gives you green. That's fascinating,' I rambled on. 'Shut up, Sherrie,' he shouted at me. 'You're a nightmare!'

As I watched him blow-dry the mess on top of his head, I tried very hard not to laugh. There was nothing more to be done. The next day Ken attended his meeting with hair that was, to put it generously, unusual. He tried to brush the green streaks under the rest but there was no disguising them. His new look must have given the Spanish Navy a bit of a start, and next door's dog wouldn't stop barking either.

I don't think Ken ever forgave me for that experiment. He certainly never let me near his hair again, not that I let that stop me. Soon afterwards I offered to dye my dad's beautiful white hair a nice shade of chestnut. 'Yes, you do that,' he said because he loved me, and so I happily mixed up my dye. Mindful of what had happened with Ken, I decided to try out the dye on a patch at the back of Dad's head first, while assuring him that he'd come out looking ten years younger – and very distinguished, too.

The patch on the back of his head came out bright green. Thankfully, he couldn't see it and he trusted me implicitly when I told him that it was fine.

'Um, not sure the colour's right for you, though, Dad,' I added. 'Perhaps we won't do the whole of your hair.'

After that I gave up experimenting on people but I couldn't resist having a go at dyeing my dog's hair. This was a little Westie called Charlie that I acquired later on, after Caius died in 1992. He also had white hair, but after I used the same chestnut dye, Charlie went green too.

Despite the good lifestyle that Ken and I were enjoying, I always knew something was missing. Deep down, I knew he wasn't so in love with me as I was with him, and I couldn't trust him. Doubts and misgivings continued to haunt me. So, what did I do? Well, I pushed them all to one side and came up with what I thought was the answer to everything.

'Shall we get married?' I asked one day.

'Oh, if you like,' said Ken.

His response wasn't anything to dance around the room about, but he didn't exactly choke over his cornflakes either or tell me not to be so daft. Taking that as a 'yes', off I went to consult the vicar of Ham church.

'Fine,' said the vicar, 'but before I can agree to marry you your husband-to-be will have to come to see me too.'

'Is that *really* necessary? He doesn't really believe …' I paused, thinking it wiser given whose company I was in to leave that sentence unfinished.

'Yes, it *is* necessary,' the vicar insisted. 'I *have* to talk to you both.'

And so we both went along, nodded and smiled, and that was that.

Thereafter, apart from turning up on the day Ken had nothing whatsoever to do with our wedding preparations. I decided on the date, booked the church, booked the hall next door to the vicarage for the reception as well as the caterers, chose the guest list, sent out the invitations and paid for everything. I would have loved him to join in and do it all with me, but I told myself that plenty of grooms have little to do with the preparations, and despite his lack of interest I began to look forward to it.

As the date grew closer, I ordered a rather grand, five-tier wedding cake and booked a 1910 white Rolls Royce to transport me from home to the ceremony. At that time Ken had a racing green DB4 Aston Martin which he loved so I decided we could also put that to good use on the day as our going-away car even though we wouldn't be going on honeymoon. Having organised and paid for our wedding, I couldn't afford a honeymoon on top. Besides, Ken was going back to work the day afterwards. The reception was to be held in an old church hall and so at the last minute I decided to hire five 15ft palm trees to add an exotic touch. I *know* … don't ask!

Having organised everything else, I set about finding my wedding dress. Even that, which should have been a joyous experience, proved quite the opposite. I went to a really upmarket wedding-dress shop, where I was unlucky enough to encounter a frosty, marble-in-mouth assistant. Having eyed me up and down, with no tact whatsoever she said: 'I hope you are not expecting to wear a white, frilly wedding dress, dear, because I think you are a little too old for that, don't you?'

I was *32*! At this, I shot her a look – I'd have said something rude, but there were children present – and walked out of the shop, making perfectly sure I slammed the door behind me. Later on, I suddenly remembered that when I was doing *My Son, My Son* with Michael Williams the theatrical outfitters in Camden where we used to go for all our costumes had beautiful vintage wedding dresses and they had kindly told me that if ever I needed a wedding dress to come and see them. I went along and spotted a 1910, full-length white wedding dress, a beautiful French veil plus a headdress made of cream wax, all of which proved to be just perfect. For my Maid of Honour (Gail Glaser, a make-up artist at the BBC and a very dear friend) I chose another lovely dress that was also a 1910 original. Sadly, I could only borrow the dresses because money was tight.

We were married on 15 May 1983 when the whole country was plunged into another heatwave. By the time the day arrived I was feeling pretty excited and thankfully, despite her continuing disapproval of Ken, Mum had come along to support me and help me get ready.

On the morning of the wedding, just two hours before the ceremony was due to take place, I said to her: 'I've got to go down to the hall to check that the cake has arrived and make sure everything's in place.'

'Don't be silly, Sherrie,' she told me. 'You need to be getting ready – it's all going to happen in two hours' time.'

'*No*, I must go, Mum,' I insisted. 'I can't leave anything to chance.'

'Well, I'm coming with you then,' she said.

And thank goodness she did. When we arrived at the hall, all boded well: the tables were beautifully arranged with white linen tablecloths and napkins, glasses sparkled and were squeaky-clean. All the staff who were putting the finishing touches to the tables looked to be over 80 – in fact, they were quite extraordinary characters and almost straight out of a comedy drama. One even resembled Mrs Overall, the character made famous by Julie Walters in *Acorn Antiques*.

As they slowly made their way back and forth between the kitchen and reception, one of the old dears wobbled over.

'Is everything all right, dear?' she asked.

'Lovely,' I told her, as she tottered off back to the kitchen.

As I went into the main hall to check on the tables, I could only see one tier of my five-tier wedding cake.

'Where's the rest of the cake?' I asked another old lady, who seemed to be in charge.

'Over there,' she told me. 'We've just taken it out of its box.'

I glanced over at the table: there was only one small tier of the cake sitting on its silver base. Bewildered, my eyes travelled slowly to the floor where, to my horror, the rest of my magnificent wedding cake was on its head.

'Oh my God!' my mother cried.

'Oh dear, oh, dear! How did it get there?' the old lady kept muttering, staring down at the heap of battered cake. She appeared so distraught that I thought she might breathe her last at any moment, the last thing I needed.

'There's no time for that!' said Mum. 'Let's salvage what we can.'

My mother's always been good when push comes to shove. She picked up the cake and jammed it back together as best she could, then dashed out of the hall.

'Come on, Sherrie!' she shouted.

We jumped into the car and in the village nearby we found a little stationer's and managed to pick up some really naff-looking silver leaves, which we took back and plastered all round the sides of the cake to cover up the holes and dust from the floor. Despite our best efforts, the cake still looked as if it had been dropped on its head. Mum kept trying to console me by saying things like, 'It doesn't look too bad,' and even 'Could be worse, couldn't it?' To be perfectly honest, no, it couldn't, but there was nothing else we could do. All the old ladies were so apologetic that I began to feel quite sorry for them.

'It's OK,' I told them. 'It's just my wedding.'

At this, they all started to sniff and I had to console them before I could go and get my frock on. At least I've got the wedding disasters out of the way, I thought, ever the optimist.

But there was more to come: the 1900 Rolls arrived to take Dad and me to the church and the chauffeur mumbled something about being late as I got in, but I didn't take in what he was saying. As we neared the turning for the road down to the church, I realised he wasn't slowing down and instead sped past at some rate. I tried to shout to him, but there was a glass panel dividing us and so he couldn't hear me. Before we knew it we were turning into another church up the road near Petersham, where a wedding was being held and the bride was already getting out of her car. As we came to an abrupt stop, Dad jumped out and nearly dragged the driver out through his window. Heated words were exchanged, we waved to the other bride to apologise, reversed and made a quick getaway. As we began our journey back to the right church we just laughed and laughed – it was just like a *Carry On* film.

We arrived safely, then Dad and I got out and waited in the church doorway for our cue. I had hired a man to make a video (quite unusual in those days) and as we stood waiting he appeared beside me. 'Hot, isn't it?' he gasped. It was about 90 degrees, so this was quite an understatement and as 'The Wedding March' struck up I noticed he looked very pale and was loosening his collar.

As Ken and I made our vows, the video man switched his camera from one of us to the other and was talking to himself the whole time, which was very distracting. While the vicar was asking, 'Do you take this woman …' I noticed the man had grabbed himself a small stool and was attempting to climb on top of it. When he fell off, I suddenly realised that he was blind drunk. As the vicar said to me, 'Do you, Sherrie, take this man …' our cameraman stood on the stool only to fall backwards, spluttering and giggling, onto a display of flowers. Luckily, Ken saw the funny side and took it all in his stride.

When we finally emerged from the boiling church it was just a stroll to the hall for our reception. As we stood in line to welcome the guests, I noticed an old boy (90, if he was a day) carrying a large tray of full champagne flutes with shaking hands. Either he was about to expire from the heat or was drunk from sampling his wares. Indeed, the latter proved the case.

With my heart in my mouth, I watched as he staggered from guest to guest, somehow hanging onto the tray for dear life as everyone helped themselves to the drinks that were sliding dangerously from one side to the other, and woe betide any guest attempting to help themselves to a second glass. 'Bugger off, you've had enough!' I could hear him repeating, over and over. Clutching the remaining drinks, he staggered back past all the guests and into the kitchen.

The next moment there was a huge crash accompanied by the sound of crystal glass splintering and smashing on the tiled floor. As I opened the kitchen door, there he was – trying to get down on his hands and knees to pick up the pieces, but completely incapable.

'We're *so* sorry,' chorused the old biddies.

'Just open some more bottles and refill the guests' glasses, please,' I told them.

As I looked down at the smashed glasses, then up again at the row of beautifully permed heads and extremely worried faces, I smiled and they all smiled back in unison.

I went back into the hall, only to discover that most of our guests looked as if they were about to expire with the heat. Worried those who hadn't already fainted in church were about to do so now, we decided to open the back doors and suggest to everyone that they should all go out into what was the vicar's garden. I felt sure he wouldn't mind, even though this wasn't part of the original deal. Clearly relieved, they flocked outside only to be greeted by washing lines filled with knickers the size of pillowcases. It seemed it was a laundry day and the vicar's wife was clearly a well-built lady judging by the size of her undies.

All wedding days are supposed to be memorable, and ours certainly was.

As it turned out, my brother Brett was the star of the show. He and his partner Annie were both wonderfully turned out: with his floppy blond hair, he was in white while Annie wore cream. They looked like a wedding couple themselves. After the lunch, Brett gave the most incredibly touching speech – no brother could have done better for a sister than he did for me that day. He also read out a poem that he had written specially for the occasion, and it was beautiful.

By the end of the day most people were flaked out, the palm trees had wilted, the old dears (including the champagne waiter) were asleep in the kitchen, the mosquitoes had started to bite in the garden and although Ken was chatting up some bird in the corner I was happy. I had achieved two of the three things I had wanted ever since I was a little girl: to pass my driving test and to walk down the aisle. Now the only one remaining was to have a baby.

Later, Ken and I left to spend our wedding night at the Richmond Hill Hotel. When we got to the room we found that my sister-in-law Annie had covered the bed in roses and there was a bottle of champagne waiting for us, which was so romantic. Ken had already had quite a lot to drink and soon fell asleep, while I sat drinking the champagne and musing on how there's nothing less attractive than a man snoring and dribbling on your wedding night.

Chapter Sixteen

It was beginning to look as though my third wish – to have a baby – might never come true. I hadn't used birth control since Ken and I got together and so by the time we got married, seven years later, I had finally given up any hope of conceiving.

I never liked the idea of fertility treatment so I did my best to resign myself to this great disappointment, although it was hard. Everyone around me seemed to be having babies, from Princess Diana to Mrs Walton in Liverpool who was expecting sextuplets, which didn't seem fair. I'd at least like to know why I'm not able to conceive, I thought – I *had* to know just how final it was and so I made an appointment with a consultant at the Chelsea Women's Hospital, who suggested they do a laparoscopy.

'What's that?' I asked.

'It's very straightforward,' he replied. 'We'll just make a small incision in your abdominal wall for exploratory purposes. This will hopefully help us to discover exactly what is causing the problem.'

I wasn't mad about the idea of the 'small incision', but on the other hand I wanted answers. So I went ahead and had it a few days later. I travelled alone to the hospital as Ken was at work, although he did pick me up when it was time to go home. At this stage things were not too bad between us and, to be fair, it didn't always occur to me to ask for extra help or support from my husband as I was always fiercely independent and so he may not always have realised when I needed it. Afterwards, the consultant came to see me.

'I am very sorry,' he said, 'but your ovaries are dormant. That means they're not producing any eggs. I'm afraid there's nothing we can do to help.'

'Right,' I said, trying hard not to show just how devastated I was, 'then I think this is the end of the story.'

But it wasn't. Almost from the moment I left the hospital I began to feel really poorly. I was constantly nauseous, often sick, and I felt weak, was bleeding all the time and generally wretched and exhausted. After a week or so I was in such a state that I phoned the consultant.

'It is possible,' he told me, 'that the laparoscopy has caused this and I suggest that for the time being you stop work, stay in bed, have plenty of rest and see how things go.'

So I did, but things did not improve.

When I returned to see the consultant, he told me, 'I'm going to give you a scan to see what's happening.' Having studied it, he turned to me and said, 'There's a shadow in there.'

'A *shadow*?' I repeated. Immediately, I thought the worst and began to imagine the big C.

'Hang on a minute,' he said, and he continued to sit there peering at the scan for what felt like an absolute age.

'Er … what can you see?' I finally asked. By this time my brow was sweating with nervous anxiety.

'I thought so,' he said, turning and beaming at me. 'It's a *baby*! The shadow is a baby, Mrs Boyd.'

'It *can't* be!' I gasped, and then slowly through my tears I managed to utter one more word: '*How?*'

'I honestly don't know,' he replied. 'As far as I'm concerned, it's a miracle. But *that*,' he pointed to the shadowy outline on the scan, 'is beyond any doubt a baby.'

'But ...' I stuttered again, 'I've been bleeding all the time.'

'I know,' he said, 'which is why we will have to monitor you very carefully. We'll keep you in hospital for a bit and then, when we eventually send you home, we'll insist you stay in bed until we are absolutely sure that the baby is going to stay put.'

When I got home and told Ken he was stunned because it was the last thing he had expected. He had never yearned for a child in the way that I did, but he liked the idea of being a dad and was pleased.

I did an awful lot of lying around over the next few weeks, but it was worth it. To pass the time, I spent hours reading baby books and pinching myself to make sure it was really happening. Ever since I was a tiny girl I had seen myself with a daughter. I used to wander round the house, back in the days when I had all my imaginary friends, and chat to a little imaginary daughter, holding her by the hand and instructing her to be careful on the stairs. We'd even go out together and have adventures. To me, she seemed so real that from then on I believed one day she would become so (these days it would be called 'positive visualisation'). Now that I was expecting my longed-for baby, I still secretly hoped it was a girl, although I know full well that I would have loved a boy just as much.

Once I got the go-ahead to carry on with life as normal, I couldn't wait to show the world I was pregnant, but I was still very slim, and the bump, when it appeared, just wasn't big enough for me. In fact, at six months pregnant I could still do my trousers up. I took to wearing billowy kaftans to try and appear more blooming. In the last seven weeks I made up for the slow start when I ate everything in sight and managed to put on four and a half stone! By the time I went for my last check-up I was waddling.

Given the consultant's initial concerns, I was remarkably healthy right through my pregnancy. It really did feel like my own special miracle. My only disappointment was that, having appeared pleased at the outset, Ken now didn't seem all that interested. He spent most of his spare time out driving his beloved cars (by then he had a Ferrari, not much use when you have a baby). But he had his priorities in a completely different order to mine and made it very clear that he didn't want to come along to any ante-natal classes or scans. I tried my best not to mind, but of course I did. Naturally, I wanted a doting husband and father, someone concerned about me, longing to hold his baby, but I had the wrong man. Ken had never doted on anybody but himself and his cars. He loved the Ferrari so much that he even slept in it one night. And if I'd hoped that getting married might improve things between us, I couldn't have been more wrong.

During my pregnancy I was still working and I had a lot of fun making a TV play called *Fowl Pest*. The director was the brilliant Michael Kerrigan and it was based on George Orwell's classic *Animal Farm* and co-starred three lovely actresses: Irene Handl, Sheila Steafel and my old friend from *Carry On* days, Joan Sims.

The four of us played chickens and we had a hilarious time getting in and out of our costumes. Irene was Mother Hen, Joan played Mad Auntie and I was Baby Chick. In the storyline the farmer was going to have us killed, so we were hiding in a caravan and had boarded up the door so that he couldn't get us. It was funny and at the same time made a political point.

In one sequence we were expected to flap our wings and jump out of the window. Worried about the effect that this antic might have on my unborn baby, I said: 'I'm sorry, but I can't do this scene – I can't jump out the window.' I hadn't told anyone about my pregnancy yet, not wanting to tempt fate, and so Sheila Steafel told me, 'But that's ridiculous, Sherrie! You're younger than the rest of us.'

'I'm four months pregnant,' I said. 'I should have told you before. I'm sorry.'

'Oh, for goodness sake – that's fantastic!' she said.

From then on Michael pampered me. In fact, they all did – the baby chick was having a baby chick! Everyone was delighted for me, and after that I didn't have to do anything more strenuous than waddle and quack.

I enjoyed my pregnancy so much that I didn't actually pay a lot of thought to the birth. Naivety and ignorance, really – I thought it would be legs up, baby out. All my thoughts were focused on the other end of the process when I would hold my child in my arms, so when I went for a final check-up around the time the baby was due and was told that I had high blood pressure and would have to go into hospital, it came as a bit of a shock.

I was admitted to Queen Charlotte's Hospital, Hammersmith, which was quite a long way from where we lived, and about ten hours after I got there I started the contractions. Well, I wondered what the bloody hell was happening.

'Shit!' I cried. 'I hope I'm not going to have many of these!'

'What's all this fuss about, Mrs Boyd? You're having a baby, you've got to expect contractions,' said the midwife, a stern young woman who was clearly not going to put up with any nonsense.

'I didn't know it would hurt so much,' I sniffed, before my next yelp.

'Believe me,' she said, and I couldn't help feeling there was a touch of smugness about the way she said it, 'this is just the beginning.'

If I was totally ignorant about childbirth before I started, I learned very, *very* fast. Within a couple of hours the contractions were coming in ever more frequent waves, and I was convinced this couldn't be right. I did try to keep the noise down, honestly, but it was like being slowly and agonisingly ripped in two. On your own, it's quite a frightening experience.

After ten hours of this I was getting desperate. Thankfully, I had no idea that there would be another thirty-two hours to go. To make matters worse, that night the midwives were all busy with other mothers-to-be who were much closer than I was to giving birth. Ken was none too keen on the idea of sticking around while I screamed the place down and had gone to the pub, so I had never felt more alone in my life.

By two o'clock in the morning I'd had enough. There was no one around, it was like the twilight zone and I was convinced no one cared, so I decided I had to get out of there.

'I want to go home!' I started to wail. 'I want to go home!'

'Well, you can't.' A rather flustered midwife had appeared and was pulling up the sides of the bed and drawing the curtains around me. 'You're having contractions, that's all, and do bear in mind there are people trying to sleep.' Well, you can imagine where I nearly told her to stick her stethoscope.

The moment she left, I somehow managed to climb out of bed, put on my coat and, stopping every now and again to double up with the next contraction, I got as far as the corridor.

Just as I reached the lift and hit the down button, the doors opened and a rather formidable midwife appeared.

'Where are you going?' she demanded, shocked.

'Home,' I spat. 'I've had more than enough of this! I'm not doing it any more.' I paused as the next contraction coursed through my body. 'Get me a taxi!' I screamed as soon as I could catch my breath.

Taking one look at me, she softened and said gently, 'OK, let's go somewhere you can wait and I'll call you a cab.'

At last the woman was talking sense. We got in the lift and she pressed the up button. When we got out she told me, 'I'll ring for a taxi – you just sit on this chair.' And so I sat there in my nightie, coat and gloves with my little suitcase perched on my knee.

A moment later she was back with a doctor in tow.

'Right, Mrs Boyd,' she said. 'We've ordered you a taxi, but before you go we're just going to check you over. So, come and get on this bed, there's a good girl.'

The doctor, having had a good probe around, said: 'Right, you can go home now, Mrs Boyd. Come with me.'

With that, we left the room and went into another with lots of equipment and, again, just one bed.

'Right,' the doctor told me, 'just wait there. Mary will wait with you till the taxi arrives.'

I had no idea I was being humoured and so I sat on a chair beside the bed, still clutching my case, hoping the taxi would arrive soon. Meanwhile, with every new contraction the pain increased and my yells became louder.

'You know, I can help you with that pain if you let me – you look very uncomfortable, Mrs Boyd,' said the nurse.

By this time I could scarcely breathe and so after she had taken my case from me I let her help me off with my coat and onto the bed. The madness had taken over.

She gave me some gas and air, followed by an injection of pethedine, but neither helped. Though spaced out, I could still feel the pain. As time passed, my pain threshold weakened and my brain became more and more addled. I started to feel very angry as if it was everyone else's fault that I was having this baby. More time passed, but I had lost track of anything apart from the overwhelming pain.

The midwife put her hand on the gas mask to reposition it on my face and I grabbed her arm and the tube with my other hand.

'Let go,' she told me, trying to yank her arm away, but I had it in a vice-like grip and wasn't about to let go. 'You're blocking the gas and air, you're holding it too tight!' she shouted, as we tussled back and forth.

At that moment Ken walked in and unfortunately got in the way, so he copped the blow on the nose that I was trying to land on her.

'You *bastard*!' I screamed.

'Oh my *God*!' he spluttered.

'Get out of the way, Mr Boyd,' yelled the midwife, shoving him aside. By this time there were two midwives with me, one each end.

'Calm down, Mrs Boyd, this isn't helping,' said one of them.

'No, it's not,' Ken piped up, this time pretty scared.

Suddenly, the one down at the rear end said, 'OK, let's push.' At this point I grabbed the nearest thing (which happened to be Ken's hand) and screamed the place down. I vaguely remember hearing him say, 'You're breaking my fingers,' but that was the least of my worries – he had another hand.

'The head's here now … one last push and you've done it!' yelled the midwife.

Oh my God, the relief! All that pain, but then the miracle happens.

'It's a girl, Mrs Boyd, a beautiful baby girl,' said the midwife, with a tired smile.

'I know,' I said.

There was never any doubt in my mind that I would have a girl. I don't know who was more relieved it was over, the midwives or me. The midwife held my baby up for me to see, but she was a strange blue colour.

'Oh my God,' I said, 'she's *blue*!'

A couple of nights earlier I'd watched *V* – a film about aliens landing on earth – and there were lots of baby ones, all blue. Just for a second, in my drugged state, I wondered if fantasy had crossed over into real life.

'Don't be silly,' she told me, 'she's just a bit blue. A puff of oxygen and she'll be fine.'

Moments later I held my baby for the first time. Exhausted as I was by the ordeal we had been through, as she sank into my arms I was overwhelmed with happiness. I gazed at that perfect little face: she was beautiful, a perfect person. Then I kissed her on her little lips and cried, my heart bursting with love.

'Someone has just fallen in love forever,' the midwife said, smiling.

I certainly had, and my love for her is still as powerful now as it was the very first moment when I met my wonderful daughter, Keeley.

That evening they were keen to take her off to the nursery, as they did in those days. I didn't want to let her out of my sight, but the nurse insisted I needed some rest, so reluctantly I let her go and fell into an exhausted sleep. The next day was a beautiful hot summer's day and for some reason I dressed Keeley in a sailor outfit to take her home from the hospital. I don't know why, but she looked adorable. Ken picked us up. By now he had sacrificed his beloved Ferrari for a proper car – I don't think he ever forgave me for that.

When we got home and had put Keeley (who was now fast asleep) into her Moses basket, I looked around the house. It was a mess. Ken hadn't bothered to do any housework while I'd been gone. The kitchen floor was dirty, the lawn hadn't been mown and he didn't even offer to make me a cup of tea. I knew I'd have to leave most of it till I felt stronger, but I've always had a thing about kitchens needing to be squeaky clean, and the sight of that dirty floor upset me.

'What does it matter?' asked Ken.

'It matters,' I replied, through gritted teeth.

Just at that moment, Caius (who had been thrilled to see me when I arrived home) went straight out of the front door, which somebody had left open.

'Oh God,' cried Ken, 'the bloody dog's got out! He's been running away a lot lately. I'll get the car and go after him.'

'I must do the floor,' I muttered, all the while feeling more exhausted than I had ever felt before. As Ken followed Caius out of the front door, I got a bucket, water and soap. Having got down on my hands and knees, I started to scrub. Suddenly my back was wracked with pain: I hadn't realised what a 42-hour labour can do to you.

Thinking I had heard Ken's car coming back along the road, I somehow managed to get up and go outside to see if he had found Caius. Just as I reached the road, though, my back completely gave way. I sank down onto my hands and knees on the tarmac and couldn't move.

'What the hell are you doing down there?' asked Ken, as he drove up alongside me.

'Washing the road,' I replied. 'What do you *think* I'm doing on my hands and knees in the middle of the road?'

'I've got to find the dog,' he told me. 'Get up and stop being so daft.'

Feeling very sorry for myself, I managed to crawl back into the house. There were no banners, no warm welcome home, just me on my knees cleaning my kitchen floor. Not exactly the humdinger of a party I'd been hoping for.

Chapter Seventeen

I know little things like unwashed floors, unmowed lawns and even leaving a person on her hands and knees in the road might not sound like big deals, but they are. Sitting in the middle of my dirty kitchen floor on the day when I brought Keeley home, something snapped inside me. I thought, This can't be right, this isn't how Doris Day would have done it – where's the romance, where's the music? Where's Cary Grant when you need him? Dead, that's where, I told myself, and burst into tears.

A cup of tea and a crumpet might have won me over, but there was nothing. It should have been the most wonderful day of my life, arriving home having just given birth to a longed-for baby: all I needed was rest and a bit of tenderness. But when Ken arrived back with Caius, he simply asked, 'What's for tea? We've got a bit of steak – do you want to shove that under the grill?' No, just your testicles, is what I wanted to say, but somehow I managed to stick the steak under the grill and life went back to normal. Ken wasn't really interested in being a father

– he wasn't a bad man, he just wanted different things – and although I know he loved Keeley, fatherhood was not top of his list.

The person who helped to fill that role in my life, and in Keeley's, was my own dad. He came to stay with us while I was pregnant, on the way to his annual Benidorm holiday, but this time he didn't go and instead ended up moving in with us. I loved him being there and Ken was happy about it, too, because it gave him a drinking companion. He and Dad both loved to play the slot machines in pubs – they would spend hours together drinking several pints and losing several pounds.

As far as I was concerned, Dad was my saviour. He was marvellous with Keeley: he adored her and would look after her while Ken and I were out working. He changed nappies, did the washing and baked pies, bread and cakes. His Christmas cake became quite famous around Surrey – we had orders for it every year. If Dad felt he hadn't been around all that much when we were children, he certainly made up for it during those years. He shocked the whole family, especially Mum, who couldn't believe he actually baked every day.

Sadly, during those same years my relationship with Ken went steadily downhill. I felt that he loved and cared for his cars more than he did his daughter and me. He still went off and bought one expensive car after another – all on 'tick', as the saying goes. Now that I had a baby girl who was the centre of my life, I no longer shared his passion for them, though. To be fair, I didn't have a lot of time or energy for Ken once Keeley arrived: I didn't ignore him, most of the time I was just knackered. She was the sweetest baby and the love of my life, so when I wasn't working I wanted to spend every minute with her, but it was still a terrible shock when I realised that Ken was having an affair.

Dad and I were cleaning out the garage one afternoon when we found a grubby plastic bag. Inside were photographs of Ken and a girl in a bed, on a bed, with clothes, without clothes, doing things together that no matter which way you turned the photo, you couldn't decipher. The photos of the girl on her own he'd actually cropped to remove her head, so I couldn't tell who it was. As I went through the bag, I found cards and letters she had written to him for Valentine's Day, Easter and Christmas, so it was clear that the affair had gone on for at least a year. How did I miss it? How could I have been so blind? I had heard of this happening to other people, but never thought it would be me.

I was beside myself with anger and Dad grew very worried. When it was time to go and collect Ken from work, he pleaded with me to let him go instead. He recognised this side of me and feared the worst. Of course I knew I shouldn't drive, but I wouldn't have any of it and so I got in the car and drove to British Aerospace. I remember sitting in the car opposite the building and waiting for Ken to come out, all the while going over in my mind how he had treated me.

'You need help,' he used to say. 'You're imagining things.' I felt utterly betrayed and humiliated and as he crossed the road to the car my blood boiled.

'What's wrong?' asked Ken as soon as he got in.

'That!' I said, slinging the soiled bag towards him.

In deadly silence, I drove off into the Kingston rush-hour traffic.

'What's your problem …'

His voice petered out as he opened the grubby bag. I could sense him shrinking, which wasn't at all the reaction I'd expected, and it made me madder.

'Well?' I screamed.

'I don't want to talk about it.'

A red mist descended on me and I pressed my foot on the accelerator, shouting and swearing at him as the car swerved, narrowly missing several vehicles.

'This is madness, Sherrie – pull over, *stop*! For God's sake, *stop*!' said Ken, now terrified.

But I was beyond caring. Consumed with anger and hurt at his betrayal, I continued to drive and scream at him at the same time. In that moment I really didn't care if I killed us both. Blinded by tears and unmanageable rage, I was out of control. I slammed my foot on the brake and so did everyone behind me, thank God.

'Who is she?'

When he didn't answer, I started hitting him with my fists. He sat there, motionless, which in my eyes was tantamount to an admission of guilt. Slowly, my fury waned and exhaustion took over; I felt completely empty. As my thoughts turned to my new baby, I silently drove back to the house with Ken slumped in the passenger seat. Thankfully, Dad was looking after Keeley and so I went up to the bedroom, locked the door and sat down on the bed, numb and very cold.

Later, I looked out of the bedroom window to see Ken burning the contents of the grimy little plastic bag on a bonfire. We didn't speak for days: he slept on the sofa and kept out of my way.

A week later I confronted him: 'I want you out of this house, I want you out of my life, I want you gone forever!'

'Why do we have to split up?' he kept on saying. 'Why can't we just be civilised and continue to live in the same house?'

Alas, he eventually wore me down and I caved in because of our money situation and the fact that Keeley was so young. It was the wrong decision: had we split then, both of us might have picked up the pieces of our lives, met other people and gone on to have new families. At the time I felt it was better for Keeley to have her dad around and I dreaded the reality of a split, which would mean selling the house, dividing everything and all the complexity that entailed. As it was, we stayed together, unhappily, for almost eighteen more years.

I was enraged over Ken's affair, mainly because my earlier suspicions proved correct but I'd let him convince me I was wrong. Soon it became obvious that he'd been playing around for a while and had had more than one affair. Now the can of worms was well and truly open.

After that, we had some terrible rows. On one awful occasion, a few years later, we were out for the evening in Spain with another couple and Ken had been drinking heavily. I picked up the bill, as I usually did, and reached for my credit card. This was normal for us (I generally paid, especially after he left his job in 1993), but this time he shot me a furious look.

On the way home in the car he started shouting, 'You *had* to do that, didn't you? You *had* to show me up!'

Terrified, I couldn't think what had got into him. After all, I had only done what I usually did: pick up the bill and pay.

Meanwhile Ken was driving like a lunatic, slamming the car across the ramps in the road. 'Stop it, Ken! Don't drive so fast. Stop it!' I screamed, but he was furious. Goodness knows how we got back to the apartment as we rowed all the way, the car lurching over speed bumps so violently at one point that I banged my head against the window.

When we got back, Ken disappeared into the spare bedroom and I lay on the other bed, hoping he'd collapsed into a deep sleep. As I lay there, feeling battered and bruised, I realised why Ken might have been behaving in the way he did. Was he having an affair with the woman we'd been having dinner with that evening? I became convinced that he was – it could be the only explanation for his fury. He must have felt that I had belittled him in front of her.

The next morning Ken was comatose and I decided to leave him. I packed my case, but there were two flights of stairs up to the apartment and I couldn't lift it, so I phoned for a taxi using a number on a card on the kitchen wall. It was a Spanish firm, they couldn't speak English and I couldn't speak Spanish. '*Donde*?' was all the operator could say and I didn't know that means 'Where?' So he kept saying, '*Donde*?' while I said, 'What?' Round and round we went. Eventually, I gave up and went back to sleep, grateful that Keeley happened to be staying with Ken's parents.

This was just one of many occasions when I realised that Ken was probably involved with another woman. Whenever I tried to talk to him about it, he made it plain that it was me who needed psychiatric help. In the end, he said this so often that I began to doubt myself and started to think that perhaps there really was something wrong with me. Was I becoming paranoid? Maybe I was imagining it all. Eventually I went to see a psychologist, who said it was Ken and not me who had the problem, but by then I doubted myself so much that I didn't want to believe her and so I didn't go back to see her again.

In some ways, I did become paranoid: everywhere we went, I was afraid that Ken would start flirting, or we'd meet someone he was having an affair with. It got to the point where I couldn't bear to go to parties or even on holiday. I was in my thirties, I had a beautiful daughter and was never out of work, yet the next three to four years were an especially disquieting time for me, and as a result of my extreme unhappiness I struggled with eating and alcohol problems.

The eating difficulties came first and they began around the time when I joined a hugely popular comedy series called *In Loving Memory*, starring Thora Hird. It was set in a 1920s funeral parlour run by Ivy Unsworth (Thora) and her nephew Billy Henshaw (played by Christopher Beeny). I had appeared several times during the previous series, playing three different roles, then I was asked to join in 1985 as Mary Braithwaite, billed as the third star alongside Thora and Chris. Mary married Billy to become Mrs Henshaw and lived in the funeral parlour with them. Ronnie Baxter was the director: one of the best, he knew everything there was to know about comedy and pathos and how the two go hand in hand. Of course there were outrageous moments with runaway coffins and dead bodies, but always tastefully done.

Being a religious woman, I think Thora sometimes felt uncomfortable with the more slapstick routines, though Ronnie was never irreverent. There was a scene that Chris and I did supposedly on our honeymoon night when he lifts me up to put me on the bed: as he lays me down, the whole bed collapses and he and I end up in a heap. Over the years, the outtakes of this made me quite a few bob on *It'll be Alright on the Night* with Denis Norden. In fact, being one of the clumsiest actresses in the business, everything I have ever been in has featured on that show.

I was delighted to land a full-time role in a series that had been a peak-time success for several years, but unfortunately there was one member of the cast who was extremely unkind to me and made my life hell. This person was a bully, but it was all done in an underhand way and I never let on. 'I'm going to get you fired,' they would whisper to me and they would also take every opportunity to put me down and taunt me just because they could. Of course I was already vulnerable because of my problems with Ken and so this affected me very badly.

During the series I literally stopped eating – I managed a chocolate bar a day, but that was about it. The weight fell off and I was in serious danger of developing anorexia. For quite a while no one realised because I walked around a lot of the time, clutching a chocolate bar. After eight weeks of filming I had lost two stone, and finally, one day on set, I collapsed and was taken to hospital. There I had tests and it turned out that I had low blood sugar levels. Seriously thin, I looked like Olive Oyle in the 'Popeye' cartoons.

In the end, it was Chris Beeny who said to me, 'As a friend, can I tell you, you look awful? Your face has aged because you're so scrawny.' At that time I weighed about seven stone and I'm five foot seven, so you can imagine how I looked. Somehow I managed to pull myself together following this wake-up call. Afterwards, I thought, why let another person do this to you? That's pathetic. And so I gave myself a kick up the backside and started eating again.

It was the same with drinking: I had never drunk very much – I was just as happy with Coca-Cola as alcohol, but as my marriage deteriorated it became a crutch, a secret friend. Of course, it was not the alcohol that I needed, it was the comfort, and if Jelly Tots had done the same thing I would have been just as addicted to them. I hated coming home and having to face the long, uncomfortable evenings with Ken, so I looked for a way to get through those hours and that atmosphere. It crept up on me, and if I'm truthful I developed a fear of alcohol. This was a complete contradiction: on the one hand, alcohol was my friend, but on the other, it became my enemy. It was an isolated world because I couldn't tell anyone – my dad would have been worried sick, while Ken would just have told me that I was a stupid cow. More than anything, I didn't want Keeley to spot anything and, thankfully, she never did. Everything was kept hidden: I only ever bought half bottles of Bacardi and gin, which fitted nicely into the large boxes of washing powder under the kitchen sink, and as I was the only one who did any washing I knew they were safe.

The funny side was that I invented the most elaborate stories to tell each person at all the off licences I visited. Of course, it was just another sale to them but I felt so ashamed that I invented all sorts of imaginary people I was buying for. There'd be a Florrie in an old people's home who had no one to visit her, then Arthur up the road, who'd just come out of hospital, and Mary whose husband had died a week ago. I'm so glad no one cared enough to ask 'How's Florrie?' or 'How's Arthur?' the next time I went in – I wouldn't have known what they were talking about.

Did my family notice? I don't think Dad and Ken did because I wasn't drunk, I just felt a nice, hazy numbness that made everything bearable and if they thought I was behaving a little oddly they never said so. When I drank in front of them I mixed the gin with orange and the Bacardi with Coke so they thought I was having soft drinks, although they were actually about 80 per cent alcohol.

I didn't drink in the morning or even during the day. It was only after work because even though Dad was around I couldn't face the evenings with Ken. I thought I had everything under control, but there was clearly a problem. At one time I believed I could fly as I'd be at the top of the stairs one minute, then I'd find myself at the bottom and have absolutely no idea how I got there. Here and there I would lose an hour or so, yet I somehow convinced myself that I could manage the situation.

By this time Ken and I were having more arguments and on rare occasions physical fights. When I look back, I feel ashamed and horrified that I let things get so out of hand. I didn't want to stay in my marriage but I didn't know how to leave it. On one occasion, as we fought and shouted at one another, I pushed Ken down a flight of stairs. As a result, he put his hand through the pint glass he'd been holding and very nearly severed two fingers. We had to call an ambulance and passed it off as an accident, but I was mortified that I'd hurt him so badly.

Thankfully he made a full recovery, but that didn't stop the fights. One Christmas Eve, when Ken's parents and my dad were staying with us, we went to a party given by some friends of ours who lived opposite. I hated parties by this stage, so I dreaded going. Ken had too much to drink and started to get really nasty. As he watched me dancing, he said some horrible things to me because although he made it clear that he didn't like me he was strangely jealous if any other man came near. It was the classic case of 'I don't want you, but no one else can have you.' 'You're being cheap and behaving like a slut,' he'd slur. 'What are you trying to prove? No one's looking at you!' – which made me drink all the more. What followed is something I have always felt guilty about because it happened in front of Keeley, who was four at the time: I slapped Ken and then stormed out home.

Furious that I'd behaved so badly, Ken followed in my wake. His parents, who had watched the whole scene, were shocked and thought I was overreacting. Meanwhile, Dad had been looking after Keeley at home. Though not usually a violent man, Ken was so infuriated that he slapped me across the face and accidentally struck my ear in the process. That stopped the fight because both of us realised we had gone too far. Now in tears, I was clutching my ear and Ken was red-faced with anger and shame. I went off to have a hot bath and try and get myself together but as I ducked my head under the water I suddenly felt the most agonising pain. Ken quickly took me to casualty, where they discovered that I had a perforated eardrum and a hairline fracture.

'It isn't serious,' the consultant said, 'but I'd like you to rest as it was quite a blow, you falling down the stairs like that. If, at any time, you feel faint or you have a funny turn, or feel a bit loopy, come back and we'll have another look.' *'Loopy?'* I said, 'I'm *already* loopy! How will I know the difference?' It made him laugh, and even Ken managed to crack a smile. We both left, knowing it was one more nail in the coffin of our marriage.

Even that episode proved not enough to prevent me drinking completely. In the end, what stopped me was the childminder's reaction when I turned up one afternoon to collect Keeley. I'd had a couple of drinks over lunch with a friend but I didn't think anyone would notice. I was wrong, though. The childminder quietly took me to one side and then told me, 'Don't come here again – I don't want a mother who's just had a drink picking up a child.' Of course she was right, and I felt sick with shame. Afterwards I swore to myself that I would stop drinking that day, and so I did.

Actually, it was not that hard to stop drinking. I poured all the alcohol away and refused to allow myself to have another drink for a long time. What was harder still was seeing my marriage slowly crumble before my eyes. It had reached the point where I was so convinced that Ken was having affairs all over the shop that I suspected everyone, even our 90-year-old post office mistress and the 20-stone local shot-putter.

I made up my mind that I had to stop driving myself mad with worry and suspicion. Having conquered my eating and alcohol problems, it was time to concentrate on the two things that never let me down and that I loved: my beloved daughter and my work. Both would remain constant and provide a source of comfort over the years.

Chapter Eighteen

I couldn't have got through it all without Mum and Dad. When I was working, Dad looked after Keeley for me and he would take her to stay with Mum in Nottingham. All the while that this drama in my life was unfolding, it seems impossible that I was able to carry on working, but I was and the offers came flooding in. Around this time I appeared in a stream of TV comedies: *Never the Twain* with Donald Sinden, *All at Number 20* (in which I played Mrs Melchett) with Maureen Lipman, *Home James!* with Jim Davidson and *Home to Roost* with John Thaw; at night I was in the West End in *Stepping Out* with Amanda Barrie and *Run for Your Wife* with Roy Hudd. Also, I was asked back onto *The Russ Abbot Show*. Meanwhile, I had a little baby at home to take care of.

I was still crossing over from TV comedy to drama, which was very lucky because in those days you were usually known for one or the other. Back then, the BBC used to put on *Play for Today* or *Play of the Month*; often it would be a Chekhov or something by Noël Coward, sometimes Catherine Cookson or

Charles Dickens. There was so much work in those days – except for the film industry, which had died in this country. *The Slipper and the Rose* was one of the last British films to be made, so you could say I had a hand in bringing it down.

I rejoined *The Russ Abbot Show* in 1988 and over the next three years I was one of the regular cast members. A mix of sketches, impressions and big musical production numbers, the series was prime-time Saturday night viewing. The other regulars, Les Dennis, Jeff Holland and Bella Emberg, were all still there but we were now joined by Blackpool comedian Tom Bright and later on newcomer Lisa Maxwell. Often we went away filming with the show. One particular summer – one of the hottest on record – we spent nearly a month in Devon.

It was around this time that I became very close to one of the other cast members. He made me laugh, and seemed to like me and found me attractive, which was so nice after feeling so rejected and humiliated. I'd forgotten how it felt to catch someone looking at you and sense that shiver of excitement, the sexual frisson when you both know you're attracted to each other – it's the best diet in the world. I couldn't eat and I lost so much weight that I was into size eight trousers, but … and there was always going to be a 'but' because, despite the problems Ken and I had, we were still married and had a child together. Although just being around this man did me the world of good, we both knew the relationship wasn't going anywhere. Still, it was a breath of fresh air and even now as I sit here, writing and remembering, I have a big smile on my face.

As well as doing *The Russ Abbot Show*, I was involved in all kinds of other projects. One of them was my first-ever pantomime: *Cinderella* at the Dominion Theatre in London, with Jim Davidson. I played the fairy godmother and Jim was Buttons. He and I were also doing a sitcom together at Thames Television called *Home James!* with two wonderful actors, George Sewell and Harry Towb. Jim had already appeared in the ITV sitcom, *Up the Elephant and Round the Castle* – his first foray into acting – in the early eighties, and this was his second. It ran from 1987 to 1990 and I think he had the potential to be an excellent actor but he didn't have the patience. He could do high comedy and pathos but he was a bugger for losing concentration.

One day at rehearsals he came in with an attaché case strapped to his arm. He unlocked the case while we rehearsed and then at lunchtime he said to me, 'I'm going to strap this case onto you whilst I go out for a meeting – I won't be long.' Before I could say a word, he'd locked it onto my arm and was out the door. Well, he was gone for the rest of the day and I had that bloody case with me right to the end of rehearsals. He sent a message via the stage manager that I was to meet him in the pub up the road with it after we'd finished.

Of course, I wasn't at all happy about this but I couldn't get in contact with him. Jim was the only one with a mobile phone in those days: it was bigger than a house brick, but it was the latest gadget and the rest of us couldn't afford one. If I could have released myself from that wretched case I would have left it at the studios. As it was, I had to go and meet Jim. Anyway, I couldn't think what all the fuss was about as he'd told me it contained only papers.

A couple of the others kindly came to the pub with me. There was no sign of Jim but he'd phoned ahead to say the drinks were on him, and no matter what other faults he might have had he was the most generous person you could ever wish to meet. When he eventually arrived, he unlocked me and then took me into the back room: 'Just want to say thank you,' he said. He opened the case and it was full of money – there must have been £20,000 or £30,000 inside. 'Got it out the bank for

Tracy's ring,' he told me. He took £100 out and handed it to me. After that, he settled the whole bar bill and took everyone out for dinner.

When he learned of Ken's affair, Jim generously offered to move me out of the house and rent me a flat in London. Of course I didn't accept, but it was a kind offer and I always knew he was there for me, should I need him. Having said that, we had a volatile relationship and on more than one occasion we actually had a stand-up fight. Jim always had to be right but he knew I didn't agree with most of his views and that I'd give as good as I got.

When we appeared together in *Cinderella*, I would stand at the side of the stage with him. In those days he'd always have a drink with him – 'just for nerves'. He'd turn to me, whisper, 'Fuck me, fuck 'em all!' and then hand me the glass, bounce on stage and Buttons would come alive. He always gave the most endearing performance: the kids loved him, the mothers loved him – he was such an enigma.

One day, Jim asked me to do a midnight matinée for charity and explained that this time it would be an adult version of the show. The night we put on *Sinderella*, 3,000 adults were there at midnight. Almost certainly, most of them had been drinking since early evening and now they were waiting to be entertained. I'd made it very plain to Jim that I didn't want any part in the smuttiness or the swearing, but I would open the show for him. I walked on stage and instead of my usual, 'Hello, kids, I'm your fairy godmother! Let's sing a song together,' I staggered on with a bottle of gin and a fag in one hand. With my tiara askew and wearing just one shoe, I started to weave my way around the stage, and the audience loved it. Then suddenly from the wings I heard a whooshing sound. As I paused, a vision of loveliness swung around over my head before she flew down and landed on her feet in front of me. It was the former child star Bonnie Langford, whom I knew very well.

'Hello, boys and girls,' she said, hands on hips and slapping a thigh. 'How lovely you all look! Would you like to sing with me? My name's Jack.'

At this, I stumbled towards her and taking a swig from the gin bottle and a drag on the fag I told her: 'Oh, fuck off, Jack! You're not even in this pantomime.'

The whole place erupted.

Delighted, Jim was jumping up and down at the side of the stage, the audience were screaming with laughter and Bonnie, bless her, played out her role beautifully and just replied, 'OK, I will. Bye-bye, boys and girls!' And off she flew.

When I came off I apologised to Bonnie, but she thought it was hysterical. As always with her, she joined in the fun, telling me: 'As long as we raise money, Sherrie – that's all that matters.'

Although Bonnie and I were only on for those few moments, the show went on for five hours in all and raised around £500,000 for charity. Jim enjoyed it so much that he extended that one-off performance into a run, though neither Bonnie nor I took part. Once was enough for us.

Naturally, *Cinderella* – the real one – ran through Christmas and into the New Year. One evening just before Christmas when we had the night off from the panto, Ken and I went out with Jim and his girlfriend, Tracy Hilton. (Later, she would become his fourth wife and was in fact the same girl for whom I'd carried all that money around in Jim's attaché case.)

The day after our night out, Tracy rang me and said, 'I hate having to tell you this, Sherrie, but your husband was making up to me all last night. He was giving me the eye. It was dreadful behaviour, Sherrie, and you don't deserve that. You've got to leave him.'

Later, Jim came to my dressing room and said: 'Sherrie, your husband is like me: we're frightened men who don't want to get any older. He wants the reassurance of knowing he's still attractive, that women still fancy him. He'll never respect you and he'll always be unfaithful – you've got to get out.'

Of course Jim's own behaviour has been well documented, but there is another side to him: he's done some wonderful work as chairman of the British Forces Foundation, a charity that entertains British troops. He's been to Iraq six times to entertain them, also to Afghanistan, and was awarded the OBE in 2001, largely for his services to charity. And while all this doesn't make his bad behaviour acceptable, I couldn't help feeling at least he'd done something very worthwhile and he was honest about himself, too: he had owned up. I really should have listened to him, but I couldn't – I just wasn't ready to walk out of my marriage, not yet. Only days later, on New Year's Eve, I had another wake-up call.

After the show, I drove over to a pub where I had arranged to join Ken for the remainder of the evening's celebrations with little Keeley. The first thing I saw when I entered the bar was my husband in a clinch with another women. It was a proper tongue-down-the-throat job, too. As I sank down into the nearest chair, still holding my daughter's hand, Ken surfaced from the lingering kiss. Obviously the worse for drink, he came over to me and said, 'Now, don't start …'

'You *bastard*!' I said, all the while mustering as much dignity as I could manage.

Indignant, he gave me a withering look and walked out of the pub. Hurt and humiliated, I hated Keeley seeing me in floods of tears once again. Suddenly, I felt a tap on my shoulder and turned to see the woman he'd been kissing.

'You want to lighten up, it was just a snog,' she told me. I stared at her as she added, 'He was good, too! I was in there.'

At this, I put my hand across her face and pushed. She landed on top of a table of leftover food – a tart covered in custard, which somehow seemed fitting. I grabbed Keeley and we went to the nearest hotel, where we had a lovely time together on our own. We spent as much as we could on the joint credit card (pointless because I would end up paying the bill, anyway), but that night I thought, what the hell?

After those two humiliating occasions, there were to be many times when I would think if only I'd taken Jim's advice and left Ken then and there, but I simply couldn't break up the family. Besides, a part of me still believed we might find a way to make our relationship work for Keeley's sake.

It was around this time that I first began to think about cosmetic surgery. After everything that had happened, I had lost confidence in myself as a woman and I felt deeply unattractive. This feeling came to a head in 1990 when I turned 40. Oh my God, what a shock! All my young life I longed to be older, I wanted to be 40, but now here it was. In those days surgery wasn't so readily available as it is now when you can have lots of procedures carried out in your lunch-hour. Botox, fillers, thread veins removal … it's amazing the things they can achieve. And in the States, where they're the innovators, you can have body lifts, liposuction … even your face lifted and replaced with someone else's – I'd want Julia Roberts's! Cosmetic surgery can be highly addictive, however, and it's a dangerous road to go down. People talk about addiction to sex, drugs and alcohol but I believe cosmetic surgery is right up there with them.

My first venture into this world was a few weeks before my fortieth birthday. Determined to ask for a facelift, I made an appointment with a cosmetic surgeon. I thought I'd done enough research, but quite obviously I hadn't. On arrival I was shown into a grandiose waiting room, all highly polished wood and chandeliers, *Tatler* and *American Vogue*. An hour passed by and I had just about talked myself into leaving when a rather disinterested receptionist came in.

'Mrs Boyd?' she murmured, and I dutifully followed her.

After being shown into a surprisingly spartan office with a desk and two chairs, I was told to take a seat. Minutes later a rather rakish young man entered the room, wearing slightly grubby white cotton trousers and a white jacket that flopped open. A cigarette was dangling from his mouth. He didn't even look at me.

'Facelift? Forty, yes?' he asked in broken English, reading the file in front of him. Of course, I should have departed then, but I was rooted to the chair.

At this point he looked straight at me and said: 'No, too young – wrong time for facelift! Do you know the things that can go wrong? If there is a mistake and a nerve is cut, your face could be black.'

I felt as if I was in *Sweeney Todd*.

'Listen to me,' he continued, 'you go, come back when you 60!'

After this, he stubbed out his cigarette and left the room.

I stared after him in horror: in my mind I'd built up the whole process into something wonderful that would make a huge difference in my life, only to find myself confronted by a chap who seemed nothing like a surgeon and who came out with warnings that sent a chill through my spine. It all sounded terrifying and I felt as if I'd had a lucky escape. Now I just wanted to get out of there as fast as possible.

Outside, I jumped into my little Renault and set off home in floods of tears. I was so disappointed and frustrated at the futile afternoon I'd just spent that I didn't notice a junction ahead and approached it too quickly. Without any time to stop, I jumped the red light and could see cars hurtling towards me on either side. All I could think was, I'm dead and I didn't even get to have a facelift! The next moment I was rammed by one of the cars.

My car spun across the road and I could hear the screech of brakes. Suddenly, it all stopped: with a thump, my head came to rest on the steering wheel and I felt an overwhelming desire to sleep. Far away, I could hear voices, shouting, 'Get her out!' and then 'Fire!' I was dragged out and the next thing I knew I was sitting on the verge. My head was spinning and there were people all around me. Suddenly I noticed my poor Renault had been reduced to a concertina, with just a small hole where the driver's door had once been. As a comforting arm went around my shoulders, I burst into tears.

'There, there, you're out now. Don't cry,' said a kindly voice. 'You're alive, that's what matters.'

'My husband will kill me!' I sobbed. 'I must get the car home.'

On that note, I struggled to my feet and lurched towards the wrecked Renault. The next moment, my legs gave way and I fell. When I opened my eyes, I was staring up at a metal lid and a face loomed over me.

'Come on, Sherrie! Stay awake now.'

The face knew my name. Slowly, I started to take in my surroundings: I was in an ambulance, wrapped in a red blanket. Apparently I'd been out for twenty minutes and we were just arriving at the hospital.

My car was a complete write-off, but I was fine and thankfully no one else was hurt. For a few days I needed to wear a neck-brace but I had survived a really bad crash with nothing worse than a few cuts and bruises to my forehead where it hit the steering wheel.

As far as surgery was concerned, however, the accident didn't dampen my ardour. A few weeks later I went to see another cosmetic surgeon, this time in London's Harley Street. I thought this would be a safer bet, but it was equally disastrous.

Arriving for the consultation, I was greeted by a very nice receptionist who purred, 'Well, hello there!' She stood looking at me and then turned and called out, 'Mary, come and look at this lady!' – which Mary did. Both scrutinised my face and clearly in agreement they began to mutter, 'Oh, *yes*! Definitely, *yes*.'

'You are *definitely* doing the right thing,' Mary told me sweetly.

'Yes,' whispered the first one, 'you are a prime candidate for a facelift. Well, you've come to the right place.' Still purring, she squeezed my hand.

No doubt they were trying to make me feel at ease and welcome, all girls together, and ensure business for the clinic, but the only thing they achieved was to make me feel much worse. I got out of there as soon as the simpering girls' brigade turned their attention to the next victim.

After those two miserable experiences I waited another eight years before considering surgery again. It was something I was to come back to – with good results but some disasters as well, of which more later. For the moment, I just had to accept that the time wasn't right.

Caius, my beloved dog, was always wonderful with Keeley. Far from being jealous that he was no longer my only baby, he absolutely adored her. He could have eaten her if he wished, but he would just sit with his nose close to her and never cease to watch over her.

I remember once going out to collect a friend from the station when I left Caius at home to guard Keeley. My friend glanced around the car and asked where she was, to which I said: 'Caius is babysitting her.' She was horrified, but by the end of her visit she agreed with me that he was the perfect gentle giant and posed no threat at all – quite the opposite, in fact.

Those of you who have owned Weimaraners will know exactly what I'm talking about when I say Caius was a very spiritual, empathetic and caring dog. He loved me unconditionally, and in the years before Keeley came along he was my baby. With their yellow eyes and ghostly, silver-grey coats, Weimeraners are quite mystical and strange, more human than dog-like beings. If I was upset, Caius would cry, and he seemed to smile when I was happy. Now I know you'll say that's very me and dismiss it altogether, but it's absolutely true. The only problem with this breed of dog is they are quite delicate and have sickly tummies – and that's just like me, too. Caius went on develop all sorts of allergies and had an eating disorder so he eventually got his own medicine cabinet, but I didn't mind – I loved him so much. At one point he developed an abscess in his stomach after swallowing a stick and had to go to hospital, where they opened him up. They had to take away so much skin that it left a gaping hole in the side of his body. Once he was home again, I sat up with him every night, bathing the wound to keep it clean, and tore up whole sheets as bandages to wrap his poor body in. Miraculously, his skin knitted itself back together again and he lived to go on eating sticks.

Weimaraners, like all large breeds, have fairly short lives, and as Caius reached the age of 9, his back legs weakened and other problems occurred. By 10 he was on numerous pills for his heart, liver and arthritis – you name it, he was taking them. I had to accept that in dog years Caius was now an old man and he wouldn't be around for too much longer – something I knew would break my heart.

In 1992 I was offered the chance to go to Blackpool to work with Russ Abbot in a live show from May to November. I had never done a live comedy show and although I was loath to leave Caius, it sounded like a fun opportunity and I did need the money.

The show was in the theatre on Blackpool's North Pier. We did two performances a day and when I looked out of my dressing-room window, I could hardly believe my eyes. Before every show, long lines of people were queuing for tickets. I can honestly say I had never seen anything like that before or since: Russ was phenomenally popular. The only downside was that while we were on stage I would often hear the sea lashing away at the columns beneath us and feel the pier sway slightly, a bit like being on a ship. I have never been that keen on the sea and ever since the swimming-pool incident when I was a little girl I have always preferred theatres on solid ground.

While I was there, I rented a flat in Blackpool. Being at least a five hour drive, it was too far to get home every night, though I did go back whenever I had a day off or a break in the show.

Bella Emberg – an incredibly funny, talented actress and a lovely person – was also starring in the show. She appeared in almost all Russ's TV programmes and was an integral part of his productions. One wild and stormy night after the show, Bella and I came out of the theatre and headed back up the pier to go home. Amid howling gales and lashing seas, both of us clung to the handrail.

Oh my God, I thought, we'll never make it to the end of the pier.

Bella is a rotund lady and as we edged our way along a sudden, fearsome gust of wind lifted her off her feet before thumping her back down on the deck, flat on her back. Every time she tried to get up the wind pushed her in the opposite direction and made it impossible for her to stand up, so she kept on rolling from one side to the other.

I was no help at all, I'm afraid, for it was a bit like a comedy sketch. Holding onto the nearest pole for safety, I was brought to my knees with laughter. I was still in hysterics when two of the guys in the show with us came tearing down the pier. One grabbed me and the other – after I had pointed out poor old Bella – ran and jumped on top of her to keep her safe. Later, I apologised to her over a large drink in our local Italian with the boys. Bless her, she saw the funny side and said: 'If one of you say I could have been mistaken for a barrage balloon, I'll push you off the pier myself!'

Another night I was in my Blackpool flat and had just come out of the shower when I looked down to see the most enormous spider. It was sitting on my leg, just below my knee. Instinctively, I flicked it off but then to my bewilderment I couldn't see it anywhere. It had completely disappeared.

The next moment a thought entered my head, clear as day.

'Oh my God,' I cried out aloud. 'Caius is dying!'

Minutes later, the phone rang.

'Something terrible is happening to Caius,' Ken told me.

At eleven o'clock at night I drove all the way from Blackpool to Surrey and reached home at about 4am. I went into my house and through to the garden (we had a big garden – you had to walk across the bottom lawn up some stone stairs to reach the top lawn). There was Caius, walking round and round in circles. When I called him, he stopped and looked at me. He then shook his head and carried on. I knew what this meant and I just sank to the grass, where I cried and cried. My beloved dog stumbled unsteadily over towards me and I could see in his eyes it was a tumour. I held him and he lay down on the grass with me. We must have been there for quite a while when Dad and Ken found us. Nothing was said; we all knew. The next morning we took him to the vet's, and Ken was so good with him: even though he never felt quite the same about Caius as I did, he really cared about him that day. As I write this, the pain feels as raw now as it was then.

One morning soon afterwards, I was lying in bed, still grieving and thinking about how much I missed Caius. I stretched out my arm and felt a sudden movement alongside me in the bed. There he was, large as life and exactly as he used to be when he was alive, with his huge head resting gently on my shoulder. It could not have been a more real sensation. I felt his wet nose, his soft, silky ears and his warm breath on my neck. He really was there, lying beside me. As I lay there, hugging him close to me, tears cascaded down my cheeks.

I can't explain such moments – I only know the visit from Caius was so comforting that it helped me come to terms with having lost him. Also, I must add that ever since that moment in the shower I believe Caius is now in the spirit of every spider. Never kill a spider, I tell everyone, because you are killing my Caius.

One day, soon after Caius died, I had another strange moment when I was still working with Russ in Blackpool: I had a sudden urge to go and see a clairvoyant. This was not something I would normally do and I certainly wasn't expecting any great revelations – in fact, I nearly turned away but I felt compelled to go ahead with the consultation. She opened the session by saying, 'You are going to be in front of cameras.' Oh well, I thought, she could have seen me on the telly – this is going to be a complete waste of £20.

'That's what I do,' I said, nodding.

'I know that's what you do,' she replied, 'but this is much bigger than anything you have done up until now.'

'Oh?' I said, leaning forward.

'It is in front of cameras and you are going to be doing it for quite some time,' she continued.

'So, what am I going to do?' I asked, pushing my luck. 'A film?'

'No,' she told me. 'You're certainly going to entertain but it's not a film, more likely to be television.'

The only other time when I'd been to a reader of cards was a few years back and she'd told me that my husband was having an affair. I'd said I didn't believe her and stormed out. This time I'd better listen, I thought.

'It is going to happen very soon,' she insisted.

'When?' I asked, desperate for more details.

'Next month,' she replied, sounding very confident this time.

At the time I shrugged it off, although I did think, Well, at least it was good news, not bad, but then I forgot about it. The only other thing of note that the clairvoyant mentioned was that I should be careful as I might get a bad chest.

Within a week of hearing her prediction I'd developed a chesty cough and I also received a telephone call from my agent.

'Good news, Sherrie,' she told me. 'I've had a call to say that Carolyn Reynolds, the producer of *Coronation Street*, would like to meet you. Can you come down in the next couple of weeks to see her? It's for a possible long-running character called Maureen, to start within the next two months.'

I did go back to let the clairvoyant know what had happened and thank her but the council had closed down her booth due to redevelopment of the area. I can't help wondering whether she had predicted that would happen, too.

Chapter Nineteen

My initial meeting with Carolyn Reynolds, the producer of *Coronation Street* at that time, was not the normal interview you'd expect for an acting role. Carolyn told me she knew my work well and was impressed that I had done such a range of comedy and drama. She then asked if I was familiar with a character in *Coronation Street* called Reg Holdsworth, played by actor Ken Morley.

Of course I was: I had grown up with *Corrie* – it had been the only soap around when I was in my teens and twenties – and it had always been one of the top-rated programmes on ITV. In 1989 Ken bounced onto the nation's TV screens as Reg, the manager of the Bettabuys supermarket, and he'd rapidly become one of the soap's most popular characters. A true comic giant, with his huge glasses and brilliant exaggerated eccentricities he was a *Corrie* icon.

'Good,' said Carolyn. 'I'm glad you know him because if we offer you this part you'll be working very closely with him. The thing is, Ken is a terrific actor but life and art mimic each other in his case: we need someone who can not only act, but who can work alongside him and stand their own ground.'

This sounded ominous.

'We know you've worked with a wealth of different types of actors and comedians – Thora Hird, Stanley Baxter, Jim Davidson and Russ Abbot – so you know all about playing the feed to a big personality and surviving. That school of learning will stand you in good stead because you would need to hold your own with Ken and that takes experience and stamina.'

Even stranger, I thought. Did they want me for my acting skills or because they thought I could handle Ken?

'Sorry, Carolyn,' I said. 'Are you trying to tell me something and I'm just not getting it?'

Carolyn laughed. 'Let me start again. You're a fantastic actress, Sherrie. We love what you do and absolutely know that you can play the part we've got in mind, that's no problem at all. I just want to let you know that you'd be working with Ken, who is quite a formidable character.'

'OK, that's fine,' I said, slightly apprehensively. 'I'm sure I can cope.'

After the meeting I rang my agent and told her all about it.

'You've *got* to do it, Sherrie,' she said. 'This is a part to *kill* for! You'd be a new star in one of the most popular programmes of all time. In fact, I'm so keen for you to do this that I've phoned the casting director and said I'll sleep with him if they give you the part!'

'Oh my God!' I replied. 'You didn't mean it, did you?'

'Let's just see if they make you an offer, shall we?' she laughed.

A little while later she rang back, saying: 'You'll be relieved to hear that I didn't need to make good my bribe, Sherrie – you've got the part!'

By this time I'd realised that the role they were offering me was Reg Holdsworth's long-lost love, Maureen Naylor. Soaps work completely differently to drama series: there's no three to four weeks of rehearsals, no time to study the script – in fact, no time to even learn the words. In *Coronation Street* the characters are developed by the actors based on the script, so I was given a pile of scripts and told to turn up at the studios the next Sunday morning at six o'clock for make-up. At the time I had dark shoulder-length hair, which they curled into a bob, and I was given a rather stern make-up, I felt. Suited and booted, I was shipped out to Eccles in Manchester to do my very first scenes with Kevin Kennedy (who played Reg's business partner and friend, Curly Watts) offering me a job in Bettabuys. Kevin was so lovely: little did I know then that Maureen and Curly would sleep together quite often but sadly only when Maureen had downed several bottles of wine.

I remember the director on that day – Brian Mills, whom I came to adore – took me to one side and asked, 'Where are you from?' 'Originally, Nottinghamshire,' I replied. He then explained: 'The first rule is never, ever try to do a Northern accent on this show: use your own. There are too many original Mancunian accents, you will sound false and you will tire of trying to keep it going, so truth always. The thing is about a long-running show like this, if you stay in it the part will become 80 per cent you and 20 per cent acting.'

Such wise words from a brilliant director: I heeded his advice and even in the height of the craziest, most farcical moments I hoped that I'd played every moment truthfully.

When I'd finished the run in *The Russ Abbot Show* I organised a hotel in Manchester, where I would need to be based for filming *Corrie*. I knew I couldn't live without Keeley so I started to arrange for her to change schools and move up there to live with me. Drastic, I know, but for me there was no other way. We started filming in early February 1993.

At first, I didn't get to meet Ken Morley as all my scenes were with Kevin but I'd heard all the stories and I thought I was ready for him. He was (and remains) a shameless, pervasive character and he loves every minute of his reputation. I knew I had to win the first round and I was nervous, but excited at the same time. Our meeting would be either a complete disaster or a total triumph.

'He's only an actor,' I kept telling myself, but it didn't really help. Ken was massive in *Coronation Street* – I knew it, and so did he.

The first time we came face to face was in the make-up room.

'Hello,' he said, staring straight at me and licking his lips.

'Hi,' I replied, staring back.

Right, I thought, go in as you mean to carry on.

'I understand you're the big, fat bastard I have to work with,' I said.

At this, he stopped licking, smiled and shook his head.

'No, no, *no*,' he told me, taking his pink glasses off and rubbing them with his handkerchief. 'You *have* to get that right!'

'Oh, *really*?' I said.

'The big, *rich*, fat bastard!' he said, laughing.

He placed his glasses back on his nose and then walked away. And that was the bond: from that day on we could say anything to each other and never offend. On- and off-screen, we were very tactile – there were rows, sulks, good times, silliness, pettiness and the whole gamut of emotions that run through a real marriage. Right from the start we understood one another, and the chemistry was perfect. Maureen and Reg became a double-act that people seemed to enjoy hugely for their comedy, pathos, endless accidents and their eternal optimism.

Back on the first day of filming, however, I was still very nervous and finding my way. Maureen appears as the new member

Left: My drug addict days in *Within These Walls*, 1975.

Below: In *Carry On Behind* with Jack Douglas (left), Carol Hawkins (centre) and Windsor Davies (right). Come on Jack, cover me up!

Right: Me with Margaret Lockwood (left) and Rosalind Ayres in *The Slipper and the Rose*, 1976. Who knew being an evil Stepsister could be so much fun!

Love for Lydia: Christopher Blake (left) and me trying to persuade Director Tony Wharmby (right) to give me a better dress.

Love for Lydia with Jeremy Irons and Mel Martin. I think I must have bored Jeremy to death – he's gone to sleep!

Above: With Vanessa Redgrave and Graham Crowden in *Lady From The Sea* at the Roundhouse, 1979.

Left: A tart with a heart: playing Letty the prostitute in *Flickers*, 1980.

Me with Thora Hird in *In Loving Memory*, waiting for a cup of tea and our chocolate HobNobs.

With Christopher Beeny in *In Loving Memory*. 'Oh, Mary, not in front of Aunty!'

The two Kates. Me as *Kate the Good Neighbour* in 1940 and Rachel Kempson playing Kate in 1980.

Making a fashion statement in *Kate the Good Neighbour*.

Left: A *TV Times* front cover for the drama series *Radio* with Clarke Peters (left) and Daniel Peacock (right). I defy anyone to look in Clarke's eyes and remember a single word of their lines.

Below: Vince Prince and The Tone Deafs. From left to right: Susie, Bella, me, Russ, Dustin, Jeff and Les.

Right: Me and Les Dennis not looking our best. But at least we make a good couple.

Above: Maud and Maureen in the corner shop on *Coronation Street*. 'Put that gun away, Mother, Reg isn't here!'

Right: Reg and Maureen. Where is Reg's other hand?

The cast of *Coronation Street*. One of the best times of my life.

Left Evil Virginia in *Crossroads.* Is that me or Lily Savage?

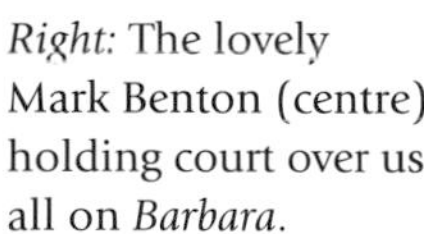

Right: The lovely Mark Benton (centre) holding court over us all on *Barbara*.

Left: Me and Karl Newton. Our one and only sober night in Thailand.

Right: Karl's dad Clifford. The sweetest man.

Above: Me and Denise auditioning for *Britain's Got Talent*.

Above: Me and Carol at the National Television Awards. Who is holding who up?

Left: The Loose Women at the TV Quick Awards. Come on, Coleen, let go!

And please welcome, Nanas Aloud!

of staff at Bettabuys. Reg (who works there, too) knew her as Maureen Grimes, but she arrives as Maureen Naylor, having been married and divorced in the interim. It's only when he sees her that he realises she is the girl he loved and lost many years earlier through her mother's meddling.

For my first scene I worked with the very lovely Lynne Perrie, who played Ivy Tilsley (later Brennan). The director told me to take over from Ivy and sit on a stool behind the till. They wanted to shoot the scene in one take and it sounded easy enough, so I slipped in behind the counter. The trouble was, I sat down rather heavily on the stool, which unfortunately had a kind of coiled spring base so I was catapulted up into the air and over the counter. I was appalled, but luckily everybody was laughing too much to care that I hadn't completed the shot in one take. It was the first of many accidents I had while in the show.

Soon after joining *The Street*, one incident almost put paid to both our careers when I thought I'd accidentally murdered Ken. It happened when he kindly offered to take me on the Granada Studios Tour (which was open to the public) and I jumped at the chance. This was a huge area where they had a props room, another room for kids, TV studios to show how they worked and a mock-up of several sets, including *Sherlock Holmes* and *Coronation Street*.

We went round after the place, vast as an aircraft hangar, had closed to the public. Apart from Ken and me, it was empty. Thoroughly enjoying the spectacle, I turned round to say something to him only to find he'd disappeared. I waited a few minutes but there was no sign of him. The place was very spooky, all on my own, and I realised that I had absolutely no idea how to find my way out.

After calling him for a bit, I started to get really worried. I'd wandered about and now I was in a little cobbled street with a red post-box and a black, fluffy cat sitting on the top of it. Suddenly, I heard him coming. Determined to get my own back, I hid behind the post-box. As he approached, I picked up the fluffy cat, jumped out and yelled 'Boo!', then threw it at him. The trouble was the fluffy cat turned out to be made of concrete. It hit Ken on the forehead ... and knocked him out clean!

Completely horrified, I stared at him. He was motionless, flat out on his back, and I was convinced I'd killed him.

'Oh my God!' I whispered. 'What have I done?'

A week into the show and I had bumped off one of its best-known stars. Already, I could see the headlines:

CAT KILLS *CORRIE* STAR

and even,

MAUREEN BATTERS REG TO DEATH

At this point I really should have gone for help, but I'm ashamed to say I did the worst possible thing – I panicked and fled. I was so shocked and frightened that I wasn't thinking clearly. All I could think was that if he was dead, then I didn't want anyone to know it was my fault. As if they wouldn't have been able to work it out.

I found my way out of the studios, ran back to my hotel and sat there all night, sick with fear and worry. It felt like the end of everything. Disastrous scenarios whirled through my mind: I was sure I'd end up in prison and never see Keeley again.

When the morning came, I was exhausted but I decided the best thing to do was to act normally, and so I arrived at the studios at seven and went to the Green Room for a coffee. By now I was a total wreck and I decided that I'd better tell someone what I'd done – I couldn't live with myself otherwise.

The first person to come in was Helen Worth, who played Gail Tilsley. I didn't know her yet, and although she smiled warmly I just didn't feel I could fess up to her. Next in was Kevin Kennedy (Curly Watts). I knew Kevin a little better, so I went up to him.

'Have you seen Ken this morning?' I asked, nervously.

'No, why?' asked Kevin.

'Well,' I began. 'I think I've …'

At that moment Ken walked in and I've never been so glad to see anyone. I wanted to throw my arms around him and shout, 'You're alive, thank goodness!' but instead I stayed rooted to the spot, staring at the huge black lump on his forehead.

'How did you get that?' asked Kevin.

'*She* did it,' Ken said, pointing at me. 'It was *her*!'

At this, I burst into tears: I was so relieved to know he was all right. Meanwhile, Kevin looked completely astounded.

Not surprisingly, it took Ken a long time to forgive me. Eventually he did and, thankfully, the story never appeared in the papers. In those days every little incident that involved the cast of *Corrie* made headlines, but no one mentioned this particular episode, I'm grateful to say.

Coronation Street was a fantastic show to be part of and it was extraordinary to be involved in something so successful and long running. At that time *Corrie* was in its thirty-third year and had become a British institution, but it wasn't just in Britain that people loved it, the show appeared all over the world. Over the years it had been transmitted in pretty unlikely places including Holland (where some children apparently learned to speak English with a Lancashire accent), Hong Kong (naturally subtitled, with Chinese characters displayed vertically down the left-hand edge of the screen), Nigeria, Singapore, Denmark, Sierra Leone and Thailand.

The level of interest in all of us who were in the series was enormous. Although I had been an actress for over twenty-two years by the time I joined, I had never experienced anything like it. Fans would wait patiently outside the studios to catch a glimpse of us and cameras would be pointed at us wherever we went. The press followed us like hawks and were always rooting round for the next *Corrie* story.

Today, plenty of other programmes attract the same level of interest. Reality shows such as *The X-Factor* make instant celebrities of people, but back then *Corrie* stars were always big news. Every day of the week you would constantly be doing photoshoots, radio interviews, chat shows, agony columns, 'at homes' with the family, 'abroad' with the family … There was the time when BA flew Liz Dawn (Vera Duckworth), her real-life husband Don, Keeley, Ken and me on a promotional visit to New York for New Year's Eve. We arrived in freezing-cold weather and had a wonderful time, ice skating at the Rockefeller Center, etc. New Year's Eve was spent in a hotel in Times Square with actual indoor rockets – only in America would that happen.

Two days later we were in the Stage Door deli when an English guy came up to us and said, 'Excuse me – I know who you both are. I don't want to intrude but I thought you should know, as I guess you will be going back to the UK to film: the snow you see falling outside now doesn't seem very heavy but this is New York and nothing is small here. Within two hours those flakes will be as big as your hands! Anyway, safe journey home. Best make a move now.' And with that, he was gone.

Well, we looked out the window and it was hardly snowing at all, so we ignored him and went back to our gigantic beef and gherkin stacks. Two hours later we emerged from the deli to find snowflakes as he had described them. From there on in, we panicked. Just to get back to the hotel was hard enough, and even though we still had two days left, we packed as we'd been advised by the hotel staff to make our way to JFK as soon as possible. All the time the snowflakes were growing. We got in a stretch limo, but the driver dumped us outside Grand Central Station for fear of getting stuck. Eventually we hitched a ride on a bus. At the airport it was chaos and we were lucky that BA had put us in the first-class lounge. That's where we stayed for four days, watching the snow rising outside the window with no food, only chocolate.

Meanwhile, the Big Freeze was declared a national emergency, but for *Corrie* it was a national disgrace that both Liz and I were going to miss our scenes and cost them a fortune. The best thing of all was when a BA representative came up to us and said: 'The quickest way we can get you back is by Concorde.' They had to push the plane onto the runway, defrost it, load it up with the allotted number of passengers (including us) and hope it got off the ground. How lucky we were to be treated to an amazing flight in the most beautiful plane ever built. Of course we arrived back to massive press coverage, declaring Vera and Maureen were lost in blizzards out in New York. I loved it, but our bosses were not so amused and we were hauled in front of them to explain ourselves as if we had done it on purpose. Eventually the furore calmed down, though we never forgot our flight of fancy.

Coronation Street is a tight-knit show run like a well-oiled machine. It's a business with a publicity machine that's second to none. With a six-day schedule, the turnaround is extremely fast. I have complete admiration for every single one of the actors involved as they deliver great performances day after day and year in, year out with no rehearsal and hardly any time for direction. They deserve all the accolades they receive, and then some. I was very proud to be part of the show and loved my character.

The storylines were of such a high standard that we all felt very lucky. The writing for Reg and Maureen's budding romance was particularly brilliant and a hugely popular storyline. Reg was thrilled to have found his love again but Maureen was strangely cautious at first. Finally, she confessed that she was living with her mother Maud (a complete harridan who had frightened off Reg the previous time) and she was afraid it might happen again.

On this occasion the two manage to resist monstrous Maud's attempts to scare off Reg. They get together and prepare to consummate their love in Reg's waterbed. This has become one of the *Street*'s best-known, well-loved and constantly shown scenes. In fact, during the fiftieth anniversary celebrations of 2010 that waterbed came in at number 10 when the viewers' 100 favourite scenes were broadcast – not bad in the history of *The Street*! We had 400 gallons of water in the bed that day and so the director warned there could only be one take. Supposedly downstairs in the shop below, Derek Wilton accidentally drills through the ceiling into the bed, bursting it. The flat is immediately flooded, seriously dampening Reg and Maureen's ardour.

Neither of us could wear any clothes because it had to look like an authentic seduction scene. Being under the duvet, I was fine, but Ken had nothing on bar a small towel. As the bed bursts and Reg gets out to check the damage, wrapping a towel around his body, Derek and Mavis enter the room. Reg rushes round the other side of the bed as I scream, desperately trying to cover my modesty with the duvet. As Reg moves out of shot, he drops his towel immediately in my eye-line. That image has stayed with me forever, and in fact, if you watch the scene back, you will notice my eyes widen and then shut very tightly.

Throughout the series, we had many more mishaps and misunderstandings during which Maureen thinks Reg is cheating on her and so she gets drunk and actually cheats on him herself: twice with Curly. Eventually, the ill-fated pair decide to get married. The wedding took place in January 1994 and by the time it aired I had already become a *Coronation Street* regular. By this time Ken and I had morphed into one: we completed each other's sentences and knew the other's every move, every speech pattern. It was a rare partnership for two actors to find and proved to be a fantastic double act. Having been offered another year's contract, I felt more secure, which was a great feeling.

By then I had rented a house and Keeley was extremely happy attending the same school as her cousin Chloe (my brother Brett's daughter), although I always felt bad about taking her away from her friends and school in London. On the strength of my new job, Ken decided to give up British Aerospace and come to Manchester, too. He rented out our Surrey home and moved up there. I had my doubts about whether leaving his job was a good idea, but I was earning enough to keep the family comfortably and I told myself that perhaps the move would give us another chance as a couple and Ken might find another job. Perhaps, after all, we could mend our marriage.

With Ken and Keeley in Manchester, Dad moved back to his Nottingham flat. He had been with us for almost eight years and I missed him so much, but he assured me that he was quite happy to go back home. I promised to see him as often as I could.

One of the nicest things about living in Manchester was that my brother Brett was also there. Some years earlier he had moved up North and started work with Peter Stringfellow at the city's Millionaire Club. He lived with his partner Annie and their daughter Chloe, who was two years older than Keeley. As they only lived a couple of miles away and Keeley's cousin was at the same school, we all became very close.

Brett and I hadn't lived near one another since we were both single so it was a real joy to see more of him. He had become (and still is) a very calm, steady and generous character, a good man. With our childhood squabbles long behind us, I felt glad to have a brother that I could turn to, if ever I needed wise advice. Still stunningly beautiful, he continued to model and did endless TV commercials. Later, Chloe started to do them with him. I think their most famous one together was for tomato ketchup, with flying sausages – it was quite well known at the time.

Back on the *Corrie* set, I was meeting people whose characters I had known for years and who were so well known that it could sometimes be daunting. The first time I met Julie Goodyear, she was all dressed up for the part of tough-as-brass, heart-of-gold barmaid Bet Lynch. Completely star-struck, I gazed at her leopard-skin tights and leopard-skin top. A huge mound of blonde hair was piled on top of her head and the longest cigarette holder I have ever seen in my life was dangling from her lips.

'Oh my goodness,' I gasped. 'You're such an icon!'

'I know,' she laughed, completely unphased. 'You're dead f****g right!'

One of the closest friends I made was Amanda Barrie, who plays Alma Sedgewick, a feisty woman who marries oily businessman Mike Baldwin. Amanda had been in *Corrie* on and off since 1981 and she became a regular in 1989, so she knew all the ropes and taught me how things worked. As I have already mentioned, we had worked together some years earlier (in the West End production of *Stepping Out*) and she was among the first to welcome me when I arrived on *The Street*. 'Keep your nose clean, head down, don't get involved; don't be late, know your lines, do your job and go home,' was her advice, and she was absolutely right. I did as she suggested, so I thoroughly enjoyed my time there and I knew what she meant: in all large corporations you should avoid confrontation, debate and disputes. Like the royal family, it's a business and rules are rules.

While most of my time on Corrie was wonderful, sadly, at one point it became impossible to avoid confrontation, when I was harassed by someone who worked on the show. I didn't tell anyone, as I thought that if I ignored this man, he might just give up and go away. I didn't want to jeopardise my job in any way, so I kept quiet. I was in the world's most famous soap and yet I was being harassed behind the scenes in a way that was so covert it was like one of the protected story lines.

The man concerned was lascivious, furtive and cunning. People liked him, but at the same time they were wary of him. Initially I thought he liked me, but as time went by I realised that he liked me in the wrong way. He would come to my dressing room and, as they were like cells, once he was inside it was hard to get past him to get out. I felt very vulnerable.

When he was in a good mood he could be good company and funny but on other occasions the demon would come out and he became convinced that anything you said – even a harmless comment – was critical. I soon learned that when he was in this mood, to keep quiet and not answer any leading questions because in his eyes I would always be wrong.

He was so difficult and unpredictable that I began steering clear of him. If he was sitting in the canteen I'd avoid going in there. But one day I walked through and didn't realise he was sitting in one of the chairs. There was no-one else around and he jumped up in front of me and started to accuse me of spreading stories about him. I had no idea what he was talking about, but suddenly he grabbed me round the neck and held me up against a wall, screaming at me. He was incoherent. He leaned in close, his face next to mine, as I stood there, terrified and unable to get away.

At that moment someone came in so he kissed me to make it look innocent. The passerby just smiled and walked out. After that, he cooled towards me – I think he realised he'd gone too far – and I tried to put it all behind me. But it left me very nervous if he was ever anywhere near me.

Chapter Twenty

It wasn't until I went on a promotional trip to Ireland with Ken Morley that I understood the true power of *Coronation Street*. As I peered out of the plane window I could see the airport was crammed with hundreds of screaming people.

'Wow!' I said to Ken. 'There must be a pop group about to land – I wonder who it is?'

I was still wondering which band it could be when a police car raced up to the plane and parked at the bottom of the steps. When I reached the bottom I turned to the nearest policeman and asked: 'What's going on? Who's arriving? What's all the fuss about?'

'*You*,' he replied, looking extremely puzzled. 'Don't you know? They're waiting for you and Reg.'

'Yeah, of course they are!' I replied flippantly, thinking he was having me on.

'No – I'm serious,' he protested. 'They're here for you two.'

Completely gob-smacked, I still thought he must have it wrong, but no, they were all waving and chanting, 'Reg and

Maureen!' I'd expected a bit of interest and a few fans, but this was beyond anything I might have imagined.

Once we were through the airport and had got into a waiting car, police outriders escorted us to the venue where we were appearing. I sat there open-mouthed, thinking this was crazy. Again, on arrival, we were surrounded by hundreds of *Corrie* fans. We were there for two hours, by which time we found ourselves in the midst of the throng and unable to get out, so, in an atmosphere that was fun and very friendly, some of the fans suggested they pick us up bodily and pass us over their heads to the police escort, which wasn't that easy with Ken as he's a big boy. It was the most exciting thing I'd ever done. That was my glimpse into the world of pop stardom – the difference being, it was all about *Coronation Street* and the characters themselves, not the real us. Throughout my years in *Corrie*, with all the fans, the hysteria, the paparazzi and the press interest, that thought kept me in good stead, with my feet firmly on the ground.

Some of the stars courted the press, others played the game to a certain extent and some refused to have anything to do with the publicity vehicle and worried about the potential intrusion into their lives. There's a fine line when it becomes about your personal life and not the show. These days, people make whole careers out of press coverage and their everyday lives: it's all about being on front covers of magazines and keeping your profile high – getting married, then divorced, and getting married again. We live in a celebrity-based world now, with huge interest in every aspect of stars' lives, and I can understand anyone who wants to stay out of it and keep their private life to themselves. I have always enjoyed a good relationship with the press, though, and have found that even in my darkest times they have been very supportive.

I've always done whatever publicity was expected while in an acting job, and *Coronation Street* was no exception. The only difference was that this was fame on a level rarely experienced in this country: everything we said or did was quoted or photographed. When I was in *Corrie* it was mainly the soaps that attracted that level of interest. I never thought of it as intrusive or bad, just part of the deal, and I enjoyed the moment. It was lovely to be recognised and asked for my autograph, but I was very realistic: I knew the interest would only last as long as the job did.

We all were expected to do promotional work, photo shoots and interviews, as well as to turn up at events such as awards ceremonies and charity functions. The award ceremonies were always very glamorous occasions. The likes of Barbara Knox, Julie Goodyear, Thelma Barlow and Amanda Barrie would arrive dressed to kill – you really had to up your game in the glamour stakes with these formidable characters. In 2010 I attended the amazing Coronation Street 50th Anniversary Ball and I can tell you that all the *Coronation Street* ladies were there along with the wonderful Betty Driver, looking as stunning as ever. It was true British Hollywood and I felt proud to have been part of that family.

There were a few occasions when the attention from the fans crossed over into everyday life and you had to handle it as well as possible. For instance, I would take Keeley ice-skating and of course there would be loads of kids, all wanting autographs, and I would sign for as long as it took. Keeley had just gone there to skate with her friends, not for an autograph session, but she would still have to wait patiently for me. I knew it wasn't fair on her, and since those days she has admitted that she hated it at the time, feeling the other children were taking me away from her. I felt very guilty about it then, but now when we look back and chat about those days she always says: 'Don't be silly! I was fine and enjoyed it, really.' However, I did find a way to make things easier by involving her in whatever I was doing. When I was making public appearances, Keeley would help out at the venues and be part of organising the day, so we felt that we were doing it together.

When I first began on *Corrie*, I had no idea that some members of the public took the storylines literally and actually believed the characters were real. For example, Maureen's mother (battle-axe Maud Grimes) was confined to a wheelchair in the programme. The actress playing Maud (Elizabeth Bradley) was perfectly fit and didn't need a wheelchair at all, but people would rush up to her in the street and ask how she'd managed to recover. I myself would make light of it and used to say to people when we were out shopping together, 'Oh, my God! It's a miracle – she can walk.' 'Stop it, Sherrie, it's not funny,' Liz would say to me. She always found it distasteful, pretending to be wheelchair-bound when she wasn't in real life, although everyone assured her that it wasn't at all offensive and people understood she was only playing a part. 'Don't get your reality lines crossed, Liz,' the producer would tell her.

I once got a cab to the airport and as I got in the driver said, 'I love your character in *The Street*.'

'Oh, thank you very much,' I replied, touched.

'I do think it's very strange, though,' he added, 'that some people think what happens in soaps is real life.'

'Oh, I know – so do I,' I answered politely.

'I think that's wrong,' he added. 'I think that's *seriously* wrong.'

'Oh well, if they want to believe …' I said.

'No, no – I think it's *wrong*,' he persisted. 'Why would they think those characters are real? It's not right, is it? You're just actors, aren't you?'

'Yeah, yeah,' I said, hoping this would be the last of the topic. But no, he was only just getting into his stride and carried on sharing his thoughts all the way to the airport.

'For example,' he continued, 'those characters don't really work in a pub or in those shops in *Coronation Street*, do they? People should get a life!'

Then, as he got out of the cab at the airport, he handed me my bags and said tenderly, 'Goodbye, Maureen, love.'

Just before he drove off, he wound down the window and said, 'Oh, by the way – if you want to go out for a day-trip with your mother, my taxi takes wheelchairs so give me a call, Maureen, love.'

I smiled. After all his protestations, it was touching that he still believed Maureen and Maud were real.

When Reg left my character Maureen and went off to Lowestoft, where he had an affair, he was threatened in the street. Not only that, but a whole bunch of my male fans wrote to me to say: 'Don't you worry, love. We've organised a bus and we're going to Lowestoft to find Reg and break his legs.'

Scared for my co-star's life, I immediately showed the letter to the then producer.

'Stop right there!' he told me. 'Firstly, what are you worrying about? One, Ken hasn't left you, two, he hasn't gone to Lowestoft, and three – more importantly, Sherrie – it's a soap! None of it is real.'

'Get a grip!' I told myself. Even I'd started to believe it was real. My only excuse was that although Reg had run off with a young bird I wanted him to retain his legs. Oh, the blurred world of soaps.

Although we didn't appear in *Coronation Street* at the same time, I got to know Denise Welch later on through different productions and she then joined *Loose Women* as a panellist in

2005. In *Corrie* Denise had played the Rover's Return barmaid Natalie Horrocks (later Barnes) and her character had an affair with married Kevin Webster (Michael Le Vell). Denise told me that while the affair was being shown on TV she was often threatened when she was out in public. Luckily I played a sympathetic character and so I didn't receive any threats, but I used to get letters saying things like, 'Your mother's horrible to you. Why don't you take her to the top of a hill, take the brake off the wheelchair and push her over?'

When I got married on screen (first to Reg and, later, butcher Fred Elliot), the fans sent me loads of wedding presents, including cash. I had to send them all back, of course, but people sent those gifts with the best of intentions. Sarah Lancashire, who was in *Corrie* at the same time as me playing barmaid Raquel Watts, used to get the most bizarre presents including American tan tights – which Raquel wore by the dozen.

The fans were very generous. Naturally, the press are always looking for a story and the juicier the better. Unfortunately, I provided them with an extremely salacious one and quite by accident. It happened in the early days when I was staying in a hotel in Manchester. On this particular day my call for the studio was nice and late (11am). After a lovely lie-in, I thought I would take a leisurely bath. Lying in the warm water facing the taps, with the bathroom door behind me, I was going over my lines. Suddenly I thought I heard a clicking noise. Later I realised it had been the sound of one of those plastic card keys being swiped through the lock on the bedroom door.

'Hello,' I heard someone say, a moment later.

I didn't reply, but sat up and turned my head to glance towards the open door. There stood about half a dozen Japanese people and they were all staring at me with extremely puzzled looks on their faces. What I really wanted to say was,

'No, *no*! I'm in the bath. I'm *naked* – you can't come in here! Go away,' but in reality no sound was coming from my mouth and for some inexplicable reason I stood up. OK, it wasn't the wisest thing to do – I just didn't think, I wanted them to go away. So there I stood, completely starkers and about to give them an earful, but instead they got an eyeful, they copped the lot. After taking one look at me, they turned on their heels and fled, stumbling into each other in their haste to get out of the room. They were obviously horrified by their 'close encounter' moment – it needs the iconic music at this point to add to the scene.

It turned out that one of the hotel porters had been instructed to show potential clients from the Tokyo Tyre and Rubber Company (you can make your own jokes up) one of the hotel's newly refurbished rooms. The porter, it seems, had forgotten to check that the room was empty before showing his guests around.

This shockingly embarrassing episode left me pretty shaken and determined to wedge a chair under the door handle the next time I had a bath. I didn't dream there would be repercussions other than me having a go at the hotel management and telling them what I thought of them, all the while hoping none of the group had 20:20 vision or bifocals. However, that afternoon I was summoned by the *Corrie* bosses.

Having fled from the tawdry scene, it transpired the porter and the tourists had hurried down to the hotel reception. The tourists then lost no time in excusing themselves, bowing politely and muttering that they did not think the Tokyo Tyre and Rubber Company would expect – or would indeed want – the kind of entertainment put on for them that morning. I suspect their rubbery bits were in better shape than mine: certainly, my tyres had lost their tread.

The porter then relayed the tale to the rest of the hotel staff, one of whom just happened to be a waitress whose boyfriend was the hotel window-cleaner, who had a mate who had recently started work on the *Manchester Evening News*. Within minutes the story had winged its way over to the editor there and on to several other newspapers, gathering momentum as it went before anybody knew what was happening. You can imagine the endless headlines:

TOKYO SHOCKED AS MAUREEN'S
SPARE TYRE DEFLATES IN BATH

and even,

MAUREEN WET AND WUBBERY,
SAYS EXCITED TOKYO REPRESENTATIVE

Naturally, the bosses wanted the full story from me. Once they knew what had really happened they realised the whole episode had been completely inflated and could do with being punctured. All right, enough already!

Photographers often followed us when we were out in public but I believed I was safe enough in the privacy of my own home until the morning when I cheerfully got out of bed and pulled back the curtains, only to see a snapper sitting on the branch of a tree across the road. He was holding a zoom lens that was pointing straight at me.

When I shouted to Ken, he leapt out of bed and rushed to the window. He bellowed so loudly that the poor chap in his hurry to escape fell out of the tree and hit the ground with a terrible thud. Ken and I looked at one another in horror and then dashed over the road to see if he was OK. He was groaning with pain and appeared to have a broken leg. Of course we couldn't leave him there, so Ken ended up driving him to the nearest hospital. It was a strange situation, but what else could we do? Life on *Corrie* was always producing surreal moments such as this.

One of the funniest occasions was when a group of us from the show were asked to do something for a royal charity night at the Theatre Royal in London's Drury Lane. So Liz Dawn (Vera Duckworth), Denise Black (who played Denise Osbourne), Elizabeth Bradley (my screen mum, Maud) and a wonderful man called Frank Lamar, who was a very famous drag act called Foo Foo Lamar, joined together to create a silly sailor's song-and-dance routine. On the day of the show we rehearsed constantly and all was well until we were given our costumes. As we were sailors, these consisted of large white shirts, old-fashioned bell-bottom trousers and big brown leather belts. Fine, except my trousers didn't have a belt and were way too big for me.

'Don't worry,' I was told and was given a piece of twine to tie around my waist. 'That'll do the trick,' they said. But it didn't, and no one took any notice of me when I kept on moaning that there was no way such a flimsy piece of twine would hold up several lengths of serge, especially when dancing 'The Sailor's Hornpipe'.

Needless to say, it was a full house that night, with Princess Margaret in the Royal Box. As is usual on these occasions, the show ran late and instead of our eight o'clock entrance we didn't actually get on stage until 11.15pm. By then the Princess had been in the box for several hours and must have been hoping the end was in sight. As it was common knowledge that some of the Royals liked a tipple in their box – and who can blame them when they have to sit through hour after hour of acts? – we guessed the evening might have been a bit of a G&T blur by then.

Anyway, when at last our music struck up out we trooped, determined to give it our all. We had only been on the stage for half a minute when, as the troupe went one way and I went the other, my pathetic excuse for a belt snapped, the trousers slithered down and ended up wrapped around my ankles. The only good news was that thanks to my grandmother constantly warning me that you never knew what might happen, I was wearing the recommended pair of clean white knickers.

The audience roared, the troupe fell over each other trying to see what had happened to cause such mirth and I was crying so much with laughter that I couldn't pull my trousers up again. Meanwhile, the music carried on and some of the others, now well and truly out of step, tried to continue with the dance, which made the audience chuckle even more. Eventually, Liz Dawn took pity on me and came over to help, but the more she tried to pull my trousers up, the more hysterical we became. We were falling on top of each other. As the music finally stopped, the whole place erupted: unintentionally, we had become the comedy highlight of the evening.

Later (and having at last composed ourselves), we lined up for the obligatory royal greeting. Not knowing what to expect after appearing on stage in my knickers, I was nervous to say the least. As Princess Margaret approached, everyone kept hissing at me: 'Say *nothing*, just curtsey!' When she got to me, she stopped and laughed.

'Ah-*ha*!' she said. 'You're the sailor! Has anybody told you you're a very funny girl?'

As she stood there, I thought I might have detected a slight sway – due, I'm sure, to the long wait she had endured in a confined space. Then, as she turned to walk on down the line, she paused again. She leaned in towards me and whispered, 'Mother always said to wear clean white knickers because you never know …' Turning, she did a slight comedy trip and gave a hiccup, then softly said: 'I think you've had one too many!'

It was a perfect gem from a princess known for her wicked wit.

And it was humour that saved me in another embarrassing situation, this time an awards dinner. Bill Roache (who played – and still plays – Ken Barlow) was due to collect a Lifetime Achievement Award. We were all of us dressed up to the nines and he was wearing a beautiful white tux. He was about to go up on stage and accept the award for *Corrie*, and as it was being televised this would be in front of at least 16 million people. I was sitting on one side of him and Thelma Barlow (Mavis Wilton) was on his other side. We were enjoying a lovely dinner when, with a sort of nervous tic, I stabbed a potato a little too hard and sent peas and gravy flying all over Bill's immaculate tux. All hell broke loose with the producers as he would look such a mess on TV and they scattered to the far corners of the room to find a borrowed tux to fit.

Horrified and apologising profusely, I started to rub his tux down with my napkin. Thelma, who was slightly inebriated at this point, told me: 'Don't worry, Sherrie – this will do it.' Thinking it would help, she threw her glass of white wine over the jacket. The tux now turned a distinct shade of grey as she and I patted and pawed poor Bill.

'I'm so sorry! Oh dear, I'm *so* sorry,' I said, as I dabbed away at his ruined jacket. With a twinkle in his eye, Bill turned to me and said 'Don't worry, it's one of the most exciting things that's ever happened to me!' and then he laughed, thank God.

With his borrowed tux, he still managed to appear onstage looking immaculate and, as always, performed his duties perfectly. I have to say, Bill is one of the most interesting men you could wish to meet. What's more, he's funny, clever and extremely sexy. I'd have given anything for Maureen to have an affair with Ken (and still would) – and that goes for Sherrie, too.

Chapter Twenty-One

Sadly, about eighteen months after I started work in *The Street* I lost my beloved grandmother, Nancy Birtles. She had lived to 98, a wonderful age. Even so, it was heartbreaking to lose her. We had always been especially close and I had been told ever since I was a little girl that I was just like her. Mentally, spiritually and emotionally, we were identical. Mum says we had the same kind of quietness, a switching-off, a shutting down. I do remember Nana doing that and I can recognise this quality in myself.

Just before she died I had the most awful time, and yet, being me, this also had its funny side. I was due to go to France on location for *Corrie* with Liz Bradley (who played Maureen's mother, Maud) and Bill Waddington (Percy Sugden). As we were leaving on the Friday, Nana had a bad fall at the home she lived in and so I said I wouldn't go. Mum assured me it was fine and when I came back on the Monday morning I could go straight to be with my grandmother. And so, reassured, off I flew. On the Saturday morning we had to film at Omaha Beach in Normandy, where all the war graves are, the storyline being that Maud had married a GI who died during the war and she wanted to find his grave.

The whole area was extraordinary and it was a really moving experience; also I had Nana on my mind the whole time so I was feeling a bit sorry for myself. But what got me out of it was Bill. He was known for having his lines strategically placed somewhere. Often they were stuck inside his cap, which is why he always took it off whenever he did a scene. When he was in the corner shop he would place them around the counter so that wherever he turned they were always there until the new girl (i.e. me) moved what I thought was an old piece of paper. Bill came on to do a scene and was horrified to find his lines missing. He called the director and I was duly reprimanded, for he was a big cheese then.

In France, we were outside with no counter to hide his lines on. After the first day's filming the director called me and said, 'I'm sorry, Sherrie, but Bill has asked for his lines to be written out for him.' 'Of course,' I said, realising there were too many to fit inside his hat, 'but *how*?' 'Well, what he has proposed as the main scene with you is that we write them on strips of paper and hang one down your back with Sellotape and then one down your front, so we do the front shot of you with him at the back and then the back of you looking at him.'

In normal circumstances I would have found the whole thing funny and just got on with it, but that evening in the hotel bar I received a call from Mum to say that Nana had taken a turn for the worse and they didn't think she would make it through the night. I never usually drink when I'm working, but I sat in the bar and drank brandy (which I don't even *like*) all through the night.

By six the next morning I was practically comatose in my room – I don't even remember how I got there. Everyone did everything they could think of to wake me, and eventually they managed to do so. As you can imagine, I was sick, shaking, unable to focus and stinking of brandy. Worse still, I had all the scenes with Bill to do and I knew he'd heard what I'd been up to and thought me disgusting. The only up side was that my mother had left a message during the night to let me know that Nana was stable again but to get home as soon as I could.

I went out to film, the whole of my back taped up with Bill's lines on it, so what you saw was me walking and him walking behind, reading my back. Somehow we got through it, although I had to be sick twice. Bill was very angry, and I don't blame him. I then had to do the front but because the eye-line was too low they had to start sticking the paper at the top of my forehead all the way down to my waist so you saw the back of my head, with Bill reading my front. Again, I had to stop to be sick, at which point Bill refused to go on filming with me. Luckily we had more or less finished. I did all my remaining lines (which should have been to him) to no one and we ended the shoot.

Afterwards I flew straight back and was able to get to Nana just before she died: she'd waited for me. Bill never really forgave me and I was ashamed of my behaviour. On the other hand, the crew never let me forget it and presented me with a sick bag the next time they saw me!

Soon after losing Nana, my wonderful dad also became extremely ill. After he went back to live in Nottingham, he had to go into hospital for a hernia operation. As it turned out, he had prostate cancer but it wasn't spotted at an early stage. Only later, when he became ill, did they find it, and by that time the cancer had spread to his bones and was terminal. Dad always used to make me laugh because he was a would-be hypochondriac and freely admitted it. He had every pill going on the market. In this day and age of the internet and medical websites,

I often think about him now. If I start looking through the lists of symptoms on these sites, I think I've got every illness known to man – he would have loved it.

Dad had a whole arsenal of medicines and medical equipment, some of it very unusual indeed. He had a really long paintbrush, which he dipped in a curious bottle of tincture to paint the back of his throat for ailments such as tonsillitis and laryngitis. Sniffers, blowers, inhalers ... you name it, he had them. 'The trouble is, Dad,' I used to say because we could joke with him about his endless complaints, 'you know the boy who cried wolf? Well, that could be you!'

He'd laugh, but sadly that day did come. Having complained of so many minor ailments, he got something serious and no one realised. Once the cancer was diagnosed, I think he was in a way relieved that this time it was for real and he felt he'd been proved right. He died in 1996, just a year after Nana, and by then he and Mum had been divorced for many years. The pain is still terrible, but I do talk to him all the time and I know he and Caius are together. I was so pleased he'd come to live with us through Keeley's first eight years and that she would remember her granddad as the lovely man he was and someone who adored her. Actually, my most lasting memory of him was at a party I gave for Ken's 40th birthday, a couple of years before Dad died. We were renting a large house in Cheshire and I thought I'd give a 1940s party. Really, it was more for Dad than Ken.

All the cast of *Corrie* came and everyone dressed as either Army or Air Force in 1940s uniforms. Dad was in his element. We had an air-raid siren, sandbags, a forties' band with singers, and the whole of the inside of the house was transformed to match the period. I even had invitations made to look like wartime ration books. My dad had too much to drink and danced with every lady – he loved it, as did Ken. The cake was a runway with miniature Harriers taking off to remind Ken of British Aerospace (even then, I was still trying hard to make our marriage work). I'm glad Dad had fun at that party before he went and I'm so pleased he lived to enjoy my success.

As I was in such a high-profile job, I expected a bit of press interest when Dad died, but one reporter proved particularly intrusive. The day after, he knocked at my door. I was about to blast him when he said, 'I've brought you flowers and there's my card,' handing it to me. Furious, I tossed the card aside and went to close the door but he thrust the bunch of flowers, at me and said: 'Sorry, I shouldn't have come.'

'No, you shouldn't,' I told him and slammed the door.

At this point Dad was still in the Chapel of Rest, where he would remain until the funeral. The problem was that I loved my father so much: I just couldn't let him go and I kept on returning to see him. Every time I appeared, the undertaker would say, 'Hello, Miss Hewson. Have you come to see your father? I'll just get him out.' A few minutes later he would beckon me into the room where Dad was lying. I would sit beside him for hours, talking away to him.

'Have you finished now?' asked the undertaker after I'd visited him every day for a week.

'*What*?' I said. 'What do you mean?'

'Oh, nothing, nothing at all,' he said hastily.

I carried on visiting for another week. No doubt the undertaker was thinking, that bloody woman, but he didn't say another word. Then one day I went in and looked at Dad's face: I could see he'd gone, that he wasn't there any more. And so I said one last goodbye and went out to the undertaker.

'It's OK,' I told him, 'you can take him now.'

In his relief, what little tact he might have usually possessed completely deserted him.

'Oh, thank God,' he said, 'because they do start to smell a bit after two weeks.'

'Oh,' I said, reeling, 'that's terrible!'

'No, *no*,' he said, realising what he had just said and now completely overcome. 'I didn't mean … It's just that we don't usually keep them this long and the weather's very hot at the moment …'

'It's OK, I understand. I'm not offended,' I told him before I shook his hand and left.

After Brett and I brought the ashes home, we both decided that, as Dad had always loved a pint and Brett had a fabulous pub in Hale Barnes in Cheshire – always packed with music, songs and lots of pretty girls – that's where he should go. We knew he'd love it, so that's where he stayed to enjoy the fun. Not everyone thought this in the best of taste, but he was our Dad, so stuff 'em.

'Where's Dad?' I asked Brett, not so very long ago.

Having thought for a moment, he replied: 'Oh, I think he's on top of our fridge.'

'*Brett!*' I exclaimed. 'He'll be *cold*.'

Anyway, that settled the matter. I took Dad home with me and put him by my fire, next to Caius. This might also be considered bizarre, I guess, but I like to think the two of them are still warm and cosy … and still with me.

I had to grieve for my dad while sticking to *Coronation Street*'s busy schedule, but I'm sure that in many ways, work helped me to cope. While Dad was always in my thoughts, I couldn't afford to just shut myself away from the world: I had to get out there and carry on.

It was not long after this when I was told that I would be getting my own dressing room at the Granada Studios. In those days we had to earn the right to a personal dressing room. Today everyone gets one, but then we shared until a dressing room became free, when it would be given to someone who was well established on the show.

As luck would have it, the dressing room I was given was the one that had been used by my best friend, Amanda Barrie. As you moved up the ladder in *Corrie* status, you moved down the stairs in the dressing-room battle. And so the bigger the star, the nearer to the ground floor you went. Amanda was a major player and had just been given a new dressing room very close to the ground floor, which was considered a great honour.

As soon as I moved in, a curious thing happened, though. While Amanda was the occupier of that particular dressing room, she had developed a problem with one of her eyes. She'd started to see what she described as 'clouds' and they were blurring her vision. Luckily, she was given treatment and this took them away altogether.

Bizarrely, within a few months of taking over the dressing room from her, I woke up with 'clouds' in my left eye and was rushed to hospital, where they discovered I had a retinal vein occlusion in my left eye. Apparently, this is a blood vessel that has been clamped for no apparent reason, causing blood and water to become trapped in the retina. They gave me an angiogram (a kind of injection) and put drops in my eye, which turned a strange yellow with a very dilated pupil. The treatment also made me extremely sick. I was then told they had to immediately laser my eye to try and drain the blood and water away. I'd no idea what they were talking about, but sitting there with my eye wide open and a laser beam shooting into it was an extremely uncomfortable and frightening experience. Unfortunately, it didn't work and I was informed that I would have to return for a series of tests and could possibly lose some sight in my left eye. At the same time, I was told it could also affect the right one, too.

Straight after the treatment I had to go back to the set to finish a scene. Elizabeth Bradley (Maud Grimes) said: 'Oh my God, you look like an alien!' And I'm sure I did, with my yellow eye. They had to film the whole scene without a close-up of me because there was no disguising that Cyclops' eye.

Afterwards, I went into the Green Room for a rest. My eye was throbbing and by then had turned an alarming shade of yellow. While I was in there, grabbing a quick cup of tea, one of the programme assistants came and told me that Brian Park, the then producer, wanted to see me. Some months earlier he had taken over and I thought he might want to discuss some aspect of the script or my character.

'We've decided not to carry your character on,' he told me, getting straight to the point.

It was such a shock that I burst out laughing – through nerves, I think. That can't be right, I thought. After all, I'd just signed another year's contract, I'd been given my own dressing room and I'd *even* become a key ring (something I'll explain in a bit).

'Why, *why*?' I kept on asking.

'No particular reason,' he said. 'It's just that the writers think the character has come to a natural end. I could change their minds, but I'm not going to.'

Naturally, I had no idea this was coming and neither the strength nor the know-how to question this decision at the time. I wanted to say, 'I've just found out I could be going blind. What do you think about that?' Of course I didn't.

'I think you should go now and work out how you will handle all the press,' he continued. 'Of course you will be given as much help with the statements as needed, and as it is only March bear in mind that you will still be with us till October to work through the storyline, whatever that is.'

I walked out of that office with no job and a broken heart. It was as if my whole world had just crashed. On my way out of the studio I always picked up a loaf of bread from the corner shop as they were thrown away at night. That evening I did the same thing and headed for my car.

Unfortunately, just as I was about to get in the car, I spotted a photographer. Somehow the press must have found out. You can guess one of the next day's headlines:

MAUREEN ON BREADLINE AFTER
BEING TOLD SHE'S LEAVING

The other thing that didn't occur to me was that I now had only one good eye. As I drove off, I suddenly realised that I had virtually no vision in my left eye. It was raining heavily and as I got on the motorway I had to stay in the outside lane and try to judge where things were. I came off onto the slip road and immediately mounted a kerb, managed to get back onto the road and at a snail's pace tried to find my way home. Just as I was negotiating a very large roundabout, I again mounted a kerb on my left-hand side; that's when I saw the flashing lights behind me. I stopped halfway onto the kerb and broke down in floods of tears.

Suspecting I might be drunk, the police had been following me. As one of them bent down to speak to me through the driver's door, he said: 'Hello, Maureen – didn't know it was you! You've had some lunchtime, haven't you?' But I couldn't stop crying, so both of them got in the car and listened to my sob story. They were fantastic: they asked me where I lived and as it was only a couple of hundred yards away they provided me with an escort there. Afterwards they came in, had some tea and I gave them autographs for their mums – they made me feel so much better. Although they did advise me not to drive for a while, that was all that happened.

Ken and Keeley were in London and so the house was empty. Trying to make sense of everything, I just sat at my kitchen table. Suddenly the lights fused and I was plunged into darkness. I tripped over a footstool while attempting to find the junction box and hit my head on the wall. Then I couldn't find a corkscrew and, as I desperately needed a drink, I used a very sharp knife, stabbed the cork, slipped and sliced my finger open. I sat and cried for some time, I can tell you.

I'd had the best of times in *The Street*. In the space of four years Maureen had been married to Reg, married to the butcher Fred Elliot (played by John Savident) and then left him for an affair with Bill Webster (Peter Armitage) – not forgetting the many dalliances with Curly – so she'd been a busy girl. Maureen and Reg were such wonderful comedy characters, but all that had ended when Reg left her. With Fred there was still quite a bit of comedy, but with Bill Webster it was a supposedly passionate affair and I didn't think Maureen was that kind of person. She was more of a comedic character and so, if I'm being honest, I think that's when she lost her way. Having said that, *The Street* is known for being a matriarchal show for women who can survive on their own. Of course Maureen could have survived, as did the wonderful Sue Nichols (Audrey), the ever-suffering Helen Worth (Gail) and the truly lovely Sally Dynevor as Sally Webster.

One of the most enduring characters is Eileen Derbyshire, who plays Emily Bishop – I absolutely adored her. She was, and is, one of the funniest people I have ever encountered. When I was there she was a big Formula One fan and would stay up all night watching the races. Betty Driver (who plays barmaid Betty Williams) is another amazing person. She had a long and interesting career as a famous singer and appeared in Ealing comedies and many other productions long before *Corrie*, where she's been since 1969.

The Street is full of colourful, interesting, watchable characters and that's why the likes of Ian McShane, Maureen Lipman and Judi Dench all love and respect the show. Indeed, the characters proved so popular that their faces were put onto all kinds of souvenirs, which were sold on the Granada Studios Tour. When you were new to the series you started off as a pencil, then graduated to a mug, T-shirt, even boxer shorts and knickers. Eventually I became a key ring, as I mentioned earlier, but I so wanted to be a fridge magnet! Among the cast, we used to say the greatest accolade you could receive was to be made into a fridge magnet. Sadly, as I walked away with my loaf of bread on that fateful afternoon I knew I'd lost any chance of that honour. Some of my best friends were already fridge magnets but now I'd never be in that exclusive club.

The history behind *The Street* was all down to one man: Darren Little. Our archivist at the time, he had a background story for every character. I used to go up to his office knowing that every question I might throw at him about the show – the characters, where they lived, where they worked, who they were related to, how many marriages they'd had, how many deaths had been in the show, how many women Ken Barlow had slept with – would all be logged. It was fascinating. On one wall he had black-and-white photos of the whole cast, but you only graduated to a colour photo on the other wall if you were staying. I can remember the day when he called me into his office and showed me my colour photo – I was over the moon! Sounds silly now but that was how it worked and you became embroiled in the machinations of the system.

I loved my character Maureen and always felt that she never quite finished her story. They decided to make her passionate and sexy with Bill Webster, and for me that didn't work as it was so far removed from her real persona.

Maureen was to leave with Bill Webster in a storyline that would see them going off to Germany to marry and start a new life. My final, beautifully written scene was with Maud, in which Maureen explained why she had to leave Fred and run away to Germany. Both of us cried a lot that day. It was so awful, getting into the obligatory black cab and saying goodbye to those cobbles. I was pleased that at least Maureen wasn't killed off – she'd simply gone abroad and could return. And indeed she briefly did so, in 2006: visiting the Websters for Christmas lunch. I loved every minute of my return to the show – would do so again in a heartbeat – and I adore Sally Dynevor (who played Bill's daughter). Naturally, I was thrilled to be part of the Webster family.

Coronation Street is one of the greatest achievements on British television. I've never liked to hear the show described as a soap opera – it's so much more than that implies and the actors are certainly not soap actors. They are amazing and should be admired and rewarded for their constant excellence. And Tony Warren, who originated the series, ought to be honoured with a knighthood, not just for his contribution to drama but for creating some truly great parts for women and changing the attitude towards their role in television.

Chapter Twenty-Two

Before I left *Coronation Street* Keeley and I bought a little Westie that we named Charlie. After the pain of losing Caius I didn't want another dog, but somehow we couldn't resist him. And when I finally left *Corrie* and we all moved back to the round, Art-Deco house in Surrey, Charlie came with us.

It was a lovely house but before I left for Manchester five years earlier it had needed some work. I had hoped Ken would organise all this while I was busy working, but as he'd moved north to be with me, the house was rented out and so none of the improvements had been carried out. We had the most stunning garden with two enormous lawns that I tended devotedly to the point of trimming the edges with scissors. Slightly OCD, I know – I think it's the Virgo in me.

I was quite excited to think that now I would have the time and money to indulge myself with mundane tasks such as gardening and decorating and I wouldn't have to say yes to every job I was offered. During the time that I had appeared in *Corrie* I'd made very good money – hundreds of thousands of pounds once all the fees from public appearances were included. However, I wasn't sure how much we had left because I didn't handle the finances, Ken did, but I was sure there must be plenty. As Ken hadn't worked for the whole five years that I was in the show, I hoped he would find himself a job and perhaps take over as breadwinner so that I could settle Keeley into school in Surrey again and spend a bit more time with her. That was the plan taking shape in my mind as we settled back into the house. I felt optimistic, but all my hopes and dreams were shattered when Ken delivered a piece of news that quite took my breath away.

We were sitting at the kitchen table, a few days after we'd arrived back. I started to talk about all the things that the house needed and how perhaps we might take a holiday and then I could have a bit of time off. As I chatted on, Ken became horribly quiet.

'What *is* it? I asked.

'We've got £10,000 left,' he told me quietly. 'That's all there is.'

'*What*?' I was so shocked that I couldn't think what else to say. How could all the money be gone?

'We've had a lot of expenses,' Ken was saying. 'The mortgage, the rent in Manchester, Keeley's school fees – and don't forget the boys.'

He was referring to our one and only foray into the music industry. We'd met two boys called Solo, who were brilliant young singers, and Ken had decided to manage them despite having no experience in the industry and no knowledge whatsoever of who to contact, how to make a demo disc, how to market them, and so on. However, my brother Brett knew something of that world and, as I have already mentioned, he had worked with Jimmy Savile, Peter Stringfellow and others in the music industry. Brett offered to help, but he and Ken are not a good match: Brett is a doer while Ken is a sitter. Anyway, you name it, we paid out for it – studios, photo shoots, publicity, promoters … They were a fantastic twosome – Simon Cowell heard them and said they were one of the best new bands of that time – but Ken refused to take any advice and soon lost interest once the glamour of being a would-be pop manager faded. It all dwindled to nothing and the money was wasted. Despite this, I couldn't believe we had virtually nothing left.

'It's just gone, deal with it,' muttered Ken, looking sheepish.

But I was horrified. What on earth could we have spent it on? I felt like a fool for not keeping a closer eye on our joint account. Of course I should have checked, I could have watched what was happening, but I'd been too busy with work. I never looked at the balance, just assumed there was money in the account. Now, when I look back, I feel so foolish. How could I not be in control of my own money? Why did I never check a statement? Hindsight can be a wonderful thing.

Ten thousand pounds sounds like an awful lot of money but I had worked in a highly paid job for five years and it was ludicrous to think that's all we had. At this point neither of us was working, and with all our living costs, mortgage and Keeley's school fees I knew the money would soon be gone. Each night I lay awake going over and over in my mind all the reasons why this might have happened until I was dead on my feet.

Eventually, my fighting instinct came back and I thought, OK, what's next? I'll get a job, but I'm going to make bloody sure Ken does, too. But we were both guilty – I knew that. Time after time, I had spoiled Ken with expensive clothes and cars. I don't even know why I did it: I didn't really love him any more, hadn't for a long time, and yet I indulged him completely. In many ways I treated him like a child who had never been able to stand on his own two feet. I was angry with myself for that – I'd put up with him not working when I should have insisted he get a job, and at the same time I bought him everything he wanted, even though I knew he didn't even like me any more. I'd spend any amount on him but would agonise over a £20 jacket for myself. It wasn't a grown-up relationship at all, it was child and mummy, but we both allowed it to be that way.

At one point I remember a friend saying to me, 'You're crazy, Sherrie! What do you think you're doing? You're his cash cow and you're feeding him all the wrong things, destroying him and yourself in the process. Can you not see that? Why are you doing it?' I have asked myself those same questions many times in the subsequent years. Why did I treat him like a child and at the same time leave our finances largely in his hands? It's not an easy question to answer. So many things we do in life are driven by emotion rather than hard practicality. I've always had a strong need to please and nurture those I'm close to, and that included Ken, even when things had gone badly wrong between us. I see this as a flaw in me and it's not to be admired: if I'd seen someone else behaving the way I did with Ken, I'd have told them to get a grip on life and get rid.

I never really got to the bottom of what had happened to all the money. I suppose it was simply frittered away, and to be honest I might not have wanted to face up to the truth, and this was something I would come to bitterly regret.

We had lived well in Manchester, but not like kings. Ken drove nice cars, but mine were free – he arranged for me to have a new Saab every year while I was in *Corrie*. I was delighted because I love Saabs. Anyway, one way or another the money was gone and we just had to face it. So, what were we going to do? I could get work, I knew that, and besides, a couple of offers had already come in, although I wouldn't be bringing in anything like the sort of money I'd made on the show.

I came to the conclusion that the best thing would be to invest our £10,000 in some kind of business that would bring us an income and give Ken a job at the same time because I was desperate to see him working again. You would think from the way I talk that Ken never entered into any conversation, never came up with any solutions and never faced the problems. The fact is, he didn't.

Lying awake one night worrying about the whole mess we were in, I came up with what felt like a brilliant scheme. We had two friends, John and Henry, who owned a lovely little restaurant in Richmond not far from us called Mrs Beetons. We'd often gone there to eat – the place was always packed, the atmosphere camp and fun. It was a highly successful business, and the last time we'd been there John and Henry had told us that they were thinking of selling up and moving permanently to their house in Spain. I wasn't sure how far our money would go towards buying out the lease, but if we could take over the restaurant then I felt it just might solve all our problems in one.

Excited and full of plans, I went to talk to John and Henry. I remember Henry saying, 'Are you *sure*? This is the hardest trade to be in, and I have to be honest, I can't see Ken getting his hands dirty or opening seven days a week from 8am till 3 the next morning. Neither of you knows anything about the restaurant trade or running a business.' As for John, he thought I was insane and that it was doomed from the start. Both knew Ken only too well, but they agreed to sell to us. The £10,000 was the deposit plus a hefty loan from the bank and a further loan from them.

The deal agreed, I was ecstatic: Ken was slightly less so, but nonetheless he was pleased and said he would run the restaurant. John, who was (and still is) a wonderful showman, knew how to entertain and treated the clientéle as his audience. We all loved his approach – it was outrageous and crazy – but it brought in the punters. He wanted Ken to go and train with him for a few weeks in the restaurant before we took over, but he refused to do so. 'He's not pushing me around, telling me what to do and how to run the place,' he said. I should have known then, but I knew the restaurant had a loyal following and all we had to do was provide continuity with the same good food and great atmosphere that John and Henry had created. I just hoped Ken would learn the ropes fast when he actually took over. A sizeable proportion of the clientéle were gay, and as Maureen had been a bit of a gay icon I thought my presence there whenever I could manage it could only help.

Preparations for the takeover went ahead and in the meantime, I started a job, appearing in *Billy Liar* at the famous King's Head Theatre in Islington. It was great to be back in a live theatre again. I played Billy's mum, while Billy was played by a gorgeous young actor called Paul Nicholls; also in the cast was Rebecca Callard (daughter of *Corrie*'s Bev Callard and a brilliant young actress, whom I adored). George Layton, a prolific writer and actor, played Billy's dad.

The King's Head is really a pub and known for still using pounds, shillings and pence. It has a little theatre at the back and the facilities are, shall we say, a bit primitive. There were no dressing rooms so the only place to get changed was in a corridor that also housed the loo. Who said an actor's life is glam? Despite the overcrowding as we all tried to get ready at once, we still managed to enjoy ourselves.

It was on the back of my performance in *Billy Liar* that I landed my next job. As so often happens in this business, a producer came to see the play and then called to offer me a part in a new family sitcom for Central Television: *Barbara*. It would star Gwen Taylor as a middle-aged, sharp-tongued doctor's receptionist married to a taxi-driver, who has two grown-up children. I was offered the part of Barbara's rather vain and air-headed sister Jean, who was engaged to a simpering chap called Phil.

It was a great offer and I happily accepted. Rehearsals began soon after we finished the King's Head run and the first episode of *Barbara* appeared in late June 1999. Less than two years after leaving *Corrie* I was back in another series with an amazing cast that included the inimitable Sam Kelly as Barbara's husband Ted, Benedict Sandiford played Neil (the couple's layabout son) and Elizabeth Carling was their long-suffering daughter Linda. The delightful Mark Benton was her husband, Martin Pond – a TV presenter with his own show, *Pond Life*. It was a small team but we all got on well together and there was always a lot of laughter when we were filming.

Despite the fact that the series was supposed to be set in Yorkshire, we filmed *Barbara* in Central's Nottingham studios but rehearsed in the barracks off the King's Road in London. This meant that I was only away in Nottingham for two days a week and so my work wouldn't disturb Keeley's life too much.

Right from the start, *Barbara* was a success. It went on to win several awards and we filmed four series in all. Although eventually axed in 2003, the viewing figures were still good but Central had been absorbed into Carlton in 1994, which was now merging with Granada to form ITV and the Nottingham studios were to close. Many Carlton shows were casualties of that merger.

As my fiftieth birthday approached in September 2000, I was feeling very unhappy about myself, partly because I was suffering really badly with menopausal symptoms: hot flushes, night sweats and tiredness. Worst of all was my burning skin. I had bought a new bed and every time I slept in it I swore it was heating up – I even went back to the manufacturer to complain. Somehow I had it in my head that someone had left a cigarette burning inside the mattress. They offered to take me to the factory where they were made. I think the factory manager must have thought we have to humour this insane woman or she will go round telling tales about the company. Eventually, they swapped the bed three times and each time I could feel burning, but then I happened to stay in a hotel where the bed was the same and at that point I realised it could be me.

Secretly, I used to call myself 'boil in the bag'. If ever I was in a supermarket and the burning began, I would stuff my hands into the nearest freezer and I'd take a big bag of frozen peas or a large bottle of freezing water to bed with me. You know, you'll do anything in that crazy state.

It was my birthday that finally convinced me to try cosmetic surgery again. Ken was in the restaurant and Keeley was at school, so I sat in the house on my own. My friend Liz had sent me a card and flowers. Of course Keeley gave me a beautiful card when she got home, but my husband had either forgotten or couldn't be bothered. There was no card or present from him.

That evening I told Keeley we would go to the cinema and, still trying hard, I rang Ken to ask if he could come home a bit earlier, say 9.30, and let the manager lock up so that we could celebrate together. He said he would, eventually arrived back at 3am and clearly had had more than a few drinks. At this point I'd had enough: I desperately needed to feel good about myself again and perhaps, deep down, I was hoping a new face might solve my problems and bring me a new life with it. Despite my earlier interest, I might never have given it a second go had a friend not recommended a wonderful cosmetic surgeon, Alex Karidis.

'You'll fall in love with him because he's so beautiful, and all his patients do,' I was told, 'and he's the very best person for a facelift.'

And so just after my birthday I booked myself in. I remember getting to the room and Alex coming in and drawing all over my face – it looked like a map of the 52 states of America. Then, as I climbed onto the trolley to be wheeled to the theatre, I suddenly changed my mind. I started to have a wrestling match with the nurse, who kept saying, 'You can't change your mind now, it's too late! We're here now, everything is ready.' Panicking, I was trying to get off the trolley, but I had one of those hospital gowns on (with just a tie at the back) and so I was desperately trying to cover my modesty at the same time.

Eventually the young nurse was pushed out of the way by a senior colleague – I'm guessing it was a sister.

'Do you want to carry on or not?' she said firmly.

'Yes,' I squeaked. And off we went.

When I came round from the operation I looked like a great big swollen turnip and felt like death. Meanwhile, my good friend Liz, who had booked in with me as a 'job lot', was already up and bouncing around.

'You'll be fine,' she kept saying, reassuringly. 'I'll make you a cup of tea.'

Big mistake. In fact, I was far from fine, and with the first gulp the tea was returned with such projectile force that it covered Liz, the bed and me.

When I was eventually sent home I was still wearing what can only be described as a pink bandage helmet, which fitted over my head and under my chin. I assumed it must be supporting my face so that, having been lifted, it didn't fall down again or my head didn't drop off. As no one told me otherwise (or so I thought), I sat there for a week and hardly dared move a muscle for fear of the helmet coming off and the potential disaster of having to pick the pieces up from the floor.

At the end of the week I went back to the hospital. In the pink helmet, I sat in a waiting room full of people.

'Why have you still got your helmet on?' asked the receptionist, talking quietly to me as if I were a child.

'I was frightened things might slip,' I meekly replied.

'Nothing will slip. You can take the helmet off now – you only needed to wear it for a few days.'

Trying not to look at anybody else in the waiting room, I quickly removed the helmet, and indeed, nothing fell off. I'm sure they must have advised me on aftercare but in my post-op state I didn't take it in.

Alex called me into his room and seemed very pleased with the results. 'I've taken a milk bottle of fat from your neck,' he told me. When I'd recovered sufficiently from this shocking announcement to look at myself in the mirror, I was really pleased with the result. I had always worried about what I considered to be my fat neck and it looked noticeably slimmer. Minus the pink helmet, post-operative swelling and bruising, my face also looked good – I was thrilled.

'It takes up to a year before everything settles down completely,' he warned me. 'Don't think about doing it again for another ten years at least – cosmetic surgery can be very addictive, so don't fall into the trap.'

And he was right. We all want to look good, and growing older isn't easy, particularly if you work on TV, so it's tempting to try what seem like magical solutions. Later on with other doctors I tried Botox, but I only ended up looking permanently surprised with a strange Gary Glitter stare. Not attractive and not good if you want to show emotion. At one point I didn't know if I was happy, sad or simply asleep. On another occasion I had fillers: now they *are* weird. After I had them done my face felt strangely lumpy and very puffy – it looked like the moon's surface without the craters. I came to the conclusion that fillers are just not for me.

My one regret was agreeing to appear in Channel 4's *Ten Years Younger* in 2004. When I met the producer she said, 'I'm not sure you ought to be doing this programme – I don't think you need cosmetic surgery.' The thing is, I never believe anyone when they pay me compliments like that. I really should have listened and been thankful, but instead I told her that I was happy to have a few more procedures.

'Well, if you're sure ...' she said doubtfully.

So no, I can't blame them – it was my decision to have a chemical face peel and a slight lift around the chin area. For the peel, acid is painted on your face (which then turns brown). Layers of skin peel off and you're left with the brand new, soft and clear skin underneath. I loved this procedure, but what I hadn't realised was that it takes quite a few weeks of peeling to get to the finished product: your brand new baby face. And the trouble was, I was due to appear in panto. I'd left three weeks for the procedure but it wasn't enough.

I was to play the Wicked Queen in Derby, and just before the show opened I had to appear in character at the press launch. It's held in the Square and usually some 5,000 people turn up, so the event is huge. At this point I had half a face on and half a face off: as my face was also still swollen, I looked more demented peeling turnip than a majestic wicked queen.

The promoters were horrified but what could they do? I put on my beautiful costume – a silk and sequined dress slit up the side, a black velvet cloak, a wig that was pure Lily Savage and long red nails. No matter how lovely it was, it still didn't disguise my face and so I donned a large pair of dark glasses to cover my eyes and nose.

The compère gave me a wonderful build-up and then I heard, 'Please give a fantastic Derby welcome to the lovely Sherrie Hewson!' The audience was deafening and so on I went. I started to say a few words but then I felt my face burning. As I turned away and touched my cheek, the huge arc lights were drying my peeling skin. The one thing the doctor had said was that I must keep it moist all the time, but now my face was cracking. As I turned back towards the crowd, my glasses fell on the floor. I bent down to pick them up, tripped over the long dress and landed on my knees near the front of the stage.

As I retrieved my glasses, I was only a couple of feet away from the audience and stared straight into a little girl's face. She looked at me and at once let out a squeal. As my skin continued to flake, she said: 'Mummy, the Queen's face has just fallen on the floor!' Her mother looked horrified and dragged her away, saying, 'Don't look!' At this point I was rushed off the stage as if I was Quasimodo going back to my tower.

Thankfully, the panto turned out fine, but for me that cosmetic surgery episode occurred at the wrong time and in the wrong place; it was also the wrong thing to do. But I had no one to blame but myself. I believe I only did it because I found myself thinking, If only I could be somebody else and not me then all this misery will go away and I'll be all right again. The truth is that whatever you do to change your face, it can't change you into somebody else. When you wake up you're still the same person, and that saddened me.

To any woman, I would say: don't do it for a man and don't do it because you think it's going to change your life. Take it from me, it won't. You may look better, but that's all – surgery doesn't solve any of life's problems.

When I started filming *Barbara*, and for a while afterwards, the restaurant seemed to be doing well. I was interviewed by *OK! Magazine* and their headline was,

THE STAR OF HIT COMEDY *BARBARA*, SHERRIE HEWSON, AND HER HUSBAND KEN LIKED THEIR FAVOURITE RESTAURANT SO MUCH, THEY DECIDED TO BUY IT

And so we had a lovely restaurant, a ready-made clientéle and now free publicity. We'd kept on the brilliant Dutch chef, and most of the customers stayed – Ken really did seem to be making a go of things there.

A few months later, however, the chef left after falling out with Ken (who thought chefs were far too expensive) over money. I thought it was worth paying for the best, but he didn't agree. We hired another chef who seemed excellent. He stayed for about four months, but then fell out with Ken (again, over money) and he left, too. We found another chef, a young guy who seemed very capable. A couple of weeks after he arrived Ken and I went down to the restaurant at two on a Saturday afternoon to check everything was OK with the preparations for the evening. We had 95 bookings (which was full capacity) and so we wanted everything to be perfect.

We walked into the kitchen expecting to see the chef busy, chopping and stirring, only to find him out cold on the floor from what later turned out to be a drug overdose. Once we realised there wasn't a chance in hell of him recovering before the evening, Ken responded to my panic by simply shrugging his shoulders and saying, 'Well, I'll just have to do the cooking myself.'

'Don't be daft!' I exclaimed. 'You've never cooked in your life.'

'I can do it,' he replied, looking round for an apron.

'You *can't*!' I retorted.

'I *can*,' he repeated and before I could protest any further he got out a chopping board and started to prepare chicken, steak and tuna for that night. I couldn't believe my eyes: he was so efficient and everything went perfectly. He cooked a whole range of dishes for all those people, with not one complaint. No one even realised there was a change of chef.

At the end of the evening, I felt stunned. I was glad that we'd been able to open and feed everyone, of course I was, but I was hurt and angry, too. I marched up to Ken, who was taking off his apron, and said: 'I've never hated you more than I hate you now.'

'Why?' he asked, sluicing down a chopping board. 'I thought the evening went well.'

'Because,' I stormed, 'I've been married to you for nearly twenty years and you've never, ever lifted a finger to help me during all that time – I don't think you've even cooked me a breakfast. Plus, if you can cook, why have we been paying for chefs when you could have done it?'

'I *own* the restaurant,' he snapped. 'I can't be seen to cook as well. I pay people to do that. I'm not working all those hours!'

There was no answer to that. It was yet another reminder, if I needed one, that I had mollycoddled Ken and he had been happy to let me so he had never fulfilled his potential, and both of us were left feeling hurt and resentful. Ken could have done so much: he was an extremely capable man, though short on motivation. I had always supported him and so he didn't feel under any pressure to work or succeed – in fact, quite the opposite.

Ken soon decided that opening a restaurant six days a week was just too much like hard work. It involved dedication, people management, organisation and, most important of all, the willingness to work long hours. The latter proved too much for him and he announced that he was only going to open on Thursdays, Fridays and Saturdays.

That was the death-knell for the business. If people try and book a table only to find you're shut, they simply go elsewhere. You've got to be superbly good for them to remember you're only open three days a week and bother to come back. To pay our bank loan, the loan from John and Henry plus the overheads, we needed to be full to the brim on those three nights – even then, it would have been touch and go. With the closure four nights a week, slowly but surely the number of bookings began to dwindle and most of our regulars started to go elsewhere.

As for Ken, I was certain he was playing around with other women. Night after night, he didn't come home until the early hours and friends told me he wasn't at the restaurant. Within months we were in a financially perilous situation: the restaurant wasn't paying and the debts we'd already accumulated from the takeover grew daily. Serious storm clouds had gathered.

What followed were meetings with the banks (who refused to help) and desperate plans to stave off collapse. As usual, Ken wouldn't take any advice or guidance – *he* knew best. Eventually, I realised it was all too late. In 2001, three years after we opened the restaurant, the bank foreclosed and we had to sell. The sale didn't make enough to repay everything and we were forced to put our house on the market, too. My big regret was losing my lovely home, and of course the profit went towards the bank loan and repaying John and Henry.

If it happened now, I would have known what to do – liquidate the man and keep the house! Seriously, I've learned so much since then and I think we could have kept our house. Back then, I blindly went ahead and sold, believing this to be our only option.

Chapter Twenty-Three

The failure of our restaurant was not, by any means, the only problem. My marriage to Ken was virtually over, but in spite of all that had happened I just couldn't bring myself to tell him to go. I knew that once the house was sold we would never live together again. We had already been in separate bedrooms for a while and the relationship was effectively over, so to ease the pain of parting I came up with a plan. After the house was sold, leaving us £20,000, I said to him, 'Why don't you take half the money we have left and put it on a flat in Spain? You've always said it's your spiritual home and that's where you would be happiest.'

Ken had once lived in Spain and had always wanted to go back there one day. The idea I suggested was that we would live between England and Spain, but I knew that once he was there he wouldn't want to leave again. Ken loved the idea: he went off to Spain, bought a flat and, as I had expected, quickly settled in there. The only thing was that as I was the breadwinner the mortgage and bills needed to be in my name, so I had to go over to Spain to sign all the papers.

After that, with Ken settled in Spain and Keeley (now 17) and me back in England, I breathed a sigh of relief. It hadn't been easy, but now we were separated. Neither of us would acknowledge the fact, though. Every now and then Ken would ring and ask, 'When are you coming over?' Each time I told him I couldn't because I had too much work on.

In the end I did go over a couple more times with Keeley. I remember being there one day, watching the TV and saying to Ken, 'This is a strange time for *The Towering Inferno* to be on,' and then I suddenly realised it was real. It was the terrible day when the Twin Towers were attacked, September 11, 2001, and watching those horrific events unfold is the last I remember of that flat. There really was no point in us going on as Ken was very distant and both Keeley and I felt he didn't want to have us around.

A few months later Ken phoned me from Spain to say he had very bad pains in his side. I told him to go to the doctor. Not long afterwards he rang and said, 'I'm in a taxi going to hospital – I have appendicitis, it's very bad. I may not live as it could be peritonitis and they don't know how long I've got.'

'*What*?' Somehow this was all I could say.

'I'm not repeating it,' he continued. 'My life insurance is in the top drawer of the desk.' And then the phone cut off. But I didn't know what peritonitis was and I certainly didn't know he had any life insurance. I rang a friend in Spain and asked him to go and check on Ken. Two hours later, my friend rang to say Ken was alive, but by the time he'd reached the hospital he'd had only an hour to live and it really had been touch and go.

I never did find that insurance policy.

That year, 2001, was awful and pushed me to the limit. I thought the nightmare would never end and at one point I truly believed the only way out was for me to end it all and have some peace at last. But as has so often been the case, while my private life was in turmoil and my heart ached, work was great. Just as Ken was making his move to Spain, I was invited to appear in the newly revamped *Crossroads* as the spiky, evil and extremely funny receptionist, Virginia Raven.

Crossroads had once been hugely popular. It ran for twenty-three years until its demise in 1988, and despite the wobbly sets, weak storylines and characters who vanished without explanation – one famously went out for a cup of sugar and never reappeared – it was much loved. In fact, in many ways its flaws became its strengths.

The 2001 revamp was launched by Carlton Television and unashamedly aimed at the gay market. We filmed two versions, the first much grittier and straighter than the second, but it was this second version – outrageously camp, with totally over-the-top characters – that worked brilliantly.

When I started work on *Crossroads* I was still doing *Barbara*. I did both series back-to-back for two years, and luckily I was able to make the schedules work, but it was a busy time for me. I absolutely loved playing the grouchy but wacky Virginia in the now rather upmarket Crossroads Motel. When I started, I had just lost quite a bit of weight and I'd had my facelift by then so I felt quite good about myself, although mainly this was because for the first time in my life I was without shackles. It was a fantastic feeling, admittedly the calm before the tsunami, but I didn't know it then.

I based Virginia on my old pal Paul O'Grady's alter ego, Lily Savage. I first met Paul when I was in *Corrie* and he interviewed me for Channel 4's *The Big Breakfast*. He was amazing – he knew everything I'd ever been in. Paul made you feel important and very special; that's one of his great gifts as an interviewer. When we met we got on really well, and we've been friends ever since.

We share an outrageous sense of humour and he is one of the warmest, kindest, funniest men I know.

One night when I was in *Coronation Street* and had gone to Blackpool to do a personal appearance at a slightly dubious-looking pub, I was in the back room waiting to go on when Paul arrived. He was late and not in the best of moods: 'Oh my God, Sherrie! Thank God you're here! It's a shit-hole. Where have we come to?'

Minutes later he was out in the pub doing his jokes. I could hear he was having a bad time of it – by now, it was really late and the punters were very drunk. He came offstage and said, 'You can't go out there – it's lethal, they're baying for blood!' But I was pushed onstage by the management, who wanted their money's worth. As I stepped out, everyone turned to stare and I thought, I'm dead, but then they started to shout, '*Maureen*, where's Reg?' They were clapping and shouting, but more to the point, friendly – at which stage, Paul put his head round the door and shouted, 'Yeah, you f***ing love her, don't you?' He came out, we did a bit together and it turned into a fantastic night – the audience were great.

Paul's creation, Lily, was brilliant. Sharp, sassy, sexy and irresistible, she was always in great demand, though these days he doesn't bring her out of retirement all that often. I think of Lily whenever I play a wicked pantomime dame, and Virginia was just the same – over-the-top, larger than life and wickedly funny. Paul had written a character into *Crossroads*, and had it gone on, he would have played my evil cousin working on the reception with me. Wouldn't that have been a great double act to be part of?

A few years earlier, Paul and I had actually been in panto together. We did *Snow White and the Seven Dwarfs* in Southampton and Paul, as Lily, played the Wicked Queen while I was Nurse, the Queen's sidekick and the butt of all her jokes. For the month we spent in Southampton in the panto Paul and I rented flats facing each other, and every night most of the cast ended up back at our place. We agreed that we would all eat in mine, then drink and smoke in his – a wise decision on my part!

By the end of the run Paul's flat was completely wrecked, splattered with alcohol stains and the carpet full of cigarette burns, while mine was spotless. Although I got food in for everyone, no one bothered to eat it – they just headed straight to Paul's to start the party. Sometimes, when I finally got back into my own flat, I would see Paul from my bedroom window, dressed in his PJs and singing at the top of his voice as he disappeared on the back of a motorbike – I never asked!

One memorable night, we all decided to have a bit of a do at Paul's flat after the show. All the cast came – including of course Snow White, the Prince and the Seven Dwarfs. It was about 11.30 when we started drinking. As was often the case, none of us had eaten. Paul and I sat in the kitchen, downing a few whiskies on empty stomachs. The next thing I remember was someone saying it was 4am and getting light outside. Paul and I ignored that piece of information, though, because by then we were onto our second bottle of whisky. By 6.30am there were two empty whisky bottles on the table and Paul had summoned his dresser to hold his arm and raise his glass and ciggie to his lips because he couldn't manage this on his own any more. Eventually, with someone either side of me, I was propelled into my own flat and off to bed. As we passed Paul's bedroom he was lying on the bed, comatose.

A few hours later, a kindly face from the theatre arrived to remind me that I had two shows that day – one of which was scheduled to start in an hour's time. As I was still drunk and couldn't focus properly, my friendly Samaritan had to help me to the theatre and then dress me so I was ready to go on. As I stood in the wings, swaying slightly, I was certainly in no frame of mind to face 3,000 screaming kids. I could hardly walk, couldn't see and my head was about to explode.

As Nurse, I would come on stage while Paul – the Wicked Queen – lay centre stage on a four-poster bed hidden behind the bed curtains. I would get the kids going by saying, 'How wonderful the Queen is – I bet her subjects can't wait to meet her! Shall we say hello and give her a big cheer?' and so on and so forth until the shouts and screams from the children rose to a crescendo.

Very gingerly, hoping the kids would respond quietly, I began in almost in a whisper: 'Hello kids, do you want to see the Queen?'

But it was hopeless. Knowing full well that Paul was behind the curtains, they started to scream and shout.

'Do you wanna see the Queen?' I repeated as quietly as possible.

'Yeah!' they hollered.

At precisely that moment I heard a kind of retching sound coming from behind the curtains. As the screams grew louder, so too did the retching. As I headed towards the bed I was aware that two stage-hands, just out of sight, were pointing at the bed and holding their noses, but the kids were in full ear-splitting swing by now and the show had to go on.

I threw back the curtain just as Paul, in full robes and wig, dived over the side of the bed towards a fire bucket and threw up! I stood there paralysed. Ignoring the audience, he straightened up from the bucket and crawled back to bed, then looked across at me and growled, 'You ... *you* did this to me!'

The kids loved it and screamed all the louder as Paul, clutching his head, made a lunge for me and missed, then flopped onto the floor.

'I'm gonna *kill* you!' he croaked.

'Kill her!' the kids screamed back, and as he heard this, Paul turned his venom on them and bellowed, 'Shut it, kids! What do you know?'

How we got through that day, I will never know. I just loved every minute and had my eyes opened to wild and wonderful things during my time with Paul and the rest of the cast. Shortly afterwards I went down to see him in his smallholding. Leaving me in the kitchen sitting with my back to the French windows while he answered the door, I was surprised by a nudge on my shoulder. I turned to be confronted by Daisy, a large Friesian cow. 'Say, "Hello Daisy" – she's come for her breakfast,' said Paul as he walked back in. That's why I love him.

Much as I enjoyed playing Virginia (and modelling her on Lily), sadly the new version of *Crossroads* wasn't to last. Again, it was the merger between Carlton and Granada that finished it. Many of us who worked on the show felt there hadn't been enough time and it might have become a cult series, had we been allowed to carry on, but we'll never know.

The show finished in the summer of 2003 on a classically ludicrous storyline in which Jane Asher's character (Angel Samson) turned out to be a till operator while the rest of the show – the cast, her hotel boss job and the hotel itself – was simply a dream! Sad as I was to see the series end, I needed a rest. For the previous few months I'd had to deal with a nightmare scenario that Ken had got himself into. At the time I'd agreed to do a play in London – *Murder Mistaken* – with the lovely Gaby Roslin and the very sexy Joe Shaw (son of Martin and the child who had been born when I was working with his dad in rep).

I was in London rehearsing when I took a call from Ken to say he was in Kosovo. The only reason I didn't fall off my chair was because our last chef in the restaurant was Kosovan and had intimated it would be a good idea for Ken to go over there and look at opening a coffee shop. I thought it was a ridiculous idea to go to a country at that time dangerous, unsettled and decidedly volatile, but I hadn't thought about it again until then. Could I send some money over, he asked, with the plea in his voice that I had to come to know so well. He was there with Tony, our ex-chef, and together they had come up with a scheme to open a restaurant-cum-bar which Ken was convinced would be a rip-roaring success. He'd be making good money in no time at all, he assured me, and would be able to repay the loan in full.

'But why on earth would you want to open a restaurant-bar in Kosovo?' I asked.

'Because there are a lot of troops here,' he explained. 'Tony's going to put up half the money if I put up the other half, and as he has contacts in the army base we could make a fortune in no time.'

So what did I do? Had I learned anything at all from the collapse of our restaurant? Apparently not, it seems, because I actually sent money to a bank in Pristina, the capital and the largest city of Kosovo. It was complete madness – I had no idea where it was going, what the money would be spent on or whether I'd see it again. I was also paying for the flat in Spain.

Needless to say, the bar was a complete disaster. Having opened it, Ken left Tony to do all the work while he continued to lead the good life. Meanwhile, I was constantly asked for more money to cover this and that expenditure at the bar. Daft as I was, I continued to send cash.

Then Ken suddenly stopped ringing. One day there was a phone call from Tony, who told me in his broken English: 'I think you must here come, Sherrie.'

'Why?' I asked, instantly alarmed.

'Because Ken, he spend all your money – no money left.'

That day I'd just sent £3,000, and so I asked him what the money was for.

'That for the coffee machine,' he told me.

'A coffee machine?' I shouted. 'For God's sake, couldn't you have bought a kettle? Where is he?'

'He not here – he in Pristina all time with women,' said Tony. 'I know how much money you send – you send lots of money, but I want you to know that the bar doesn't see this money. Ken, he bought Range Rover.'

'Why?' I asked, feeling faint. 'Why on earth didn't he get a van? Oh my God, so what's happening to the bar now?'

'I try to run it, but it's no good any more – the building is rented and is owned by the Mafia. They not interested if you can't pay, they just shoot you and that is what will happen to Ken and me.'

I thought this was rather melodramatic but he clearly believed that he and Ken were about to be killed.

'So, how much do you owe?' I asked weakly.

'Twenty thousand,' he told me after a long pause.

'*How* much?' I gasped, quaking at the knees.

After that call I tried all day to get hold of Ken but he was not answering his mobile. Eventually, I gave up and rang a number that Tony had given me. A girl with a very young voice answered.

'Is Ken there?' I asked, feeling instantly sick.

'No, he not,' she replied in broken English, 'but he back soon …'

'*When*? What time? Are you *sure* he's coming back?' I persisted.

'Yes, we live together – he goin' to marry me. Then we go Spain, live there and have many children,' she told me.

That's funny, I thought, as he had never wanted any.

'Is that what you think?' I asked, trying hard to remain calm.

'Yes – who you?'

'Never you mind who I am! Where is Ken now?'

'I not know,' she replied, sullenly. 'Are you Marie?'

'No, I'm not. Who is she?'

'Oh, she is other girl, but he doesn't like her much no more – he loves me now.'

Unable to take any more of this, I slammed the phone down.

Slowly but painfully, after more calls from Tony I learned that Ken really had got on the wrong side of the Kosovan Mafia and if he didn't pay some of the money now due to them both he and Tony could lose their lives. I tried my hardest to find Ken, but to no avail. The last I heard he had made his way back to Spain via Bulgaria and Tony had handed the restaurant over to the Mafia.

After the Kosovo fiasco Ken returned to Spain to live with his parents, who had settled there. Obviously too ashamed to phone me, he made no contact – not even to thank me for sending the money.

As for me, it was time to take stock. My marriage was well and truly over and both *Barbara* and *Crossroads* had ended, one after the other. Meanwhile, I was tired, disillusioned and hurting. Things couldn't get any worse, I felt, until one day when I washed my hair and discovered a clump of it had come out in my hand. I rushed to a doctor, who told me that I had alopecia as a result of stress.

The break-up of my marriage had taken everything I had, it seemed – even my hair.

Chapter Twenty-Four

It was while I was at my lowest ebb in 2003 that I made the crazy decision to go and visit Ken in Spain. Keeley came too and somehow I managed to convince myself that we were going so that she could see her grandparents, but the truth is I wanted to see Ken one more time. Even now, I'm not sure why I felt the need to see him. Perhaps just to ask why and finally achieve some kind of peace between us.

Unfortunately I was not in a good state. As I have already mentioned, my hair was starting to fall out and so I had extensions to try and disguise it. Also, I had put on more weight than usual. Of course, I was worn out and hurting from everything that had happened and all the revelations. The shock had hit me hard and I felt I was only just surviving, yet I had never once confronted Ken or made him answer to anyone: I'd let him walk away from all responsibilities to his daughter and me, not to mention his debts.

So, did I say any of this? Did I hell!

Keeley and I stayed in a hotel, where Ken came to meet me while his parents spent some time with their granddaughter.

'Now, don't let's discuss things – I don't want to get into all that, it's over,' he told me.

And I agreed with him. How insane was that? My first mistake was in going there at all and my second was to let him off the hook. What was the point in going over everything – the affairs, the money and all the heartache? Of course I had every reason to do so, but I had never confronted him before and in my low state I didn't have the strength to start then.

To add insult to injury, Ken began to comment on my appearance.

'I've got to say, you're not looking great, Sherrie,' he told me. 'You've always been such a good-looking woman, but you've lost your looks. I'm only telling you this for your own good and because I still love you in my own way.'

Why do people do that? Putting someone down while pretending to be 'helpful'. What a load of s*** it is!

And things did not improve the next day when I agreed to meet up with Ken and his parents. They were looking very strained and I couldn't help but wonder what he might have said to them.

That night I foolishly met up with Ken again, this time in a bar. I couldn't help it – I still wanted to tell him the things I'd never said. Pathetically, I tried to do my hair as best I could, wore what I thought was pretty, and I was careful with my make-up. I wanted him to see an attractive person, not the broken-down, dreary woman I felt I'd become. It wasn't that I wanted him back – I didn't – but I still wanted him to care. After all, we'd been together for twenty-seven years and I suppose I still hoped that I could salvage a little pride and dignity from the wreck of our relationship and that we could part as friends.

Sadly, the reality couldn't have been more different. On that last evening together Ken inflicted one last parting shot that really hurt and shocked me to the core. He mentioned a long-standing friend of ours, asked how she was and added, 'She was always very hot, she's never let herself go – *I* should know!' I didn't want to know what he was implying. I left it at that.

As Ken strolled up to the bar to pay, I walked out into the night. I had no idea where I was going, I just wanted it all to stop – I'd had enough. I knew we were close to the motorway and so I walked slowly towards it, filled with pain and sadness and a terrible sense of loss. I had tried so hard and for so long to make my marriage work, but suddenly it all seemed completely pointless.

For a split second I seriously contemplated throwing myself into the traffic, but luckily there was an eight-foot fence between the motorway and me. As I stood staring at it, I thought, What are you doing, Sherrie? You have a beautiful daughter just starting out in the world and she needs you. Why would you let him drive you to this? He's not worth it. And so I turned back, collected Keeley from her grandparents and caught the first plane out of there.

When I got home, Ken sent a card, saying, 'So wonderful to see you. Let's see how the next few years go. Maybe in 2010 we can be together again'. I tore the card into tiny pieces and tossed them in the bin. But I can't say life suddenly became easy after that – far from it, in fact. I had to face financial meltdown, battle my way back to health, come to terms with being alone and take a long, hard look at my life and the choices I'd made. However, I never again thought about suicide (I was ashamed of that) and I made up my mind to live and to enjoy and appreciate all the good things in my life. I also realised how lucky I was to have such a fantastic daughter and family around me – never again would I be that selfish. And within weeks of my decision something came along that was to become such an important, wise, funny and special part of my life.

Not that I knew it when the phone rang that spring day, back April 2003. It was my agent.

'You are being asked to become a Loose Woman!' he announced, matter of factly.

'*Really?*' I said. 'In what way "loose"?'

'It's a daytime magazine show called *Loose Women* – four women discussing the day's news, men, life ... that sort of thing,' he explained.

'Oh, *that* kind of "loose" – gossip, chat, women's talk? I can do that – I do it every day, anyway!' I laughed.

'*Exactly!*' he said. 'I think it's right up your street, Sherrie.'

I had to confess I hadn't watched the show. At the time I was still working on *Crossroads* from 6.30 in the morning to eight every night, so I seldom had the chance to see any daytime TV.

'It's a great show,' my agent continued. 'It's going to be filmed in Norwich and they want to see you.'

It seemed that Karl Newton, the producer, had phoned my agent and said he'd followed my career for years, knew my work well and thought I might make a good 'Loose Woman'. So, off I went to meet Karl at the London studios and do what I guess was a kind of audition with several different presenters plus the anchor, Kaye Adams. This was something I had never tried before: it wasn't an acting job and the idea was to be myself and hopefully be entertaining, chatty and funny.

Kaye introduced topics and we all had our say on them. I decided that I would just be honest and say what I really thought. Soon I began to thoroughly enjoy myself.

I was trying to look reasonably composed, sitting on a stool beside the others, all of us behind some kind of desk, when suddenly one of the legs on my stool buckled, then gave way and broke. Having flailed about windmill-like for a moment or so, the inevitable happened. I landed with a bump on my backside on the studio floor, all of which was captured on tape.

I thought it was hilarious and I couldn't stop laughing. As I explained to the others afterwards, things like that just seem to happen to me so often – I've had so many on-screen calamities that Dennis Norden once told me he had more out-takes on me than anybody else in the business! When he retired, he sent me a tape of them all plus a personal letter to thank me for providing him with such good material for his show and a beautiful silver star.

I once appeared on *Pebble Mill*, the lunchtime talk show, and having smiled at the audience from the top step as I made my entrance, I fell down the other six, to the consternation of the presenter, Judi Spiers. She rushed over to help me, tripped and fell on top of me! And I did the same thing on Dale Winton's show. There was a door through which his guest was supposed to make an entrance. As he announced, 'Ladies and gentlemen, welcome my favourite person in all the world, Sherrie Hewson!' I opened the door and fell out onto the set – thankfully, with nothing worse than a bruise or two.

On another occasion I appeared on *This Morning* to help with a cookery feature. Before the take I had said that I didn't believe the ovens were real – I was convinced it was all pretend. I was assured they were real, but I still thought they were having me on. Anyway, all I had to do was talk to Susan Brooks, the cook presenting the feature, and then go to one of the ovens and take out a cake.

When it was time to do my piece, live on the show, Susan said, 'OK, Sherrie, go and get the cake out of the oven.' As I opened the oven door, the heat was intense. Picking up the cake was difficult enough, but holding onto it proved impossible. I dropped the whole thing on the floor and spent the rest of the time on my knees, throwing pieces of cake to Susan. We were laughing so much that we couldn't go on with the item.

There was another of what I call my 'moments' on *Ready Steady Cook*, this time with the lovely Ainsley Harriott. I was wearing quite high-heeled boots and in the middle of cooking I decided to take them off because I couldn't work very well in heels. As I bent down, Ainsley asked what I was doing. As I straightened up to explain, I accidentally knocked over a bag of sugar, which fell off the work surface. As I tried to catch the bag it sprayed sugar all over the floor, which I then slipped on. I ended up flat on the floor and Ainsley was beside himself with laughter – he couldn't continue and had to stop filming.

On *Corrie* I had a string of mishaps, starting with that memorable first scene in which a stool bounced me onto the shop counter. Then there was the time when I walked into the shop with Ken Morley, tripped and fell on my back. As he came over to help me up, I accidentally kneed him in the balls. Poor man, he was in agony! But that wasn't as bad as the scene I did with Kevin Kennedy, who played Curly Watts. He was sitting on a sofa and I was supposed to be drinking red wine (we used Ribena). I got so carried away that I actually felt drunk. Instead of gently lowering myself into his arms as I was supposed to do, I misjudged it and dive-bombed so that my knee landed right between his legs. However, I didn't realise what I'd done and poor Kevin couldn't speak – he had tears in his eyes. I thought what a good actor he was, showing so much emotion. It was only later when we had finished the scene and he managed to squeak, 'I'm going to kill you!' that I realised he was in agony.

I could go on – the list is endless – but the good news was that, having tumbled off the stool in my *Loose Women* audition,

I was promptly offered the job. I was delighted because I knew it was something I would enjoy and the timing was perfect as *Crossroads* and *Barbara* were just ending.

When I joined *Loose Women* the show had been running in different guises for a while. At one stage it was renamed *Live Talk*, and a new team came in to revamp it when the name was changed back to *Loose Women*. I joined just as the programme was beginning to make a name for itself, and right from the start I was convinced I'd landed somewhere that felt good. Carol McGiffin was on the team and we soon became good friends. I love her honesty and quirky humour. In the beginning I felt a bit intimidated by her – not because she's almost six foot tall, but because she's a strong character and a highly intelligent woman. In time all that changed – *not* Carol being intelligent, just our relationship, although sometimes I wonder. I'm only joking, Carol! *Loose Women* (and Carol, in particular) taught me that us women have to stop underselling ourselves and playing the martyr while letting others undermine us.

What I loved about the show (and still do) was that, as well as commenting on the stories and issues of the day and interviewing guests, we talked about ourselves and our own lives: the good, the bad and the downright embarrassing. At the beginning this did take some getting used to because it's not the same as acting a part. You're being yourself and that can be liberating and scary, exciting and nerve-racking at the same time. For some of us it's almost like therapy. Often I receive messages on Facebook or Twitter saying, 'I'm glad you mentioned that today,' or 'I've just been through the same as you,' and even 'You've made me feel so much better.' We thrash out so many different problems, some hard to face on your own, and it's good to know there are people who care – not just my fellow panellists but the millions of viewers, too.

Almost from the start I received some lovely press coverage. One paper said, 'Sherrie Hewson: eccentric actress can always be relied upon to offer a unique point of view'. Another wrote, 'The off-the-wall panellist has been a hit with the *Loose Women* audience, thanks to her quirky outlook and self-deprecating sense of humour.' I liked that – it was as though I had found exactly the right niche, somewhere I could really be myself and be appreciated for just being me.

We've always had amazing celebrity guests on the show, such as Robbie Williams, Neil Sedaka, Bette Midler, Bryan Ferry and Jackie and Joan Collins. In the early days one of my favourites was singer David Essex, who has since been on several more times. The last time I'd seen him was when he was in *Godspell* at the Roundhouse and I was a student at RADA, watching him with Bob Lindsay. Thirty years on he was just as sexy and gorgeous.

When we went to the commercial break he leaned over to me and whispered, 'Could you not mention that I've just become a granddad because that won't be good for my image? Somehow rock stars and granddads don't go together – goodness knows what the fans would think if they knew!'

'Of course,' I told him. 'I won't say a thing.'

We came back from the break and were chatting about this and that when David suddenly astonished me by turning to the audience and saying, 'I just want to say to everybody out there that I've just become a granddad.'

'Hey,' I said, 'I thought you told me not to mention that?'

'I know,' he replied, 'but I suddenly feel so proud of my daughter and my grandchild.'

And that did it for me: I fell in love with him all over again. He really was the sweetest man.

But the man who has become my dearest friend on the show is Karl Newton, the producer who first rang my agent and asked me to come along for an audition. From the start we've had a lovely friendship. Karl is a visionary: one of the team behind the revamp, he rose from way down in the pecking order to become an executive producer. He's a brilliant programme-maker who can really see into the future: he took *Loose Women* and moulded the series into what it has become today – a hugely popular show that attracts excellent ratings every weekday.

Not everyone loves *Loose Women*, but thousands watch the show and talk about it. The internet buzzes with chat forums asking questions like 'Is *Loose Women* a triumph for feminism or a disgrace to women?' and that's what I love about the programme – it can be controversial, funny, clever and informative, all at the same time.

It was Karl who instinctively knew how the show should develop and just how honest we girls on the panel should be, and he knew there should never be any scripted material or acting – it's all genuine, off-the-cuff reaction and interaction.

As well as admiring Karl, I absolutely adore him. He has become a most loyal friend and colleague and I have so much to thank him for. As far as I'm concerned, for the last ten years he has run the world for me, and since he left *Loose Women* in late 2010 I have missed him terribly. I'm so grateful to him not just for thinking of me and bringing me onto the show, but for all the help he has given me with my personal life. Throughout the last few years Karl has been patient and supportive – he's always helped me out, given me advice and picked me up when I was down.

I think he came to regard me as a second mum, which is a great honour for me. I have even been on holiday with him – we went to Thailand together for Carol's 50th birthday, which was amazing. If I'd had a son, I would have loved him to be just like Karl.

In 2005, when Keeley turned 21, I gave her a birthday party at The Mulberry in Conwy, north Wales – the restaurant and bar my brother Brett had bought. We had indoor rockets, 600 pink balloons, magicians, singers and a stretch Hummer to take us there. Karl and all the production staff came from London and Karl's dad, Clifford Newton, and his niece, Charlotte Jones, came too. His dad had such a great time and I felt very close to him – he was kind and loving, also extremely funny and much like my own dad. I'm so pleased he came, especially as he died not long afterwards – Karl and I have such fond memories of him at the party.

Loose Women picked me up and put me back on my feet after the heartbreak and fallout of my marriage breakdown. If ever there was a time when I wondered if I would laugh again … Well, the show soon proved to me not only could I still laugh, I could also be outrageous, go out on the town, flash my knickers like Carol (or my Spanx like Denise Welch!), or just relax with Jane McDonald, with her cup of tea and pork pie. We've had some fantastic times and I love and cherish everyone on the show, behind as well as in front of the cameras.

As mentioned, I joined the panel of *Loose Women* in April 2003, just as *Crossroads* was coming to an end. On average, I have appeared three times a week from the start and it's an hour-long lunchtime show. Although this didn't leave me a lot of time, I still continued to be offered acting roles.

One of my closest friends in *Crossroads* was Lucy Pargeter, who played Helen Raven, my daughter. She also appeared in *Emmerdale* as Chas (Chastity) Dingle, a loud-mouthed, in-your-face barmaid. After *Crossroads* was axed Lucy called and said, 'Sherrie, come up to Leeds for dinner and meet Steve Frost, the *Emmerdale* producer.' So, up I went to Manchester and booked in at the Malmaison before going out for dinner that night with

Lucy, Steve and his wife Hayley, whom I also knew from *Crossroads*.

One of the rules I try and stick to is not drinking when social occasions are anything to do with business. That night, however, proved to be an exception. The evening began at seven and continued until five in the morning. In ten hours a fair amount of alcohol was consumed and all I can recall is that when morning came I felt extremely ill. I remember sitting on the bathroom floor, trying to focus through a fog and groaning, 'Oh *God*, I'm never going to be able to get out of this hotel!' Worse than feeling like death warmed up, however, was the realisation that I couldn't remember a single thing from the night before. What did I say, or do? I tried to think, but all I could remember was being in the restaurant and then in the nightclub – the rest was a complete blank.

I didn't hear from Steve Frost, so I spent the next week worrying and wondering whether I'd done something awful, like pole dancing or playing strip-poker – now that would have got the local dogs barking. But no, my memory was frustratingly (and perhaps mercifully) blank. Unable to stand the suspense, I sent a text to Lucy, saying, 'Put me out of my misery! What did I say or do that night?'

'Don't ask me!' the answer came back. 'I've no idea. I can't remember a thing.'

At least it wasn't just me then, but as I was the one being considered for a job I really should have been on my best behaviour. Thankfully, my worst fears were unfounded. A few days later Steve asked me to audition for a part in *Emmerdale*, Britain's second longest-running soap after *Coronation Street*.

On arrival, I discovered that I was one of five actresses competing for the role of Lesley Meredith, the unscrupulous mother of lovable fishmonger Simon. It's always daunting to be up against good competition, and the other four were all successful actresses, whom I really admired. When Steve called to say he would love me to play Lesley, I was thrilled – it was a hat trick, my third soap!

The next time I saw Steve I took a deep breath then plucked up the courage and asked him, 'I have to ask you, did I do or say anything outrageous that night when we went out?'

'Don't ask *me*!' he said, laughing. 'I don't remember a thing about it.'

In June 2004 I joined the cast of *Emmerdale*. My son Simon was played by Dale Meeks – such a good actor, a really lovely man and a joy to work with – in fact, we got on so well that he became yet another contender for the 'Son I Never Had' award. We're still friends and when he rings me he always says, 'Hi Mam, how are you?' Such a sweetheart!

I had a really good time in *Emmerdale* and it wasn't quite so pressurised as *Coronation Street*, where we could hardly breathe for journalists lying in wait. *Emmerdale* has its own loyal following and is full of excellent actors and great production staff. Anyone who joins the cast is welcomed wholeheartedly. However, in some ways the pressure is just the same as in *The Street*, with no time to learn lines, rehearse or take direction. Instant acting, we call it. Just as in *Corrie*, the cast deliver brilliant performances, day after day. I had my favourites, such as Mark Charnock (Marlon Dingle) and Dominic Brunt (Paddy Kirk) and of course Lucy Pargeter and Charlie Webb (Debbie Dingle), but they were all lovely.

Lesley Meredith was the interfering mum who comes to stay and disapproves of her son's choice of girlfriend. Eventually she ends up running his company into the ground, then steals the money and runs off with an old flame. I really enjoyed the role, which lasted for two and a half years until early 2006.

After the break-up with Ken, I felt I needed a change of scene and so I relocated to a house on Conwy Marina, North Wales, with Keeley. I moved there to be close to my brother Brett, who had gone there with his family to run The Mulberry. Although I really liked living in Wales, once I got the job on *Emmerdale* I had to make a journey to Leeds that was at least two and a half hours there and the same back (I only stayed overnight in Leeds if I was filming into the evening).

At the time I was also commuting to Norwich to do *Loose Women* and so all the travelling became quite exhausting. I decided to leave Wales and rent a house in Pudsey, near Leeds. As the local saying goes, 'The birds fly backwards because of the dust,' although to be fair I think that comes from when there were pits in the area. Anyway, it's a lovely little place.

Then Keeley met a wonderful man and fell in love. Simon was a property developer, and right from the start I could see that he really cared about my daughter and would look after her. He came from Lancashire, where he was building his own house, so Keeley moved there to live with him. When she and Simon told me they were expecting their first child in 2006 my time on *Emmerdale* had already come to an end and so I moved to a remote little cottage in Ashley, Cheshire. I'm not sure why – to be close to nature? Or perhaps it was just those lovely country pubs.

By this time my finances were beginning to go into meltdown. For years I'd been shelling out cash and I simply couldn't keep up with all the loan repayments. I felt very vulnerable where I was and I didn't want my landlord to know that I was in trouble. Unsure of what to do, I met the most wonderful lady called Anne just by chance. She lived in a beautiful old nunnery, not far from Keeley. We started to talk and I felt compelled to tell her my life story, which is strange as I would never normally talk so openly to a stranger. She offered me sanctuary in her beautiful house until I found my own home. There was, and still is, something very tranquil and serene about Anne – I knew I'd met someone special. In the end I stayed with her for several months, and I believe she healed things in me at that time and gave me the strength to cope with what was to come.

After staying with Anne, I made the decision to move into a house down the road from Keeley and Simon. It was wonderful to see my daughter so happy and settled and I was thrilled at the thought of having a grandchild.

Loose Women had now moved from Norwich to London, so I could easily shoot down to the ITV studios for my appearances but be back in Lancashire by teatime. Around this time, I was offered the part of Martha Brewster in the wonderful play, *Arsenic and Old Lace*. It was to tour (something I had never done) and also starred Louise Jameson as Abby Brewster, while Wayne Sleep played Dr Einstein. In such great company, it seemed like a lovely opportunity and who would have thought that 35 years later I'd be reunited with my former flatmate.

Both Louise and I needed to age to our mid-70s and I even had to wear a fat suit with a white wig and horn-rimmed glasses. Just imagine it, I looked gorgeous! The tour was going well and in October 2006 we were appearing in Lincoln when I received a call to say Keeley had gone into labour. I'd just got to the theatre and so I said to the stage manager, 'Sorry, my baby's having her baby – I have to go to her!' and promptly left. I drove like a crazy person and got to the hospital a few hours later – and that's where we stayed for the next three days until Oliver decided to appear. He took his time, but he was worth it – my grandson is the most beautiful boy in the world.

It was an extraordinary feeling, to see my child become a mum and to have another little person join our family. Keeley took to motherhood with real joy and I have been a besotted Nana from the moment I laid eyes on my Ollie.

At this time my hair was still falling out, but I'd finally given in and started to wear wigs. I wore them on the tour, on *Loose Women*, and now I'd been asked to return to *Coronation Street*, so I knew that I would have to wear one for that, too. And as my hair fell out, my confidence plummeted.

As for *Coronation Street*, I still had great affection for the show and the people I'd worked with there, so I was thrilled to make a return visit. The story was that Maureen married Bill Webster in Germany. He had returned to Coronation Street to visit his family and Maureen decides to come over for Christmas to surprise him. The trouble is, she doesn't know that Bill is in the midst of a torrid affair with Audrey Roberts (Sue Nicholls). When all is revealed by David Platt (busy stirring up trouble), Maureen is left heartbroken and returns to Germany alone. I loved every second of it, especially working with Jack P. Shephard, the actor who played the evil David Platt.

Of course I would have loved it had Maureen been brought back for longer, but it was not to be. Even so, it was a real pleasure to reappear in those two episodes – even if I did have to disappear just as before in the back of a taxi.

Chapter Twenty-Five

While many good things had happened to me since I parted from Ken, the fallout from our collapsed restaurant business and the money I had subsequently given him for the ventures in Spain and Kosovo continued. Although I was still earning, there was not enough money to repay the debts I had been left with, and in 2007 I took the decision to declare bankruptcy.

It wasn't an easy decision by any means, but by this time my debt repayments had risen to £12,000 a month, which was ridiculous and more than I could possibly manage. It had reached the point where I felt I was going mad. As ever, Keeley was extremely supportive and my friend Bobby Gee (from Bucks Fizz) helped me a lot, but at the end of the day I knew bankruptcy was inevitable – no one could sustain the amount of overheads I had.

I took advice from several experts and some suggested an IVA (Individual Voluntary Arrangement), which is an alternative to bankruptcy. Others recommended borrowing from friends on a fixed interest rate, but those in the know told me the best way forward was to declare bankruptcy and relieve myself of all the pressure. With hindsight, I'm not so sure this was the best choice: bankruptcy proved to be a gruelling experience with enormous repercussions. Since then I've learned a good deal, and would almost certainly handle things very differently now. In those days I didn't even know the rudimentary workings of a court or debt collection, let alone my legal rights, and so when the court-appointed bankruptcy administrator insisted I hand over my Mini at a certain time on a certain day to two men in macs, that's exactly what I did – and it was a shocking experience.

Of course Ken was liable for the debts, too, but I chose to carry the burden myself. Looking back, this was also crazy. The main reason for this was that Ken's mum was not well at the time – he didn't really keep me informed about her illness, though. She was still living in Spain with his dad and I didn't want them to be upset or frightened by a knock on the door from bailiffs looking for Ken – they would have been so ashamed.

To be bankrupt, I discovered, is like suffering from some dreadful contagious disease. Take my advice, as someone who has already been there: never tell people if it should happen to you. If you do, you'll see a change come over them almost instantaneously. One minute they'll be laughing and joking with you, the next they will be backing away or, worse still, feeling sorry for you. All right, maybe I'm exaggerating a little, but believe me, those people you tell about your bankruptcy would far rather you didn't talk about it and some of them won't even want to be around you just in case they get it themselves. Saying that, my friend and fellow actor Gary Webster went through the same thing and was very helpful to me (I didn't tell people about my troubles and only talked about the bankruptcy if they happened to find out). Sadly, in these tough times bankruptcy is becoming the only option for a lot of people, and while the stigma is nowhere near as bad as it once was it's still a very difficult thing for anyone to go through.

I thought I was being very discreet when I chose to go to Wales to declare myself bankrupt. Hoping against hope that no one would recognise me, I arrived at the court wearing no make-up and dark glasses plus a long coat with the collar turned up and a flat cap. I looked like a demented version of Andy Capp. Having waited in my car until I was absolutely sure the coast was clear, I slid out of the driver's seat, keeping low. In this strange, crouched posture I shuffled towards the court entrance. As the coat now covered my feet, I must have looked like one of those stuffed animals on wheels. But I couldn't see where I was going and as a result I bumped into a bollard just outside the main doors, hitting my knee with such a thud that it brought tears to my eyes. Never mind, I thought, at least no one will point and say, 'It's Maureen from *Corrie*!'

I reached the reception and, glancing up cautiously, I spotted a wall with a sliding window in it. Feeling quite pleased with myself since the disguise seemed to have worked, I straightened up and looked around. Thankfully no one else was waiting, and so I stepped over to the open window. At this point the lady clerk seated behind the desk turned, saw me and said, 'Oh, hello, Maureen! Fancy seeing you here.'

My humiliation was complete.

Scarlet with embarrassment, I explained what I was there for. 'Oh yes,' the clerk said. 'Here it is – Mrs Sherrie Boyd, the bankrupt state of, case number 07.'

And so I had become a case number, something I was to remain for the next three years.

A short time later I was summoned to enter a small room. Inside was just a desk and a telephone, which rang as soon as I entered. As there was nobody else there, I realised the call had to be for me and so I picked it up. It felt like *Big Brother*.

'Hello?' I said.

'This is your Court Official speaking,' replied a man's voice. 'Please state your name and address.'

After I had done so, he outlined my duties and commitments to the court, then asked me for a telephone number where I could be contacted at any given moment.

'When you have seen the judge,' he went on to explain, 'I will need to speak to you again to tell you how the next three years will unfold. I can arrange that meeting now, if you wish, or we can do it over the phone.'

'Over the phone, please,' I said.

So far it hadn't been too bad. From there I was directed up a rather stark staircase, all very 1970s with lots of brown paint. At the very top was a long, bleak corridor with a few chairs lined up against the wall. A sign suggested I should sit and wait and warned that if there was any disturbance or threatening behaviour, then I would be removed from the building forthwith. And so I sat and waited, feeling very alone and highly ashamed, yet all the while knowing that I was only partially responsible for the mess I was in. I wanted to say out loud, 'This isn't my fault – I'm not the perpetrator of this mess! It was *his* fault. I'm just taking the rap, Guv,' but there was no one within earshot and even if there had been they would probably have said, 'Yeah, yeah – they all say that!'

Moments later a glass door swished open and a slight, grey-suited woman with a kind face appeared. 'Mrs S. Boyd, case number 07?' she asked. There it was again, that case number.

She disappeared, with another swish of the door closing behind her. Suddenly, it occurred to me this was the same noise that the *Starship Enterprise* makes and the thought made me laugh out loud. Still smiling, I followed her through the doors.

'I hardly think this is a laughing matter,' a voice from inside the room muttered as the door closed behind me with another swish.

I was in a courtroom with a long wooden desk and in front of it rows and rows of wooden benches. That must be where the jury sits, I thought. And the large chairs to left and right were for the Prosecution and Defence.

'Are you coming in, Mrs Boyd?' asked the same voice.

'Oh, yes,' I walked forward. 'Case number 07,' I added helpfully.

There was a grunt from the rather stern-looking man sitting behind the desk.

'Sit down. Let's get this over with,' he said gruffly. It sounded as if what he meant was 'I have better things to do.'

Me too, I thought, tears filling my eyes.

All the courtroom dramas on TV have big fans on the ceiling, raised platforms for the judge's bench and a judge sporting a red gown, a white wig and a black square hat and ready to condemn the likes of me to the firing squad. But this courtroom was bare, bleak and colourless. The judge was equally disappointing, wearing only a grey suit and tie.

'Mrs Boyd, please sit down,' he told me. 'I have to be at the vet's in ten minutes.'

Ah, he did have better things to do. I felt like saying, 'While you're there, I know a pair of testicles that need chopping off – in fact, you're about to read about that very person!' Of course I didn't say it – I didn't have the balls, and that would have made two of us, if you think about it.

So the judge opened the file to dissect my life and discover the reasons why I was sitting in the cold, unforgiving courtroom.

He flicked through two pages of what looked like a 20-page document, then took his glasses off, looked at me and harrumphed.

'Let me tell you a story,' he said, closing the file.

This took me completely by surprise and I stared at him as he continued, 'Young girl meets boy, falls in love, knowing the boy is wrong for her, takes no notice of her instincts or her mother, organises the wedding, the house, the baby, everything … She works all her life, trusting this man whom she knows is untrustworthy and probably unfaithful. She never checks what's happening to her money, becomes famous, the man enjoying the fame and the money. Years go by, the cracks show, the man disappears and she is left with nothing as he has manipulated her whole life. She wakes up too late …' He glanced at me before adding, 'It's the oldest story in the book.'

By this time I was in floods of tears. In a softer tone he said, 'It's going to be fine – no one will know about this. It's not as if you're in Manchester, is it?'

Little did he know, the jungle drums could easily pass the message over hundreds of miles, especially if someone might make a few bucks from selling the story. The judge might have been a little glib, perhaps, but he was also honest and understanding, for which I was grateful. Our meeting was over in well under the ten minutes he had available: he told me that I could go, and so I went back downstairs to sign a document entitled 'The Bankrupt Estate of Mrs S Boyd, (and yes, you've guessed it) case number 07'.

Once the whole miserable business was over, I went home. I felt subdued and humiliated, but resigned to my fate. The repercussions were enormous, however – I had to learn to live with no bank or credit cards, no cheque book and initially no bank account. In other words, everything had to be cash – which can be pretty awkward these days. On the other hand, it's a great way to see what you actually spend. Having to hand over cash for everything really does stop you buying things.

You can't do everything with cash, though: I needed a bank account, if only to pay my household bills. I was told of one High Street bank that will give you a simple account with a cash card only and so I went along to see if I could open an account. Sitting in the waiting area, I felt like a criminal coming up before the parole board. I hoped to be seen by someone discreet, sympathetic and experienced.

'Mrs Boyd?'

It was the voice of a child. I swung round to be confronted by a scrawny young boy, who looked very unsure. First he directed me to a small table with two chairs in the middle of the bank, where everyone could see and hear us. He then opened a notebook, which I was sure he must have brought with him from school. He had three angry-looking spots on his face and a red nose – clearly, he must have had a cold and so I suppose he wasn't having the best of days either.

'What can we do for you?' he asked.

Before I could answer, he dived for his trouser pocket and dragged out a handkerchief, which was followed by a packet of Smarties that spilt all over the floor. I helped him pick them up.

'I need a bank account, please,' I told him once we were back on track.

'A bank account?' the child repeated.

'Yes,' I said, 'you know, this being a bank.'

'In that case I will have to ask you a series of questions,' he said, looking increasingly nervous. 'Er, I'll have to go and find them. Just hang on a minute, please.'

Thankfully, the boy disappeared only to be replaced by a kinder-looking and definitely more mature gentleman.

'Mrs Boyd?' he asked. 'I'm so sorry – Mr Jenkins is new, he's only been with us for a couple of weeks. We're very short-staffed and you slipped through our professional net. Let me start again.'

Big smiles. He started to go through the basic questions – address, age, work, etc. – but as he got to questions about my financial history my hands started to sweat. I knew the question I dreaded most was coming up.

'Have you ever declared bankruptcy?'

He didn't even look up, he was expecting an instant no. When I didn't reply, he raised his eyes to me, his pen still hovering over the form, and started to tap.

'Yes,' I said quietly.

He glanced at me with a pitying smile and I so wanted to squash that smile all over his face.

'Well, Mrs Boyd ...' he said, before some coughing, 'you can have an account, but you can't have a bank card, a cheque book, a credit card, an overdraft or a loan of any sort. No credit. You can have a cash card, which you can only use to withdraw cash. Is that clear, Mrs Boyd?'

At 56, with a long and wonderful career behind me, I accepted the paperwork he handed me with which to claim my cash-only card. Following this, I said a stiff goodbye, walked out to my car and wept like a baby with the humiliation of it all. As I dried my eyes, I looked up and saw what I thought was a parking ticket on my windscreen. Suddenly blind with rage, I got out of the car and grabbed the wretched thing, only to see it was an invitation to, 'Call Suzanne, make yourself £50 a night and more, learn to be a nude pole dancer!'

For a split second I thought about it, but at my age, I reckoned, I'd probably have to pay *them* – and what about the thread veins and cellulite? Yuck, get that image out of your head right now! I then travelled home, feeling sadder, wiser and wistful for the days when money wasn't a problem and life seemed so much less complicated.

Needless to say, because I am in the public eye it proved impossible to keep my bankruptcy a secret. In October 2007 it made a full-page splash in the *News of the World*. Under the headline,

EXCLUSIVE: BUBBLE BURSTS FOR SOAP LEGEND TV SHERRIE: STAR BANKRUPT AFTER 30 YEARS ON BOX

the copy apparently supplied by 'a pal' of mine read: 'I took one of the toughest decisions of my life. I declared myself bankrupt before my creditors could. I have a lot of creditors. I feel terrible about it, but people will just have to hold their breath while I work things out. I have lost the lot and am back at square one after working 30-odd years. But so be it – I'm determined not to let this break me.'

I felt stripped naked and completely exposed – and still do so at times. However I dress it up, this has been a sobering experience: a leveller, an eye-opener, a wake-up call, call it what you will. For me it's been a stomach-churning time – a time when I was forced to face my worst fears. I describe it as my 'wildebeest moment'. You know the moment when the lion chases the poor wildebeest, who has stopped a little too long to take a drink without realising all his pals have gone? When it looks up, there's an 'Oh, no!' moment before it starts to run. You see the whites of its eyes followed by the dreaded slow-motion shot when the lion grabs the poor beast by the flanks and sinks its claws in. I've read that in that moment God provides the poor dying creature with the ability to release some sort of drug from its brain that renders it anaesthetised. In my despair I felt that God had forgotten me and left me flailing about, wounded.

Of course I would have coped better had the so-called 'pal' not sold my story to a tabloid. As it was, the story included so many wrong details that it hurt not only me, but also my family. After reading it, I felt I had no choice but to give another interview to put the record straight. With the help of my agent I chose *Hello!* magazine and they published a really honest factual piece, but it didn't stop my tears of frustration at knowing the other story was still out there and being discussed and quoted *ad nauseam*.

These days I've discovered that being bankrupt is rather like those moments when you're abroad and you meet someone from your home town. The conversation goes like this:

'Where are you from?'

'Nottingham.'

'Oh, my *God*! I'm from there!'

When it comes to bankruptcy, it's: 'So, you're bankrupt? Oh, my *God*! So am I. What a coincidence! Where did you declare? Oh, no, *not* Wales! Oh, my *God*! So did I.' You exchange phone numbers, arrange a dinner date – practically agree to go to bed with them – all because they've had a wildebeest moment too.

We all have words we don't like saying. For me, they include 'snot', 'bogey', 'nipples', 'crotch', 'penis', 'toilet', 'tax man' – and now 'bankrupt'. Just the word makes me go all sweaty. What more can I say, other than that I've been in enough plays about Churchill to know that one of his most frequently quoted sayings is: 'When you're going through hell, keep going.'

Well,Winston ... I've been there, I kept going and I have to say I hated every minute of it.

Chapter Twenty-Six

Having been through all of that and come out the other end still standing, I'm very aware of how lucky I am: I have a truly wonderful family, my health and a brilliant job, which I love.

In fact, *Loose Women* – the show I have been a part of for eight years now – has gone from strength to strength. In 2004 filming moved from Norwich to the London studios, where we've been ever since. The panel in Norwich had been Kaye Adams, Carol McGiffin, Kerry Katona and me. In London it changed, as Kerry went off to do other things and Karl became the editor, with great plans for the show. We all liked and trusted him, and we knew we were in safe hands.

As the show evolved and more women joined the panel, we started to gain recognition and respect. We could be frivolous, crazy, hard-hitting and poignant, but we still had to keep on proving ourselves as a vehicle worthy of a permanent slot on ITV. It took quite a few years to gain that status, and Karl fought long and hard for us. Always innovative and original, what he did worked. The show took hold and the nation loved it – they might shout at it and have a go, but they watched the programme and they could see we loved doing it.

All of the girls are larger-than-life characters. It's a bit like a soap – you may like one more than another or disagree with one of them or sympathise with someone. Whatever you think, you always want to know what they are saying. As I said earlier, I liked Carol from the start. Her mum was terminally ill when we first met and Carol was going through a very tough time, which she dealt with bravely and with such dignity. On the show she was opinionated and political, but always funny. Kaye used to be the anchor: bright, feisty and formidable, she kept us all in line. Coleen Nolan joined us and was often non-committal about her opinions in the most hilarious way, at the same time very bright and extremely aware.

By 2007 the show was being broadcast all year round, apart from a brief break at Christmas and a longer one in the summer. Kaye left to have a baby and Andrea McLean and Jackie Brambles took over the job of anchor, sharing it between them. When Jackie left in 2009, Kate Thornton joined us. Along the way the panel was joined by Lynda Bellingham, Zoe Tyler, Denise Welch, Jane McDonald, Lesley Garrett, Lisa Maxwell, Sarah Millican and the hilarious Cilla Black (who is great on a night out, by the way – in fact, it's hard to keep up with her!).

We are asked to do all sorts of things. Carol and I trained dogs, I went off to train as a hairdresser at Toni & Guy (remember that hairdressing dream I had?), Carol and I had a liver test (to see if Carol still had one!) and then Carol, Denise, Lisa and I travelled to New York to make a *Loose Women* DVD and follow the trail of the *Sex in the City* girls. Now that was an amazing experience. One day I lost the others and ended up wandering around New York. I was accosted by a lady who lured me into her shop, gave me a candle and a crystal to hold and told me I had lived in the sixteenth century, died when I was 20 years old and my spirit had been wandering ever since. She added that if I gave her $400 she could save me. As Karl said, when he eventually found me, 'It could only happen to you, Sherrie!' Another adventure with Karl was when, in 2009, along with our series editor Emily, I was asked to make up a panel for our competition to find a new Loose Woman. That brought us the lovely Rachel Agnew, who has been a great addition to the show.

Another time I was sent to the States to interview Helen Mirren and Bruce Willis for a new film, and while I was there I went to Las Vegas to join the Stiletto Spy School. It seemed like a fun idea, but when I got there I found myself working with ex-mercenaries, wearing camouflage combat clothes and pretending to be in a war zone.

Loose Women has been amazing for me, and Carol is a true friend. Last year, along with Karl, we went to Thailand for her 50th birthday. One night, Karl and I went out for dinner with two lovely boys we had met there, and I decided to splash out on some nice wine. I didn't really understand the local currency (the baht) but as far as I could see the wine was 1,700 baht (about £30 a bottle) – a lot, I know, but it was a special night and we were in a beautiful country. Unfortunately I had misread the wine list, though, and it wasn't 1,700 baht: it was 17,000 baht (or £300 a bottle)! By then we'd had three bottles, so it left us with a bill of £900. We were all paralysed with shock and needless to say I've never been allowed to order wine again.

A couple of years ago I was involved in a reality show called *Murder Most Famous*. There were six of us taking part, including ex-*Sun* editor and media executive Kelvin MacKenzie, actress Angela Griffin, garden expert Diarmuid Gavin, dancer Brendan

Cole and the presenter Matt Allwright. Crime writer Minette Walters was our mentor and judge.

The idea was to learn to be a crime writer. One by one we would be eliminated until there was a winner, and that person would be able to write a book and have it published. Every day we had tasks to help in our understanding of crime. We worked in morgues with bodies (not real ones, but very realistic); also with scene-of-crime officers, police dogs and car chases – we even stayed in a prison for the night and had to interview a murderer. For every episode we had to write a different crime story.

From day one, I didn't think I stood a chance, but I loved the challenge. Day after day I wrote dark, macabre and disturbing stories, which astonished me – I had no idea where they were coming from. And to my amazement I won the show and indeed had a book published, called *The Tannery*. My only gripe was that it was very short – a quick read of only 20,000 words. I'd written 70,000 words, so the editing was harsh and I felt my story had been very diluted. Nonetheless, I know how lucky I was and it gave me an amazing boost.

The *Loose Women* regulars are recognised in public and we're part of people's lives much in the same way as actors in a soap. I know it looks easy but we work very hard just like the actors in any of the soaps – we don't turn up at 12.30 and sit on stools, talking about any old thing. At 8.30am we arrive for planning meetings (which can go on all morning) and are interrupted by make-up and hair with Lee Din, who is a life-saver for all of us except Carol, who won't let anyone near her – she can't stand make-up or combs. I'm always telling her to at least get her roots done. The show finishes at 1.30pm and we're all gone. We rarely socialise together as a group, which is perhaps why we go mad when we go to awards or other events together. One or two of us are usually a little worse for wear and for some strange reason want to show off knickers, bras or even more!

Not me, I hasten to add – apart from the National Television Awards in 2010, when I wore a sheer top. It wasn't deliberate – I just didn't realise – but goodness, what a fuss the papers made. They always pick up on the fall or the trip or the snog: Carol's thong, Denise's bra, Coleen's boobs ...

On one occasion Lisa and I managed to trip and fall over on a red carpet and we were snapped sweeping up the free goodies we were taking home. Well, why not? Then there was the time Denise was pictured with her hands on Cilla's bottom, shoving her into a cab after a night out. Somehow we manage to survive it all, and come out laughing. We have fantastic, loyal fans and they come to see the live shows over and over again – they are brilliant. And of course, we've had our share of outspokenly honest viewers. One said to me, 'You look lovely in real life, but you look a bugger on TV'!

Then there was the time when two little old ladies came up to me in Blackpool and said, 'We know who you really are.' 'Do you?' I asked. 'Who am I?' Extremely pleased with themselves, both said in unison: 'That Sherrie Hewson on telly is your mother, isn't she?' Before I could say anything, they added, 'Don't deny it – you're the spitting image!' 'Thank you,' I said, and they went off happy.

All the Loose Women support each other. We cheered for Coleen and Denise when they appeared on *Dancing on Ice* and Lynda in *Strictly Come Dancing*. Most of the girls have written books and we're delighted when anyone has a success – there's no envy or jealousy. On the actual show we will argue – and it genuinely gets very heated sometimes because we're all very opinionated women and we can clash – but it's forgotten after the show and we all live to see another day. Our series editor

Emily knows us all very well and is very good at calming things down!

One thing I get very angry about is the obsession with age that we have in this country, and I'm very proud that *Loose Women* is one of the most non-ageist shows on TV. In fact, we embrace age and we have some heated debates about it, too. Zoe Tyler and I clash because she thinks it's OK to ask anyone their age and I think it's not. We have lots of older women guests on the show, too – we've had Stephanie Powers, Bette Midler, Stephanie Beacham, Dionne Warwick and many others – and I think it's rude to say, 'So tell us, exactly how old are you?'

But Zoe is young and not concerned about her age – I felt the same when I was young. Now I know how hard it is growing older: to look in the mirror and realise, to your horror, that the young person has gone and in her place is an ageing woman.

My dad used to say, 'You wait, Sherrie' – bear in mind that he was a hypochondriac – 'You wait till you're older – your back aches, your teeth come loose, your hair weakens, you can't sleep at night, even your bowels struggle.' I used to think, Oh God, will he ever stop going on? But he was right: things do drop off, everything aches and I haven't slept well since 1993.

In 2005 I was out for a walk with my dog one day when I had a funny turn. I thought I must be having a heart attack, and so I called Keeley. She took me to hospital, where eventually it was discovered that I have an underactive thyroid, which makes you feel lethargic and put on weight. You have to take medication and it can take time to get the balance right, which resulted in a bit of a scary moment on *Loose Women*. Denise and I were having a heated debate about something really trivial when we (thankfully) went into a break. Suddenly I felt blood come up into my mouth and start to pour out of my nose. I was taken off the set and couldn't return for the last half of the show. The next day the tabloids had a field day suggesting Denise had punched me on the nose and I had fled in tears – we still laugh at that. It was simply that my medication was too high and had to be adjusted.

All of us on the show have had lives and the lovely messages I get from my Facebook friends and all my lovely Tweeters tell me that they're so pleased to hear someone talking openly about life and love, heartache and loss. And I just love it when I get messages because viewers tell me they've been through these things, too, and it makes me feel I'm not the only one.

When I fell over on the ice on Christmas Eve 2010 and cracked my ribs I never knew how painful this could be, but the advice and care I received in all those messages was overwhelming. Thank you, everyone, for being there. Being on telly for so long – forty years now – is the only life I know and it can be lonely at times. I've always tried to keep changing and challenging myself, reinventing myself and looking ahead – I'm also extremely grateful to have enjoyed such an amazing career.

I'm also grateful for some wonderful friends. Someone I met only recently (and who has since become a great friend) is David Gest, former husband of Liza Minnelli. In 2010 I did a Christmas *Come Dine With Me* special with David, Diarmuid Gavin (again) and Hannah Waterman and it was the most bizarre show I have ever done.

As you probably know, everyone gets to cook and at the end one person wins £1,000 for a chosen charity. When it came to my turn, I decided to do a traditional Christmas dinner. I dressed up as Mother Christmas in a long red dress with a fur wrap and I made Diarmuid dress up as a Christmas pudding, Hannah came as a Christmas tree and David dressed as a pixie. David took it all in good part, but Diarmuid and Hannah were so horrified that they decided to do a runner to the pub and left me alone with David.

Now I can cook a turkey, but by the time they filmed me serving it it was two o'clock in the morning and the whole meal was ruined. Not only that, but after feeling cross with Hannah and Diarmuid for going off, I'd had a few drinks. The meal was a disaster but I was determined to make up for it with the pudding. I'd made a Christmas pudding from scratch and I was very proud of it. All it needed was some ice cream on the top so that it looked like a snowy mountain. The trouble was, the ice cream had accidentally been left out and of course it melted, so when I poured it over the pudding it dribbled onto the floor! As I went to carry it to the table I slipped in the ice cream and both the pudding and I went up in the air, landing on our bottoms. I was so upset that I picked it up and put it back on the plate. Not surprisingly, they were having none of it.

David's night was extraordinary – good-humoured and kind as he is, he just laughed when things went wrong. He's very special, and what's more he knows everyone. When he cooked for us we walked in to find Mickey Rooney sitting there. After the show we stayed friends and Carol and I have been to his big Mowtown extravaganzas with all the bands from my youth.

These days I have a split life: my work is in London but my daughter and her family live in Lancashire so I seem to live on a Virgin train, where the staff are always lovely. I have two grandchildren now – Ollie and Molly – and along with my daughter Keeley they are the greatest loves of my life.

I'm so proud of Keeley, who is the loveliest person you could ever wish to meet. She is all the things that I knew she would be – strong, wise, loving, extremely loyal and the best mother any little boy or girl could have. Simon and Keeley are fantastic together: they have a good relationship and you can tell it's forever. They are going to marry soon and we're all looking forward to it. There I'll be, in my hat!

Little Ollie is four now and he's funny, bright, inquisitive and loving. He can be a little rascal, too – as all four-year-olds can be. At the weekends he often comes over to me and we spend time together: playing football, trampolining or swimming. I'm hoping to take him to karate soon – he is a very active boy and I am determined to keep up with him if it kills me! I love it when he stays over and we cuddle up in bed.

Molly was born in January 2011 and so she's still very small and so beautiful. I was there for both my grandchildren's births, and afterwards I relived them on the show as the viewers went through every emotion with me. Ollie weighed 10 pounds and his birth was a bit traumatic, but little Molly was just 6 pounds and her birth was very simple. I didn't realise babies could be that small – I couldn't stop gazing at her, and it's going to be a joy watching the two children grow up together.

Brett and his family still live in Conwy, North Wales, and it's only an hour and a half away so we do try to see each other as much as possible. Keeley and Brett's daughter Chloe are very close – more like sisters than cousins – and both have two children now. Then there's my mum, my inspiration. She is extraordinary and full of energy. She's always swimming, dancing, seeing friends, dressing beautifully and enjoys being a great-grandmother. Mum has always been there for me and I love her very much.

It's been four years since I declared bankruptcy and I've come a long, long way. It wasn't easy picking up the pieces of my life afterwards. For a start, my self-esteem was on the floor. At 56, it's humiliating to find yourself separated and without much to show materially for all those years of hard work. For a while I felt very low and I couldn't help but wonder what it had all been for. Gradually I began to see things differently and to stop feeling sorry for myself.

For a start, I have a work record to be proud of and no one can take that away from me. As an actress, I've worked non-stop for my whole adult life and appeared in some wonderful productions, on-stage, film and television. You have to recognise what really matters – to laugh in the face of adversity, that's the expression, isn't it? Also, to realise that stuff doesn't matter, only people do. Most importantly, as Carol keeps on telling me, you have to learn to love yourself or you'll never find love again.

I am often asked if I date or whether I have a boyfriend, but that sounds weird to me. It makes me feel very silly, as if I'm a girl again. At the moment, the answer is no. After everything that's happened I do have a major problem with trust. Will I ever conquer it? I hope so. If Robert Redford was available, it might help, but I'm not falling over myself to share my bathroom with a man again (all those grubby socks, and the loo seat permanently up) or to have to let someone know where I am all the time. I'm not worried about being without a partner. Most of my free time is spent with Keeley and her babies, and most of my love is for them. When I wake in the mornings and think of them, they make my heart beat. How lucky am I.

Having said all that, last year a friend persuaded me to try a dating website. It was great fun and I did get chatting to a guy who sounded nice but he was a bit too young for me (twelve years my junior) and I wasn't sure I could cope. Still, it just goes to show you can start your pistons again after a long cold winter.

I'm not suggesting that life is perfect now. I'm still riddled with fears, doubts and hang-ups just like everybody else, but I know I've been very lucky. I've come out the other end – scathed, but still in good working order.

So, here's my wish list for the best years to come:

- I want to play the piano properly – I can manage 'Little Donkey' but it doesn't go down well at parties!
- I want to be in a musical, although I have a whole industry begging me not to do so. Maybe I should write my own and call it 'Little Donkey'?
- Finally, I would like to have that body-lift they all have in America. They start at the ankles and pull up the skin on your legs and thighs, stomach, chest and arms until the whole thing is smooth and reaches the top of your neck. Afterwards, they secure it with a bulldog clip at the back. *Voilà,* a whole new body! The only downside is that you end up with a small, curly black beard.

Cheers, clink!

Acknowledgements

I'd like to thank my Mum, firstly for her love and secondly for reminding me of things long ago that needed to be said. To my Nana, Granddad and Dad: you inspired and encouraged me throughout my life. Thanks to my brother, Brett, for being such being an amazing power and to his lovely family, Annie, Chloe, John, Spencer and Olivia. I hope I never let any of you down. Thank you to all the special people in my life who I am very proud to call friends and who have always believed in me. There are too many of you to name here, but you all know who you are.

I'd like to thank everyone at Harper Collins for encouraging me and being excited about the book, we all got a bit giddy. A special thank you to Anna Valentine, who was always calm and always had a solution.

Thank you to Neil Howarth for your loyalty and friendship, and for your belief in me and this book.

Thank you to Wigan A&E for nursing me, without you I would never have finished the book!

Thank you to the amazing Loose Women who give me such great material every day that I could now write a second book and a third.

And of course, thank you to Simon and his lovely family.

But most of all thank you to my wonderful daughter, Keeley, who makes my heart beat every day, and my truly adorable grandchildren Ollie and Molly. They are the reason I exist, and they are the reason I have written this book, so it can sit on their shelves for ever and they can say, 'That's my Nana.'